POPULISM
ON TRIAL

POPULISM ON TRIAL

WHAT HAPPENS WHEN TRUST IN LAW BREAKS DOWN

INIGO BING

Biteback Publishing

First published in Great Britain in 2020 by
Biteback Publishing Ltd, London
Copyright © Inigo Bing 2020

ISBN 978-1-78590-575-9

10 9 8 7 6 5 4 3 2 1

A CIP catalogue record for this book is available from the British Library.

Set in Minion Pro

Printed and bound in Great Britain by
CPI Group (UK) Ltd, Croydon CR0 4YY

MIX
Paper from
responsible sources
FSC® C020471
FSC
www.fsc.org

For Mary

'Liberty lies in the hearts of men and women; when it dies there, no constitution, no law, no court can save it.'
BILLINGS LEARNED HAND

'The British Constitution presumes more boldly than any other the good sense and the good faith of those who work it.'
WILLIAM EWART GLADSTONE

CONTENTS

ACKNOWLEDGEMENTS

Many friends and colleagues, too numerous to mention, have contributed to the thoughts and ideas that make up this book. From my time in chambers I would especially like to record thanks over the years to Winston Guthrie-Jones QC, Tom Pigot QC (who became Common Serjeant at the Central Criminal Court) and Philip Singer QC, who demonstrated to those below them the fundamental ethical foundations of law. During my service on the bench Sir Peter Badge and Lord Judge, under whose leadership I served at different times, taught me and my contemporaries qualities of reason, objectivity, humanity and kindness, which have greatly contributed to the formation of the ideas for this book. I owe a particular debt of gratitude to my post-graduate supervisor at Birkbeck College, Professor Joanna Bourke FBA, who provided the inspiration to embark on a book which attempts to discuss the relationship of law to politics.

Thanks are also due to my agent, Robert Dudley, who encouraged this book from its first rather tentative beginnings. I also wish to thank my editors at Biteback, Olivia Beattie and James Lilford, who have seen the book through to press with calm efficiency.

The librarians at the Inner Temple and the British Library have always been on hand to provide help and advice when most needed and the staff at the National Archives have provided original sources when required with their customary speed.

I wish to record special thanks to Howard Riddle CBE and Dr Sarah Pemberton, who read earlier drafts and have provided me with helpful comments and suggestions for improvement. I am most grateful to them both.

Last, but by no means least, I wish to thank my wife Mary, who not only endured the long periods of research and writing with stoicism and patience but read every word and provided some valuable thoughts of her own to the arguments advanced in the book. This book is dedicated to her, with love. Errors and omissions are entirely down to me.

London
July 2020

INTRODUCTION

In the last week of August 2019, when judges were on their vacation and many others were abroad or by the seaside, an event of constitutional importance was taking place in London and in Scotland. A delegation of Privy Councillors, led by Jacob Rees-Mogg MP, went to Balmoral Castle and, on the instructions of the Prime Minister, asked the Queen to prorogue Parliament. The subsequent prorogation let loose a barrage of pent-up emotion either in support of this bold move to ensure that the result of the EU referendum was honoured or in denunciation of it as an outrage against the constitutional apparatus of the United Kingdom.

Yet to summarise the opposing reactions to the prorogation decision in this way immediately exposes the gulf between the two sides. One side was talking about the need to honour the decision by the electorate to leave the EU, the other was talking about how prorogation was the equivalent of detonating a bomb to silence Parliament debating it. The dialogue of the deaf over the pros and cons of the prorogation decision exposed a growing crisis about the nature of British democracy. Those who supported the decision to prorogue congratulated the Prime Minister for being willing 'to do whatever it takes to carry out the people's will'.[1] This side blamed the 'shameless plotting' of the anti-Brexit forces and the outrageous behaviour of the 'parliamentary Remainers'. On the other side, prorogation was all about the 'constitutional chicanery' of a Prime Minister who was daring to choose a revolutionary path to implement the referendum result.[2]

These completely opposite opinions about the prorogation decision revealed a chasm about democracy and law that went far beyond being for or against leaving the EU. The chasm was the gap between two opposing views about the source of power in the United Kingdom. One side, which wanted above all else to deliver the result of the 2016 referendum, believed that real power lay in the executive. The other believed that our constitutional heritage, with a supreme Parliament to make or unmake law, could not be messed about with for short-term political gain. Occupying the ground between these two firmly entrenched views were the judges who within the space of a few weeks would be asked to make a decision on where legitimate power resided. The 2019 prorogation process engaged the three sources of power in modern Britain: Parliament, the executive and the judiciary. This book attempts to examine the origins of this power struggle with a particular focus on the driving force behind the attempt to provide simple answers to complex questions – populism.

The purpose of this book is to argue that populism, as it has emerged in the United Kingdom, is a threat to our notions of liberal democracy and points our future towards authoritarianism. Liberal democracies must address the distribution of power within a society that is bonded together by trust. If the bonds of trust in any institution deteriorate there is a danger that the delicate balance between trust and power will also collapse. What are the proper limits to power in the hands of the police? Do we trust the executive to have powers that are not overseen by rules of law? Is the threat of terrorism an emergency that justifies giving more power to those in authority without any legal restraints? These are some of the dilemmas discussed in this book. Legal arguments which are rarely heard outside the courtroom are told for the benefit of the general reader to explain the judicial decisions which have, despite being legally sound, encouraged populism.

If we are to avoid unquestioning obedience to the authority of a powerful executive, the need for trust in the rule of law is essential to preserving our democratic way of life. Modern-day attacks on judicial power are unjustified and only seek to undermine trust in an independent judiciary. The scourge of populism can only be defeated if values which uphold individual rights and liberties are protected. The protection is provided, on the whole, by trust in an independent judiciary.

At its heart, populism in Britain claims that if elites, such as MPs and judges, listened more carefully to what ordinary people want then the country would be a better place. Why do we have human rights? Surely, they are only for murderers, criminals and rapists who soak up public money in legal aid to exercise their 'rights'? Why can't we just deport foreigners quickly if the government think they threaten our country? Why do the police have to contend with so much 'red tape'? Why can't they just get on with keeping our streets safe and catching criminals? What is stopping the government from carrying out the will of the people? Why are judges always getting in the way?

The new government of Boris Johnson began by appearing to confront these questions with a gusto that took civil servants by surprise. It was only the arrival of the coronavirus in the spring of

2020 that halted an agenda which was going to challenge important traditions of constitutional law. Behind the sound and fury of the highly charged debate about the merits of Brexit – the demonstrations outside Parliament, the campaign for a second 'people's vote' and the counter-chants of 'let's get Brexit done' – there were important constitutional issues at stake. The Prime Minister's platform was to persuade the electorate that the power he wanted 'to get Brexit done' was what the country craved. The people did not want a Parliament that dithered and delayed. The Conservative Party leader gambled on the country putting strong leadership before an indecisive Parliament.

This argument won the day as Boris Johnson's party benefited from, among other things, a growing lack of trust in the British political system. In January 2020, the Centre for the Future of Democracy at Cambridge reported that voters' faith in the democratic process had declined sharply in the seventeen years since the Iraq War when Tony Blair was unpopular (although he recovered and went on to win the next election). Over 30 per cent were dissatisfied then, but at the time of the 2019 general election 60 per cent of the people were dissatisfied with the political system.[3] This unhappiness about the ability of democracy – as practised in the United Kingdom – to satisfy the public coincided with the Hansard Society Audit of Political Engagement, which reported in 2019 that people wanted radical solutions. Fifty-four per cent of the public said that Britain needed a strong leader who was willing to break the rules.[4]

The mood of the country which helped the Conservatives in the 2019 general election was not just or even mainly about delivering Brexit. Professor John Curtice said that if it had been just about Brexit the result would have been 53 per cent for Remain and 47 per cent for Leave.[5] The election was not, exclusively, the Brexit election. More complicated forces were at play. Johnson had tapped into a prevailing mood for the simplification of democracy where decisions could be taken quickly and decisively without tiresome arcane parliamentary procedures getting in the way and where judges could not frustrate the will of the people.

In one sense it was a despair about democratic processes that propelled Boris Johnson into Downing Street, but he was able to take full advantage of this by styling himself as a populist leader who did not want to tolerate dissent. Shortly after his election as leader of the Conservative Party and therefore Prime Minister, he withdrew the whip from twenty-one Conservative MPs who supported the EU Withdrawal (No. 2 Act), which became known as the Benn Act (named after the MP, Hilary Benn, who introduced it), about the timetable for Britain's withdrawal from the EU.

After his election in 2019, Johnson spoke from a lectern in Downing Street which bore the masthead 'The People's Government'. In January 2020, he let it be known that he was contemplating moving the chamber of the House of Lords to York. The Conservative Party chairman, James Cleverly MP, went on television to say the plan would demonstrate that 'we are going to do things differently'.[6] Perhaps this was an attempt to try to make us believe that when Johnson spoke, he meant what he said. If true, moving the House of Lords well away from the House of Commons would abolish the joint committees of peers and MPs who are free to comment on and criticise government policy. These have traditionally applied a restraining brake on the use of executive power in their recommendations. It would also do away with the ceremony and pageant associated with the Palace of Westminster, so beloved by Jacob Rees-Mogg. It is therefore possible that the plan was an example of gesture politics.

On the other hand, if Johnson really meant what he said then there is not a feature of our constitutional system that his ambitions would not contemplate changing. The signs of populism are evident. Either it was a statement of intent he had no intention of actually implementing – reminiscent of the promises that were made in the referendum campaign – or it was a bold attempt to draw power away from his opponents and claw it towards himself.

The writer and historian Ferdinand Mount described this initiative as being reminiscent of the Roman leader Pericles, who neutered the upper house, the Areopagus, which had acted as a restraining influence over the popular assembly in the fourth century BC.[7] Boris Johnson allegedly keeps a bust of Pericles on his desk in Downing Street; perhaps a reminder of the imperative of drawing power towards oneself.

Liberal democracy in Britain is now in crisis and there is a scepticism about the traditional norms which provide the glue to hold societies together. Liberal democracies depend upon society being vibrant, where a responsible free press reports true, not fake, news; where public debate and discourse is polite; and where critical thinking is an occupation to be encouraged not reviled. A liberal democracy values the neutrality of key institutions – like the civil service and the judiciary – and acknowledges that citizens have rights not just responsibilities.

The foundation of all of these elements, however, is levels of wealth which are accepted at the time as being comfortable, and an expectation that succeeding generations will be wealthier than their predecessors. The liberal method of delivering high standards of living has been an economic theory which embraces globalised trade and a minimum level of intervention to the free market. When these foundations of liberal democracies fail, populists have a genuine point which needs answering.

The liberal consensus that international structures, global free trade and the reduction of tariffs could meet an excessive demand for coal, steel, textiles, shipbuilding and cars was wildly optimistic. Far from dealing with excessive demand and, with it, over-capacity, the liberal solution, supported by democratic governments, only seemed to lead to a destruction of communities. In the process, people were robbed of their dignity and self-respect. The working class at home lost their jobs to provide employment abroad. At the same time the free movement of labour seemed only to help the middle class, who were benefiting from globalisation with jobs in finance, technology, medicine and communications. The financial crash of 2008 proved to be a tipping point. The conventional wisdom was to impose austerity for working people while excusing 'elite' bankers of all blame. The scene was set for a populist alternative.

Few would disagree that a serious reappraisal of the liberal economic model in Europe and the United States is overdue. Unfortunately, populists have been floundering when it has come to suggesting credible economic alternatives. For example, Boris Johnson, an important figure in any discussion about populism, said in 2013 that 'the free market is the only show in town. Britain is competing in an increasingly impatient and globalised economy, in which the competition is getting ever stiffer.'[8] This was not exactly what people in Tyne and Wear or Wakefield who had lost their jobs to free market liberalism of a global economy wanted to hear.

To make up for their paucity of economic ideas, populists blamed the institutions and values of liberalism. In doing so they have spectacularly missed the mark in their recipes for change. They aim at the wrong target in identifying human rights as a problem, or by insisting it is judges exceeding their authority that is the problem, or that civil servants tendering impartial advice is the problem, or that a rule of law which upholds standards of pluralism, tolerance and broad-mindedness is the problem. This book will try to explain that these targets are not the problem. Populists have chosen to attack aspects of modern political and legal culture which are actually improvements to the way we did things in the past. They are improvements that should endure irrespective of shifting economic circumstances. You cannot have human rights when the going is good, only to abandon them when the going gets tough.

Shifting the blame on others is a typical tactic of the populist who is seeking power. At the time of his assessment that the free market was the only show in town, Boris Johnson was Mayor of London, but he was sharpening his populist pen in the pursuit of power at 10 Downing Street. Like all populists, Johnson identified himself as an outsider, but he realised that if he was to claim power and hold on to it he needed to change the character and style of his administration.

In a liberal democratic Britain, Prime Ministers usually hold power fleetingly and uncertainly. In the period covered by this book, 1950 to 2020, there have been sixteen Prime Ministers in 10 Downing Street. Six have been Labour (Wilson's two premierships were interrupted by Edward Heath's tenure), nine have been Conservative and one has been the head of a Conservative-led coalition. Nearly all of these Prime Ministers held power for short periods. Only Margaret Thatcher and Tony Blair commanded all they surveyed over sustained periods. Politicians in liberal democracies *must* make an appeal to voters in order to retain power. If they don't, they are out. It is a fundamental misconception to believe that Britain has been governed by out-of-touch elites who ignore voters.[9] The price to pay for attempting to heed the voice of voters is that you may not hold office for very long. But that is a feature of a democracy that is underpinned by liberal values.

Politicians of all parties since the Second World War, up until the arrival of Boris Johnson, have relied to a greater or lesser extent on a shared consensus. This is the belief that there was a way of doing things which was *political*. This involved a reliance on facts, a respect for institutions, a dialogue that did not challenge the legitimacy of your opponent's arguments and a Cabinet government involving trusted colleagues. For example, during Margaret Thatcher's premiership, Lord Carrington, Geoffrey Howe and William Whitelaw wielded power. In Harold Wilson's administrations, Denis Healey and James Callaghan held similar power and, until Gordon Brown sought the Prime Minister's position for himself, he had immense power as Blair's Chancellor. Under David Cameron, the country was ruled under a coalition where, inevitably, prime ministerial power was shared with his deputy, Nick Clegg.

These traditional features of politics drain away under populism. The 2016 referendum campaign fundamentally changed the political way of doing things. First, there was precious little reliance on facts. Any 'facts' presented by the Remain side were dismissed as 'project fear' that was created by 'experts', and respect for the arguments from the other side had virtually disappeared by the time the public voted. In the general election of 2017 which followed the referendum, Jeremy Corbyn was demonised as a completely illegitimate politician.

Populists want to challenge the traditional norms of democratic government, on the grounds that the democracy we have become accustomed to has failed the people. Populists reject the idea that there can be a shared consensus because some parts of the population are excluded from consensus politics. This may be true and there are complicated cultural and economic reasons for this. Populists are poor at analysing the reasons for social exclusion, disillusionment and despair. Instead they are very good at exploiting disappointment and claiming to represent those who are excluded from the political process.

There is an innocent virtue about this claim to represent the unrepresented. The populist seeking power does not want to accept any responsibility for the ills of society. They are the innocent outsider. Much better to place the blame for our misfortunes on those who caused it in the first place, the bankers, the European Union, out-of-touch politicians and the system in general. The system in general, according to populists, encompasses civil servants, diplomats and judges. But this deliberate tactic of creating distance between a virtuous people and a corrupt elite is, in reality, the populist's chosen route to power. It was the route chosen by Hitler, Mussolini, Chávez, Castro, a host of African dictators and Donald Trump in the United States. We are not there yet, but this book attempts to identify the danger signs that populism poses to the rule of law. As the title asks: what happens when trust in law breaks down?

The first signs of a fracturing between politics and the rule of law is when politicians appear to disown important aspects of our democracy. When the 2016 referendum result was being debated in Parliament, Jacob Rees-Mogg said, 'Let us obey the result of the referendum.' For him, the result of the referendum was a blank cheque in the hands of the executive to leave the EU at the time and on the terms it thought best. For Rees-Mogg and later Boris Johnson, Parliament was a bit of a side-show when it came to the serious business of leaving the EU. When Theresa May was facing obstacles in Parliament to getting her EU Withdrawal Agreement approved, she blamed the democracy which produced an election result of a 'hung' parliament for her misfortunes. She went on television to make a direct appeal to the people, saying: 'I'm on your side.' By doing so she was rebuking the institution of Parliament as the forum for representative democracy. When a bench of senior judges, including the Lord Chief Justice, ruled that it was for Parliament, not the executive, to authorise the triggering of Article 50 to begin the process of leaving the EU, they were branded 'enemies of the people' by the *Daily Mail*.[10] The populist in power wants to implement the will of the people by pretending there is a hotline between the people and the leader who has the privilege of obeying their will. Anybody who wants to block this process is an enemy.

These utterances and arguments are based on a fundamental misconception. When we use the word 'people', it can mean one of two things, but not both. It can mean the people comprising a common body, such as members of a club, a congregation in church or an audience at a play. Or it can man the collection of individual people who have chosen to become joined as a common body.[11] If the word is used in the first sense then it does not carry with it an understanding that the people within the common body are diverse and that they may hold different views, because their collectivity is represented by their presence in the club, church or theatre. In the second sense, where people have chosen to live in a particular town or locality, they carry with them their own personal individuality, opinions, prejudices and voting preferences.

Populists conflate the two meanings of 'people' and by doing so confuse important constitutional and legal principles. If it is true that in the United Kingdom Parliament is supreme, how can the 'people' be more in control of the body which makes laws on our behalf? Along with this constitutional confusion, populists are often uncertain about whether they are bold in their plans for the future or nostalgic for a past that has been lost.

Populists in power claim to be modernisers, but underneath the veneer of daring modernisation and radical rethinking lies a belief that somehow things were always better in times past. This was the past when judges did not stray into politics; when we didn't have to obey laws made in the European Court of Human Rights in Strasbourg; when we did not have as many foreigners in the country to start with and when the police could give young thugs a clip around the ear without a solicitor running off to a judge claiming that his client had been assaulted.

This book is a polemic. It attempts to confront the populist outlook and to retell the stories about human rights, foreign criminals and police behaviour in the past in a different way. It will argue that Britain was not a better place when judges sat in their courtrooms determined not to upset the executive, when the police were unrestrained by legally enforceable codes of behaviour and when discrimination, gender inequality and privacy rights were not admitted to exist. The arguments in this book concentrate exclusively on populism in the United Kingdom, or, to be precise, England. Populism has taken hold in some European countries, notably Poland, Hungary and Italy, but it is beyond the scope of this book to discuss the origins of populism outside England. The threat to the rule of law which, as this book argues, is posed by populism is a threat in England and Wales. Scotland and Northern Ireland have their own distinctive legal regimes and populism has not taken hold in devolved regions to the extent that it has in England. There is no reference to Scottish nationalism in this book, which some might try to argue is a populist phenomenon. I do not intend to enter the discussion of whether Scottish nationalism falls within the definition.

Immigration is another subject which is avoided. It is undoubtedly the case that fears and apprehensions about immigration into the United Kingdom contributed to the rise of populism. It was one of Nigel Farage's main concerns and he made it a central plank of his Brexit Party policy to oppose immigration. Some have argued that fears about immigration are false and exaggerated. Others claim that people's anxieties about immigration are genuine and must be addressed.[12] I do not attempt to take sides in this debate. My purpose is to examine the causes of populism and its consequences for the rule of law and the conventions of the Constitution. The book therefore has a discrete, narrow focus on the subject of populism in modern Britain.

I do not claim to pick apart all the flaws in the populist recipe book. I do not deal at all with economics, nor do I discuss any threats to a free press that the rise in populism may pose. I concentrate on the rule of law and the Constitution in the United Kingdom. There are only passing references to the rise of populism in Poland, Hungary and the United States. There are many books on these features of populism that have been released around the world. Inevitably, a large amount of space is dedicated to the work of judges and the way the meaning of the words 'the rule of law' have evolved over the period the book covers, 1950 until the present day. As historians are fond of saying, to understand the present we must know the past. Some of the narrative in this book is historical as it is necessary to understand how we got to the place we are in now.

When dealing with the rule of law and any threats to it, we need to begin at the beginning. The starting point is to identify what every child at school learns about the bedrocks of our society, the foundation stones which uphold the three pillars of our constitutional democracy: the elected legislature; a free press; and the rule of law. The next step is to ask: is there a danger that any of these are being undermined here in Britain? Although populist dangers, if any, to a free press are beyond the scope of this book, it cannot be overlooked that Boris Johnson has given instructions to his ministers not to talk to tough interrogators, like Andrew Neil, on the BBC. At the same time he has restricted lobby access to briefings at 10 Downing Street. This book concentrates on the constitutional checks and balances which keep the essential fabric of democracy in good repair.

We are a long way from becoming a country that is defined by populism, but there are trends that are relevant to law and justice, pointing in this direction. Senior legal figures have already spotted the trends. Lord Hodge, Deputy President of the Supreme Court, gave a speech in 2018 entitled 'Preserving Judicial Independence in an Age of Populism'[13] and in the same year the former Chief Justice of Canada gave a speech at Cambridge University entitled 'Where Are We Going? Reflections on the Rule of Law in a Dangerous World'.[14] In his valedictory address in September 2017, the President of the Supreme Court, Lord Neuberger, said 'misconceived attacks on judges undermine the rule of law domestically and the international reputation of the legal system'.[15]

The relationship of law to politics – and politics to law – is now a subject of interest to many outside the legal establishment or the 'Westminster village'. The choice by the BBC to invite Jonathan Sumption, a senior lawyer and former Supreme Court Justice, to deliver the Reith Lectures in 2019 reflects a growing interest in the interaction between law and politics. In the course of this book I find myself in disagreement with Jonathan Sumption on a number of topics. I hope that I have set out the arguments with sufficient objectivity for readers to make their minds up for themselves about the merits of these differing points of view.

When Lord Bingham, perhaps Britain's greatest judge of modern times, published his book *The Rule of Law* in 2010, it was a bestseller. There is obviously an appetite among sections of the British public to grapple with a very real contemporary issue. Are judges stepping too far into the realm of politics and overreaching themselves, or are politicians justifiably fearful of a strong, independent and independent-minded judiciary? If so, what is it that politicians fear?

This book is for the general reader. The overall aim is to attempt to repudiate the dogmas of populism and to suggest that judges are now so routinely attacked that the case for the defence needs to be made. Judges themselves are usually reticent about expressing their own views too readily. They are, after all, a privileged group whose day job is to give judgments which bind the parties who have contested the case. Traditionally, the judge earns his or her reputation by the quality of the legal judgment handed down, not by his or her personal views. The process by which an individual judge or a bench of judges hearing appeals reach a decision is a closely guarded secret. It is the judgment, not the process by which it is reached, that matters.

It is important that a judge does not get involved in political controversy, unless the controversy raises a legal point which requires a decision. When senior judges are invited to give lectures or speeches, it is usually in order to promote a greater understanding by the public of the role they perform. Usually these lectures or speeches are given to a self-selecting audience who are predisposed to agree with the judicial outlook in the first place. Persuading or converting the public to their point of view is something judges cannot do unless the persuading is low-key, cerebral and delivered in coded language.

In current times, therefore, the debate about whether judges are moving too far into the territory occupied by politicians tends to be a bit one-sided. Politicians and the media are free to say what they like about judges, subject only to the laws of libel and contempt of court, but judges are constrained from answering back. The freedom to speak and write what you want about a legal judgment has been eagerly taken up by some politicians, and their gripes and complaints about judicial decisions are often read without rebuttal.

One of the purposes of this book is to try to put some of the judicial decisions which have caused controversy into a proper context. I have chosen areas of law where differences of opinion between politicians and the judiciary have been most acute: criminal sentencing, constitutional law, laws about terrorism and laws on the European Convention on Human Rights.

Tensions between law and politics have ebbed and flowed and sometimes the tides are whipped up by the strength of wind behind them and the arguments are not especially edifying. The tensions involve *trust* and *power*. In ordinary life we usually place trust in those whom we allow to have power over us, otherwise the use of power becomes overbearing and the trust we have bestowed on the one having power is betrayed. This book covers three distinct phases of our history where power and trust between politicians and the judiciary has ebbed and flowed.

The first phase was when power was firmly held in Parliament and the executive. Judges were expected to keep well away from trying to make law. Their job was to apply the law made by Parliament. Alongside this judicial timidity, too much power and trust were placed in the hands of the police. Judges joined hands with Parliament and did very little about it, but this phase included many miscarriages of justice when people were executed or imprisoned for crimes they were judged later not to have committed.

This was the second phase when judges came to terms with the errors of their ways in being complicit in miscarriages of justice. They recognised their own mistakes and many wrongful convictions were quashed. This phase coincided with a new judicial assertiveness when scrutinising the power of the executive became a feature of judicial work. This was the use of judicial review by individual citizens who claimed they were disempowered by an overbearing executive. In this phase politicians began to complain that now the judges had too much power. The final phase examined is the fallout from the Brexit referendum. This provoked a constitutional crisis when the executive seized power over Parliament and the judges restored power to Parliament.

THE FIRST PHASE

In the first phase, which covered the period from 1950 until around the early 1980s, there was a deference towards the men and women who led institutions or who stood for office in a democracy. Deference was accorded to judges, civil servants and elected politicians, but such courteous and obedient regard instilled a culture of complacency among the elite. A by-product of complacency was a woeful unwillingness for judges, politicians and civil servants to recognise and remedy injustices within the system. In this phase the administration of criminal justice was overseen by an overarching institutional culture which was especially shameful. Institutions responsible for justice closed ranks and protected themselves against criticism from outside their own cloistered environment.

During this phase it is beyond doubt that judges were conspicuously apprehensive and deferential towards Whitehall and government ministers. After the war Lord Chancellor Jowitt believed that judges should not be creative; they should simply interpret and apply the law as it was laid down by Parliament. The judges took their cue from the Lord Chancellor and were content to accept a subservient place within the Constitution, deciding disputes between citizens and faithfully interpreting the statutes passed by Parliament, with a simple, literal meaning being given to the words used.

There was a cosy, rather chummy relationship between judges and senior civil servants, who were from the same class and background as the judges themselves. Judges regarded them as being their intellectual equals. This was not a happy time for minorities in society, who did not enjoy equal treatment; for consumers, who had little redress against an overweening state apparatus; or for those with disabilities, who were barely able to leave their own home for lack of facilities, recognition or support. It was a good time for government, however, and ministers did not need to look over their shoulder to see where the next troublesome judge was coming from. These were the bad old days not the good old days.

The structure of this book is built around the staple diet of all lawyers, the real cases with their real facts. Lawyers, on the whole, do not need theories about law. They are too busy litigating about the vicissitudes and misfortunes of the clients with whom they come into contact. This book will retell some of these real-life cases about how and why trust in law broke down and how and why trust was restored. The restoration of trust happened because judges became *more* assertive, not less, and politicians were prepared to give *more* discretion to judges, not less.

The book begins by asking, 'What is populism in modern Britain?' For most of the time, since populism first surfaced in the guise of the United Kingdom Independence Party (UKIP), populists in Britain defined themselves as outsiders; an insurgent anti-establishment force standing up for ordinary people against remote and detached elitists. Populists styled themselves as representing the ordinary voter, or 'the people' as populists invariably describe them. Populists believe these people possess a shared truth that conventional politicians fail to spot. Conventional politics is too out of touch with ordinary folk to be able to represent them properly. Populists must convey this point with a shrill tone, reflecting an anger that is felt by those who are ignored, with solutions that are simple, straightforward and different. The definition and meaning of populism in modern Britain are discussed in Chapter 1.

Following this general description, the book follows a chronological pattern. Chapter 2 deals with some real cases of miscarriages of justice. It starts with the Timothy Evans case, which involved an illiterate van driver who was hanged for a murder he did not commit on the strength of a confession that could not be true. The chapter continues by discussing the Craig and Bentley case. Craig, the principal in a burglary of a warehouse, carried a gun. Bentley was his accomplice. When the pair were caught, Craig shot a policeman, but he was too young to be executed. After a flawed trial, Bentley was hanged on the strength of a few words that he had uttered to Craig before the shooting, which were ambiguous to say the least. Both Evans and Bentley were the victims of gross miscarriages of justice which went uncorrected for many years.

These cases are important when considering the consequences of trust in law breaking down. Timothy Evans and Derek Bentley both suffered terrible miscarriages of justice and they went to their deaths under a flawed legal system which judges and politicians at the time believed was infallible. There was a misplaced trust by lawyers and judges in the processes of criminal justice, which could not be seen to fail. The alternative was that the whole edifice on which criminal justice rested would start to collapse, and this could not be permitted by an establishment that included politicians, civil servants, judges and barristers.

The system was trusted, but the system let these two men down. By contrast, the Challenor affair concerned a corrupt detective working in London's West End in the early 1960s. He invented a story, which he swore on oath was true, that a demonstrator at a protest outside Claridge's Hotel in 1962 had a brick in his pocket which he planned to throw at a member of the Greek royal family. The 'brick' case occupied the attention of the press and a full inquiry was conducted to find out why this completely dishonest and corrupt police sergeant was allowed to continue on duty when he was clearly not suitable to serve in the force. The Claridge's case was not an isolated incident. Challenor himself never stood trial, on the grounds of mental illness from which he later made a complete recovery. The Challenor affair is important because the inquiry into it found no fault whatsoever in the practices and procedures of the Metropolitan Police.

Just as criminal justice was considered infallible, it was also deemed that nothing was fundamentally wrong with the methods of the police in London. Similar refusals by judges, civil servants and politicians to acknowledge that anything about criminal justice was in need of change occurred in the Irish cases: the 'Birmingham Six', the 'Guildford Four' and the 'Maguire Seven'. The stories of these cases are told to expose what many at the time refused to admit was possible: that the police could not be trusted to treat suspects under interrogation fairly. Once again there was a wall of silence from the legal and political establishment to resist changes to the system. It was only after persistent campaigning from those outside the legal establishment that eventually the convictions in these cases were admitted to be unsafe and unsatisfactory. The 1950s, 1960s and 1970s were a gloomy time for criminal justice in England and Wales.

During this phase a Nelson's eye was turned in the direction of police conduct. Everybody knew that the police had a difficult job to do and the public were grateful for their efforts. Everybody also knew that there were good utilitarian reasons for criminals to be caught and put away, but not everybody knew the methods that were sometimes adopted to achieve this. In fact, it was impossible for anybody to find out what methods were used by the police, as police stations were secret places where only the police themselves and the villains they brought in were allowed access. Only the judges who tried criminal cases became acquainted with allegations of police misconduct, but there was no appetite to do anything about it. Judges invariably accepted the police account of the circumstances in which confessions came to be made and once a disputed confession went before the jury the accused had little chance of being acquitted.

In this period all the pillars on which the pediment of justice rested looked firm and the podium seemed to be stoutly upheld. However, the pillar marked 'police' was the weakest part of the structure and its marble began to crack in the mid-1960s.

This set in motion some wholesale changes. When the collapse of the old edifice was inspected by an enquiring public, it could not be repaired. It had to be rebuilt on different foundations and with different values. When the collapse began with the distrust of the police in the 1960s, the values inherent in the words 'rule of law' were found to be wanting as miscarriages of justice began to be exposed. Huge changes to the way the police were required to behave and the manner in which criminal trials were conducted were introduced.

It was not the powerful establishment of judges, civil servants or parliamentarians who spearheaded the changes. It was campaigns from outside the legal establishment which exposed police malpractice and miscarriages of justice.

The cosy atmosphere that existed between the organs of government and the judiciary was based entirely on trust. There was an unspoken understanding that the common good was being served by criminals being arrested and sent away. The methods of achieving this result were not as important as the result itself.

Challenging these assumptions were a new breed of barristers who were from mixed social backgrounds and not exclusively from Oxbridge, and who were prepared to challenge an entrenched and decaying culture. Lawyers such as Michael Mansfield, Tony Gifford, Rock Tansey, Peter Thornton, Helena Kennedy, Patrick O'Connor and Courtenay Griffiths helped transform criminal justice by confronting its shortcomings. Many miscarriages were recognised and wrongful convictions were quashed. The barristers, instructed by an equally dedicated body of solicitors, are now leaders of the profession and highly respected. They were once pilloried as 'the alternative bar' who often had to start their own chambers in order to advance their careers.

The point is a simple one. It was fearless lawyers who were properly funded for their work who sent the signal to Parliament that change was inevitable. Parliament reacted to these events by introducing legislation which corrected flagrant flaws in the system. It was not 'the people' who were sending a message to a strong leader that they wanted change. On the contrary, without the work of courageous lawyers, trust in criminal justice might have broken down completely in the era between 1950 and 1985. Had 'the people' been the headwind, nothing would have changed. The police were trusted and capital punishment for murder was consistently supported. It need hardly be stressed, but if we had had populism in Britain during the forty years following the end of the Second World War, this country would undoubtedly have been a worse place in which to live than it actually turned out to be under the semblances of the post-war consensus.

THE SECOND PHASE

The second phase could be called the period of reform. Curbing unregulated police power and restoring the trust that had been betrayed required strong action. The solution lay in the rule of law. Instead of the police *being* the law in the minds of many people in a culture of trust, the solution lay in placing them *under* the law. This was a huge change which meant that police conduct became subject to Codes of Practice created under laws made by Parliament. Every police officer investigating an offence had to use methods that were compliant with the Code and every judge trying a criminal case had a responsibility for ensuring the Code was used properly. This reform, spearheaded after a royal commission, was necessary because there was too much trust and too little law in defining the acceptable limits for police conduct. Trust had broken down, but law came to its rescue. Judges now had more power when they tried criminal cases. They had to decide, on the facts of each case, whether the actions of the police in their investigations complied with the Codes of Practice. Do we really want to go back to the days before police methods were regulated under law and before judges were given responsibilities for ensuring this law was applied?

A similar gloom had descended on the civil courts. In the 1950s, when this book begins, a politician, Douglas Jay MP, could seriously say, 'The man in Whitehall really does know best.' In the years that followed a new realisation became apparent. If the faceless bureaucrat in Whitehall really did know best, he had to have a legal basis for this opinion. There was a gradual transition taking place in judicial attitudes towards the use of executive power. This was partly in response to cultural changes as citizens became less deferential of authority, particularly the authority of officials acting on instructions given to them by laws made in Parliament. Judges would decide whether the power used in the name of the elected government had actually been authorised by those elected representatives.

During this phase there was a new judicial awareness that citizens might actually have rights against the nameless man in Whitehall who claimed he knew best. It began to dawn on judges that an over-powerful executive might overstep the mark in restricting a citizen's liberty without parliamentary consent. The judiciary was beginning to emerge from its sheltered existence from the period when there was a unified 'establishment'. This was the united front of judges, civil servants and politicians in power who claimed our legal system was perfectly calibrated in the allocation of responsibilities between the judiciary and the legislature.

The turning point for a new era in the tensions between law and politics began in the mid-1970s, when one of Britain's most far-sighted and clear-headed senior judges gave a series of lectures in 1974.[16] Sir Leslie Scarman, as he then was, took a broad view of lawyers and the law in 1974 and concluded that the rule of law was shut away and cocooned within its own archaic practices. Unless the law developed with new principles, new remedies, new machinery and new entrants into the profession then the practice of law would be threatened by the formidable forces of social change. Scarman took comfort from the fact there were international and European models that England might follow. These models pointed to Britain embracing entrenched rights as an ingredient of law. This was revolutionary, as the British tradition – stemming from Jeremy Bentham and Albert Venn Dicey – maintained that there were no natural or fundamental rights in the British Constitution. Liberties were protected by the common law and these could only be abridged by Parliament. Every citizen in the kingdom could do as he or she liked unless and until Parliament forbade it. Trust in law was ebbing away, but only a development in law itself could provide the solution.

Sir Leslie Scarman's prescriptions for the way forward proved highly controversial. New words like 'values' and 'rights' entered the vocabulary of lawyers. A new interest in the concepts of privacy, censorship and equality of citizenship irrespective of gender or ethnicity was developing. Deference towards elites and those who held the levers of power was being replaced by a healthy scepticism of authority. People were asking why they couldn't read or watch what they wanted and questioning why censorship on the grounds of obscenity was being imposed by some remote official whose name nobody could remember. Alongside these changes, people were beginning to recognise their own potential power to bring about change by challenging the authority that had previously been obeyed uncomplainingly. Once again lawyers were leading the way. A cadre of barristers such as Stephen Sedley, Nicholas

Blake, Geoffrey Robertson and Ian MacDonald were taking up the cudgels on behalf of the citizen to confront the exercise of power by the elites. Like the radical criminal specialists, these barristers also achieved eminence in their later careers.

There was one crucial difference between the developments taking place in criminal law and the cultural changes informing the views of judges in the civil courts. While politicians acknowledged that power needed to be shifted away from the police to a rules-based culture of policing where less discretion lay in the hands of the police officer, the opposite reaction was happening for civil law changes. Instead of recognising that a growth of judicial power would be in step with society's expectations, politicians interpreted the new judicial confidence as a power grab. They resented the changes.

Politicians recognised the power that the judiciary had once refused to use in relation to curbing an over-zealous executive was now being exercised by a new breed of judges. The unspoken trust between elected politicians and unelected judges which had worked so well when the judiciary was so deferential was breaking down. A new 'rights' culture became evident in the courts of justice. The European Convention on Human Rights 1998 was made part of British law in 2000. The decision to pass the Human Rights Act was made by Parliament, but when judges began applying the principles of the convention they were routinely attacked as being 'crazy' or 'mind-boggling'. The attack was so relentless that when Theresa May was Home Secretary she felt that she could entertain her audience at the Conservative Party conference in 2011 by ridiculing the stories 'we all know about the Human Rights Act'.

When these features of the criminal and civil justice systems are put together, it is clear that a fearless legal profession and a fiercely independent judiciary were giving new life to the words 'rule of law'. It was taken for granted that law, like society itself, should be tolerant and broad-minded, respectful of individual rights and of choices made by the exercise of personal autonomy. But no sooner had values that many people would celebrate as being civilised and necessary in a mature democracy been established in the courts than they came to be undermined by the press and politicians. When trust in law breaks down, trust in civilised and tolerant values are at risk of being challenged.

THE THIRD PHASE

Current populist ideas about clipping the wings of the judiciary are entirely misplaced. It was the judiciary who came to democracy's rescue by upholding the power of Parliament – the cornerstone of our Constitution – during the fallout from the referendum in 2016. This is the third phase of the tension between law and politics. The central constitutional issues arising from the 2016 referendum are discussed in Chapter 4. The key question was this: if the referendum vote was a 'mandate' or an 'instruction', how is the supremacy of the referendum decision to be reconciled with the constitutional fact of a parliamentary supremacy? This question is tackled head on with a description of the origins, theory and practice of the law and conventions of the British Constitution. The chapter also argues that despite the constant refrain made by politicians about the need to 'Take Back Control' it will be quite impossible for the doctrines and practices of parliamentary sovereignty to return to the status it enjoyed prior to Britain joining the European Economic Community (EEC) in 1973. There is something of a void opening up and it is a territory that could be occupied by a breed of populism. This book attempts to identify the dangers that a growth of populism in

Britain would pose to our democracy. Populism thrives on undermining trust.

Many of the signs of danger are found in the debate about the values or the hindrances that the subject of human rights poses for the power balance between law and politics. This is discussed in Chapter 5. Judges have been repeatedly vilified over their interpretation and application of principles enshrined in the European Convention on Human Rights. There was a time when hardly a day went by when the tabloid press did not seize on a story to expose, in their view, the irrelevance and stupidity of human rights. But the source of this distaste must be pinned down for their arguments to be answered. Is it that human rights emanate from a foreign court, the European Court of Human Rights which sits in Strasbourg and consists of judges who are not, with one exception, British? (The United Kingdom is a signatory to the treaty which set up the court and we have one permanent judge, Tim Eicke QC, who sits on all cases which involve the United Kingdom.) Or is it that the values inherent in the convention have been too widely interpreted by the judges sitting in Strasbourg, so human rights have got out of hand? Or is it, as the more extreme critics argue, that there is something fundamentally unnecessary about having human rights as part of our law in the first place? In attempting to answer these questions, I find myself in disagreement with Lord Sumption, whose Reith Lectures gave the sceptic's interpretation of convention rights now being given by judges here and in Strasbourg.

Chapter 6 deals with the legal and ethical problems thrown up by terrorism. In a post-9/11 age when the threat of terrorism is now with us every day, we expect our government to protect us, as best it can, against the risk of being harmed by extremists. Most people would expect a democracy whose values are under attack by terrorists to take extraordinary measures to provide this protection. Many would say it is a price worth paying to curtail some of our individual liberties in order to save the greater good of protecting our society as a whole. But where should the line to be drawn? The relationship between the individual citizen and the state is delicate and ill-defined until a real live case comes up in which the boundaries have to be drawn. This is a task for judges. The ethics and dilemmas thrown up by the need to protect us from terrorism while not turning us into a state without liberties are discussed in Chapter 6.

My own conclusions about how the threat of populism should be tackled are set out in Chapter 7. I pose two simple questions. If, as some believe, judges are too powerful, human rights are too invasive and the police are too hamstrung by bureaucracy, then to what period in our post-war history do these critics want to return? The Human Rights Act has been on the statute book for over twenty years; the Police and Criminal Evidence Act, which has made police behaviour subject to enforceable legal rules, has been with us for thirty-six years. Senior judges have been holding the executive to account by applying principles of judicial review for more than thirty years. The period that pre-dates these developments were dark and shameful days for civil and criminal law. There is no better yesterday which can magically be restored to our public life.

The second question that I pose is, in a way, more fundamental. If, as many senior judges and some commentators fear, the building blocks of a mature liberal democracy are starting to crumble, will this be hastened or retarded under populism? Are there forces within our political society that make it more or less likely that we, in Britain, will import methods used in Poland, Hungary and the United States that undermine the rule of law? These are the questions that put populism on trial.

Populism can only be defeated if there is a strong, vibrant civil society embracing rights and mutual obligations underpinned by a strong and respected judiciary who occupy a public domain of equity. This route does not lie in judges admitting that they have overstepped the mark by intruding into politics. The tide of history and the social developments which have been hastened by individual expectations have moved the judiciary into a territory they did not previously occupy. The consequences of the Human Rights Act 1998 which obliged judges to add a new dimension to their reasoning have been evolving for over twenty years. It is a simple fact of legal history that judges have, in a sense, become more political than they used to be, but there is no need for judges to impose restraints upon themselves. To do so would simply put the clock back and the question again recurs: to what period, exactly, do they want to return? When was the better yesterday?

The arguments in this book are as much about the distribution of power in modern Britain as they are about politicians making unfounded and ill-informed comments about judges. In essence, this book argues that there can be no challenge to populism that does not uphold the legal rules that judges and politicians should apply. Legal rules are, at heart, managing agents for 'suppressing, confining, limiting, guiding, directing, standardising, integrating and adapting changing behaviour'.[17] Underpinning these rules are certain fundamental principles which are called the 'rule of law'. These exist independently of the judges who apply and enforce them, but attacks on the judiciary are an indirect attack on the fundamental principles of law. That is why trends within populism which undermine judges are a veiled attack on principles which make our society liberal.

There is another attack on the judiciary which does not originate from populism. This assault comes from some academics in universities in Britain and the United States. In a recent book, the American academic Michael Lind argues that judges are part of a privileged 'overclass' or 'juristocracy' from elite backgrounds who, along with executive agencies and transnational bodies, have helped shift power away from working-class people. Lind argues that the working class can only have their views expressed in legislatures, not the courts: 'Government by judiciary tends to be a dictatorship of overclass libertarians in robes.'[18]

The British political scientist John Gray makes similar points. He suggests that to deal with the anxieties and concerns of communities who have been 'left behind' is to admit that the Enlightenment project is dead, as it is grounded in a political morality of universal principles of justice and rights. He maintains this universalism is no more than an abstract conception with no 'definite cultural identity or specific historical inheritance'. Its core belief was to displace local, customary and traditional morality with a rational morality projected as a basis of a universal civilisation.

Like Lind, Gray claims judges are too overwhelmed by the rights of individuals to think about the rights of communities. It is a positive falsehood, he argues, to believe that progress is achieved by abstract individualism 'in the service of a legalist or jurisprudential paradigm of political philosophy'.[19]

More recently still, Nick Timothy, Theresa May's former adviser in 10 Downing Street, has taken up the same theme by suggesting that the problem with modern society is that 'markets trump institutions, individualism trumps community and ... legal rights come before civic obligations ... and universalism erodes citizenship'.[20] One of the more reflective and thoughtful Conservatives in Parliament at present is Danny Kruger MP, a former personal secretary to Boris Johnson and speechwriter to David Cameron. He has said the government's central purpose is to re-establish 'democracy and the common good', which he describes as 'the well-being of local places'. One of the priorities in pursuit of this ideal is 'the restoration of politics to its proper place at the apex of our common life', including a 'reform of legal rights and responsibilities ... Politicians, on behalf of the people, should take the decisions and make the rules: civil servants and judges should implement the decisions and apply the rules. That balance will be restored under this government.'[21]

There are two aspects to these new prescriptions. The first is the claim that it is legitimate to identify judges as being part of the problem, the privileged 'juristocracy' or the outdated 'jurisprudential paradigm'. The second aspect is the assumption that the solution to problems within society can be resolved politically, with minimum resort to law. The role of the judiciary, it is claimed, is to decide disputes between citizens and to apply the laws enacted by Parliament. If judges stray beyond this then they find themselves embroiled in politics and this should be discouraged, or, better still, prevented by law from happening.

Drawing the line between stepping onto the forbidden turf of politics or staying within the boundaries of your own lawn is not easy to define, especially as the expectations of citizens and the broader interests of society are constantly changing. If facial recognition is possible in a camera so that the identities of individuals can be picked out in a crowd, who has the right to this information, and how may it be used? If a prominent politician has an illegitimate child, is this purely a personal matter or is there a public interest in revealing the name of the politician? Both these questions arose in real cases, but the resolution can only be a legal one, despite the fact that they might both be described as political questions.[22]

In a multi-ethnic and multi-cultural society, conflicts between the interests of the individual weighed against the interests of society as a whole arise constantly. For example, if a Sikh boy wanted to attend a private school, could the school prevent the child from wearing a turban, an important part of Sikh identity, and refuse him admission if his parents insisted he wear it? It is hardly surprisingly that the House of Lords found for the boy and ruled that the school had discriminated against him on racial grounds.[23] But would the result be the same if the facts were slightly different? A Muslim girl insisted she wear a jilbab to school, which is a loose garment concealing the shape of her body. She wanted to wear it as she was entering puberty and some schools permitted it. Her school, however, offered Muslim pupils the option of wearing the kameez, a sleeveless smock which did not hide the collar and tie of the school uniform, and loose salwar trousers. When she was sent home and told to remove the jilbab, she claimed that she had been unlawfully excluded from school. On these facts the House of Lords upheld the school's decision. It was decided that the policy on uniforms, and the additional clothing option offered to Muslim pupils, was a legitimate policy adopted to foster cohesion rather to prevent the creation of sub-groups within the school. The justices also agreed with the Muslim headteacher and the governing body that the school should not offer too much discretion to children to identify themselves along racial lines.[24] Once again, a solution which some might say should be reached through conciliation could only be resolved legally.

There is a central point underlying all these real cases. A truly free society is one where there are conflicts and disagreements about ideas and theories and a resolution of such conflicts can often only be achieved by judges making a decision because society's conflicts are frequently reflected in the cases brought before a court of law. It is a myth to suppose that there is some 'common good' which citizens themselves will strive to attain and that judges are, in some way, irrelevant to the aspirations within society.

The cases on surveillance, privacy, multi-culturalism and terrorism arose because as citizens in modern Britain we have actually lived through and experienced the issues the cases have raised. In every case there is a choice that judges have to make about which of the arguments placed before them they will prefer and whether the law allows them to prefer one choice over another.

Any challenge to populism must involve trying to capture a civic ideal within a public domain where citizenship rights trump market power. The public domain is a domain of trust where a restoration of trust must be its foundation in order to incorporate values of equity and citizenship. Underpinning this challenge to populism must be the rule of law, a truly independent judiciary and a disinterested non-partisan civil service.[25] These are presently under threat and this threat must be exposed and prevented from taking hold as a permanent fixture in modern Britain.

CHAPTER 1

WHAT IS POPULISM IN MODERN BRITAIN?

Fifty-two years before Boris Johnson spent the summer of 2019 in a barnstorming tour of the country during the hustings for the leadership of the Conservative Party, a group of academics from Britain, France, Italy, Poland and the United States were meeting at the London School of Economics. Their purpose was to try to define what they called 'a spectre haunting the world'. Its name was '*populismo*', '*populisme*', or '*narodnichestvo*' if you happened to speak Russian. Their discussions lasted several days and two years later a book appeared recording their debates and conclusions.[1] The scholars spotted certain features which were common to all the nations where populism had developed. Most of the features were historical. There was a phenomenon concerning apprehensions about unknown outside forces, a dislike of bankers and a history of xenophobia and anti-Semitism. There were learned discussions about the influence of Marx, Lenin, Herder and Mao-Tse Tung and special attention was paid to populism in North and South America, Russia, Eastern Europe and Africa. There was absolutely no discussion about populism in Britain. The spectre haunting the world was not present in Britain in the late 1960s.

Populism in Britain is, by world standards, a recent phenomenon and, by pure coincidence, it also started at the London School of Economics. Dr Alan Sked, a historian specialising in the Hapsburg Empire, was fearful of a federal Europe. He had played a part in the Anti-Federalist League set up to oppose the Maastricht Treaty in 1991. By 1993, a small group of dedicated followers used to meet in his room at the LSE. They included Robert Kilroy-Silk, a handsome daytime television presenter and former Labour MP; Paul Nuttall, a former footballer with Tranmere Rovers who went on to become an elected politician; and a young City of London commodity broker called Nigel Farage. It was this group that founded UKIP in 1993.

As a single-issue pressure group opposed to the European Union, UKIP made little headway until 2005, when Nigel Farage became its leader. A combination of circumstances were working in UKIP's favour. A few MPs in both main parties had been exposed in the expenses scandal which followed shortly after the financial crash of 2008. There was widespread disillusionment with politics and politicians. UKIP took off in the European elections in 2009, achieving 16 per cent of the popular vote, although this fell back to single-figure support in the 2010 general election. But Nigel Farage was not disheartened. He had spotted the trends that the mainstream politicians had failed to notice.

He had observed that there was a growing disconnection between the outlook of all the leaders of the mainstream parties and the concerns and insecurities of a very large number of ordinary voters. Political leaders were all highly educated, middle-class, socially liberal and comfortable with a culturally and ethnically diverse society. The people Farage was interested in were less educated, older, economically disadvantaged and insecure about their future. They were fearful of a cosmopolitan Britain and a globally integrated economy.[2] They were resentful of an elite who had not suffered from austerity or the financial crash and politicians were pursuing an agenda of human rights at home and global justice, in the form of international aid, abroad. The elite and ordinary folk appeared to be speaking in different languages. Farage enlarged the objectives of UKIP from being a single-issue pressure group to a movement which articulated opposition to Europe, opposed immigration, promoted a sense of national identity and expressed the views of those who were dissatisfied with the democratic process. He did this with supreme self-confidence and eye-catching publicity campaigns. 'Sod the Lot' was the slogan that UKIP billboards proclaimed in the 2010 general election. The three words were printed in large letters under photographs of the leaders of the three main parties.

His success lay in outflanking both Labour and the Conservatives simultaneously. While the Conservative theorist Tim Montgomerie was warning his party that Farage's position on human rights, gay marriage and foreign aid was taking support away from the Conservative Party,[3] Farage himself was gaining support from 'white working-class Labour voters who feel abandoned'.[4] Farage was becoming something of a phenomenon who had plenty of charisma and was able to get his message across in short, staccato-like sentences.

What was unclear was whether UKIP was really a political party in the ordinary sense of the word. UKIP could not readily be defined in conventional 'left' or 'right' terms. Farage was giving vent to a mood of disillusionment, anger and despair. He was gathering support from a section of the population, drawn from both the left and the right, who believed conventional politics were not dealing with their concerns, hopes and fears.[5] It cannot be denied, however, that Nigel Farage was, and remains, a populist.

Populism thrives when liberal democracies display features of failure. One perceptive analysis of the Farage phenomenon is entitled *National Populism: The Revolt Against Liberal Democracy*.[6] Populism must be *against* the features of the society in which it seeks to thrive. In Britain, this means being against core ingredients of the society we call a liberal democracy. A definition of populism in modern Britain must therefore entail consideration of what we mean by our liberal democracy. But first, we must understand populism.

To understand populism, we must know how populists define themselves. They see society through a prism where there are vertical divisions between the ruled and the rulers. On one side of the line is an organic entity: the people. On this side of the divide is a heartland, occupied by a virtuous people with a common heritage who are ignored by those on the other side. On this side are the ruled. The other side belongs to the rulers and is made up of a privileged gang, a usurping elite who wield a hidden power out of view from the people on the other side. There is little that the two sides have in common. If the elites are intellectual and internationalist, then the people are isolationist and anti-intellectual. The 'establishment' on one side must be challenged in a way that is 'anti-establishment'. Populists do not plan to keep the dividing wall up. Populists want to tear it down, so that the values and outlook on the one side permeate through to the other. In time there will be no wall of division and populist ideas will occupy the side with the power, the side of the rulers.[7]

Populism, at its most basic level, is the indignation of those who are resentful of change or the risks that change involve. As the philosopher A. C. Grayling has put it, populism is a claim to speak in the name of the people and to convey a shared truth.[8] Populism thrives on disappointment and promises solutions for those who feel excluded from the political process. Populism is, in a sense, a catchword to describe any new political movement which challenges entrenched values, rules and institutions and democratic orthodoxy. Populism is an insurgent anti-establishment force which attacks the legitimacy of established parties for being corrupt, elitist and detached from the ordinary voter.[9]

There is a claim for legitimacy for themselves, while denying a legitimacy for established parties. This feature of populism can be readily understood by glancing at Nigel Farage's 'Contract with the People' that was released for the 2019 general election. The Brexit Party, which Nigel Farage formed after leaving UKIP in December 2018, published a 'Contract with the People' instead of a manifesto, explaining that 'the old mainstream parties have made "manifesto" a dirty word. Everybody knows that a manifesto is little more than a set of vague promises that its authors have no intention of keeping.' The Contract stated that:

The way the political Establishment has conspired to frustrate democracy over Brexit has highlighted the need for fundamental political reform. The Brexit Party can deliver real democratic change because we are not part of the Westminster status quo. It is now time for a debate on a written constitution. We pledge to:

- Reform the voting system to make it more representative.
- Abolish the unelected House of Lords.
- Make MPs who switch parties subject to recall petitions.
- Overhaul the postal voting system to combat fraud and abuse.
- Reform the Supreme Court – judges who play a role in politics must be subject to political scrutiny. Ensure political balance by broadening participation in the Selection Commission or conduct interviews by parliamentary Committee.[10]

In these few sentences all the central beliefs of populism are expressed. The 'Westminster status quo', in Farage's view, cannot deliver democratic change as it is infected by a conspiracy to frustrate democracy itself. This 'establishment' conspiracy is aided and abetted by the judges who, Farage promises, will in future be subject to 'political scrutiny'. He wants a written constitution but does not tell us what it will contain. As a coda, Farage pledges to combat voting fraud. However, individual allegations of fraud number the few hundreds among the millions of citizens who cast their vote, and it exists occasionally and sporadically in close-knit communities. Farage became obsessed with allegations of voting fraud in the Peterborough by-election, which his party contested, and is an area which has a strong South Asian community.[11] By highlighting a statistically insignificant blemish in an otherwise properly observed system, Farage placed emphasis on something relatively unimportant to make an appeal to those who believe that close-knit communities have the ability to distort the democratic process. It is difficult not to conclude that Farage is alluding to race in this policy commitment. But, as with populist attacks on the rule of law, it is done obliquely and indirectly. Such oblique references always allow Farage to deny charges of racism.

The 2019 'Contract with the People' was unvarnished populism, encouraging people to be suspicious of 'establishment' institutions. If institutions have failed or are in disarray then it is not 'the people' who have allowed that to happen. The wall between 'the people' and 'the elites' absolve the people of all responsibility for society's ills. 'The people' have been shut out from the processes which have moulded society but, at the same time, are prevented, by democracy, from finding any remedies. This is why one of the central tenets of populism is to promote direct representation, via plebiscites and referendums, on the grounds that democracy only produces elites.

The sort of democracy favoured by populists proclaims that the will of the people is supreme and prevails over the standards set by traditional institutions which protect those who did not form the majority in the election.

For populists, the vote is the single most important thing, as it is the way that ordinary, righteous, law-abiding and undemanding people are able to participate directly in the making of law. Populists respect the result of the vote on the grounds that the vote will always be right. It is to be obeyed as the result reflects directly what the people wanted. This provides the moral argument for the will of the majority prevailing over the interests of minorities.[12]

Farage's 'Contract' demonstrates that, at its heart, populism is illiberal. Populists blame the system, not just the policies of their opponents. Recent populist utterances have stated, with complete conviction, that the media represents 'fake news', elections are 'fraudulent', political parties are 'dysfunctional', public demonstrations are 'rent-a-mob', the commissioners of the European Union are 'Brussels bureaucrats', intellectuals are 'arrogant liberals' and judges are 'enemies of the people'.[13] Making extravagant claims based on flimsy evidence is not just a preference for those on the right of politics. For Jeremy Corbyn, whose demons are 'greedy bankers', 'dodgy landlords' and the 'privileged few', populism also provides him with the language to push his message.[14] What each leader has in common is a shrillness of tone and complete confidence in the remedies they are proposing.

This sort of language, beloved by every demagogue, undermines trust and challenges the orthodoxy of the liberal democracy we value in Britain. The objections to populism are: first, it undermines trust in traditional democratic values and the role of independent institutions; and second, populist solutions are fundamentally illiberal. Populism challenges some basic tenets of liberal democracy.

Liberal democracies around the world are mostly republics with a written constitution. Britain is a constitutional monarchy with the sovereignty of Parliament at its apex, which derives its legitimacy from periodic elections. It is, however, a liberal democracy in every sense of the word. British parliamentary democracy is sustained by the rule of law embracing certain fundamental values. Features of a liberal democracy include a recognition that there are differences of opinion between different groups and classes with competing needs and aspirations. Liberal democracy seeks dialogue and an understanding that there may be differing points of view on any given subject, and it seeks consensus. Liberal democracy recognises that pure majoritarianism within a legislature cannot always protect minorities whose interests need independent courts of law and an independent judiciary to protect them. This is a political philosophy and tradition which does not believe the will of the people must be supreme. A liberal democracy exists through representative, not direct, democracy as it recognises political decisions are complex and are taken at many levels: local, national and international. A liberal democracy is constructed around liberalism itself which believes individuals are imbued with certain rights enjoyed within a society where power is separated between the legislature, the executive and the judiciary. A liberal democracy recognises there is a plurality of social divisions which must be accommodated, if possible, by consensus. Above all, a liberal democracy sustains and is sustained by the rule of law.

In a recent book, the philosopher A. C. Grayling has explained that democracy is the right of the electorate to choose its government, but a liberal democracy must also oblige those who are chosen to govern within structures, institutions, conventions and practices of the constitution. This places a particular responsibility on elected representatives, whom Grayling calls 'plenipotentiaries', to provide good government between elections.[15]

Populism has taken a hold in Britain because the bedrocks of British society – elected legislatures, independent judges and a free press – are now threatened by intolerance, mistrust, online bullying and a cacophony of noise and conspiracy theories. We cannot assume our cherished institutions will necessarily survive intact unless populism is confronted and the falsity of its doctrines exposed.

There is a very strong argument to suggest that, judging by experience of populism in other countries, we now have a populist government in Britain. One trait of populism is to centralise power around an elected charismatic leader who will attempt to draw more power to himself than is allowed by convention, ethics or law. This is often done by emasculating independent institutions, such as the civil service, or embarking on bold constitutional change to shore up power. In its most extreme form, populism will seek to recalibrate the relationship between an independent judiciary and the executive. In other words, once a populist has won power through the ballot box, the leader will seek to hold on to that power through illiberal measures.[16]

These claims to power, legitimised by the 'will of the people', must be resisted if Britain is to retain its reputation for liberal democracy. But populism cannot be defeated or resisted until we know how and why it gained ground in the first place. The origins of populism add a certain piquancy to the appreciation of Nigel Farage's ostentatious Englishness, his fondness for draught beer, cavalry twill trousers and brown brogue shoes. For populism is an international phenomenon and a strongly European one. Jean-Marie Le Pen,

former leader of the National Front in France, was already an elected member of the European Parliament and a well-known figure
throughout France before Nigel Farage sat at the feet of Dr Alan
Sked in 1993. Populism is the result of fractures on a global scale
which have affected every community in the European Union,
Britain included. Now, in a perverse way, Britain must stand alone
in any endeavours to defeat it. Standing alone to defeat a menace
which is haunting Europe is where the story starts.

THE FORCES THAT PRODUCED POPULISM

At the end of the Second World War, populism, which had
grotesquely morphed into fascism and Nazism, had been defeated
not just militarily and strategically but also ideologically. The
Italian dictator Benito Mussolini had boasted that his fascist state
represented the sovereignty of the people because the state was the
highest and most powerful form of personality which had a spiritual
and moral character of its own; the state needed to remake the
character of man, and the state required discipline and authority to
govern unopposed. This view was not only redolent of oppression
and tyranny but also inherently un-British. Fortunately, by the end
of the war Mussolini was dead and his perverse vision had been
defeated.[17] Populism had been wiped off the map of Europe and
in the Federal Republic of Germany the year 1945 was known as
'*Jahr Null*' (Year Zero) as a new constitutional court was created to
ensure Nazism could never reappear. The device for doing so was
to confer a large amount of judicial authority in the 'Basic Law for
the Federal Republic of Germany'.

The idea of the Basic Law was that there could be no democracy in
a post-war Germany without fundamental rights, and the new Basic
Law had rights enshrined in the Constitution. The root-and-branch

replacement of a constitution that permitted Hitler to be elected legitimately in 1933 with one which contained a constitutional court was part of a general distrust of unconstrained parliamentary sovereignty in Europe. This fear of absolutism was built into the DNA of post-war European politics.[18] The deliberate breaking up of the source of political power after the Second World War was a necessary reaction against the totalitarian populism of fascism.

In Britain, on the other hand, there was no fear of absolutism and no need whatsoever to start thinking anew about the Constitution. Britain had been the victor in the war and the country was content to rest on its laurels with an unwritten Constitution which had emerged gradually through custom, practice and a respect for authority. The United Kingdom was unique: it had a monarchy and a parliamentary system which was both mutual and separable. As George Orwell had observed, England had its own distinctive culture of solid breakfasts, winding roads, red pillar boxes, policeman who did not carry revolvers; the Englishman had a suspicion of foreigners and believed in the 'all-important English trait: the respect for constitutionalism and legality, the belief in "the law" as something above the State and above the individual, which … is incorruptible'.[19] This was the comfortable and dependable England which had no need for fundamental rights; Great Britain had law, whereas the tyrannies that had been defeated in the war only had power. When the Conservative politician David Maxwell Fyfe drafted the European Convention on Human Rights in 1950 to be 'a beacon to those at the moment in totalitarian darkness', he did not imagine for a moment that human rights, a 'basic law' or a constitutional court could possibly be needed in Britain.

Forty-five years later, when John Major stood on the steps of 10 Downing Street in November 1990 after becoming Conservative

Party leader and Prime Minister, he told the nation that he wanted a country which was 'at ease with itself'. But even as he spoke those words global changes were taking place which would propel populism into the arena of British politics.

In the 1980s, when John Major's career flourished under Margaret Thatcher, there was a worldwide over-capacity for steel, textiles, shipbuilding, cars and coal. A liberal consensus was confident that this problem could be fixed by international trade deals buttressed by structures. Tony Blair told the Labour Party conference in 2005 that to debate globalisation was futile, as changes in the world economic order were as inevitable as autumn following summer. Globalisation has done much good, but it has had a dreadful consequence for people in unskilled or semi-skilled jobs in settled communities, the towns and cities in England who voted Leave in the EU referendum. Blair was tacitly admitting that governments no longer had a role in protecting employment, sustaining growth and ensuring that wages grew faster than inflation. Monetarism, or neoliberalism, vaunted the consumer as king, proclaiming that it was markets, not governments, which ensured prosperity and contentment.

The obvious consequence was that the state, as a provider, should be slimmed down, but international institutions, consisting of unelected officials, appeared to be thriving. The European Union, the European Central Bank, the World Bank and the International Monetary Fund seemed to be the servants of the markets instead of being the servants of the people in a democracy. The Keynesian post-war social peace was also threatened by cultural changes. Newly created civil rights, the rise of feminism and fluid movements of a workforce between nations all appeared on the political stage around the same time. These trends were perceived by some as taking precedence over the aspirations of those trapped in communities that were overwhelmed by the pace of change. A new confident middle class, which included those bringing their skills to Britain from abroad, were taking jobs in finance, technology, medicine and communications. There was resentment that it was the middle class who appeared to be benefiting from cultural and economic change. By contrast, those communities who had lost jobs and their own self-respect were being marginalised and ignored. The country seemed to be irrevocably divided between those who had done well out of globalisation, the 'exam-passing classes', and those who had not. The losers were often the white working class who felt excluded from a conversation which was increasingly about the identity of minorities.[20]

The effect of globalisation on communities and cultural identity was likened by one leading political scientist to 'Maoism of the Right ... the permanent revolution in unfettered market processes'. This turned globalisation into an economic doctrine that was insensitive to basic human needs for community and cultural identity. If progress and contentment were to be judged only on the successes of pure free markets then it opened a 'window of political opportunity for avowed enemies of liberal civilisation'.[21] An American commentator predicted in 1994 that this window of opportunity could be occupied by fascists. Edward Luttwak observed that globalisation allowed any production to expand anywhere, far beyond the limits of domestic markets. This meant that the workforce in any nation state could be replaced more cheaply somewhere else in the world. In Britain, many working lives were displaced in this way and a new political challenge presented itself. How do you deal with personal economic insecurity? It was a new problem as the people affected were not especially poor, dependent on benefits and were not political activists interested in redistribution. They simply wanted some security in the jobs they already had. 'This is the space that remains wide open for a product-improved Fascist party dedicated to the enhancement of the broad masses of (mainly) white-collar working people.'[22]

State institutions which were there to translate the electorate's views into public policy and act as a brake to extremism had been complicit in the failures of globalisation. John Major's mission to be Prime Minister of a nation 'at ease with itself' was doomed to failure from the outset. A nation at ease with itself is one where there is trust in a political process. Trust allows institutions to deliver values that are shared by the population as a whole. This was the society that Orwell was describing in the late 1940s, but when society becomes fractured, trust, the structural cement sustaining peaceful cooperation, collapses. Change is perceived as a threat, and the economic progress of some at the expense of the many is resented.

The political tradition in Britain is for politicians in both major parties to enjoy trust and to face challenges without breaking the rules. But this culture of liberal democracy has involved many stresses. Sticking to the rules means politicians must confront the fears and insecurities of the citizenry with honesty. Solutions must be achieved by respecting the rule of law. Political choices must accommodate the rights of minorities and be framed within a rules-based world order. Neither of the competing liberal ideologies will pretend to possess 'canonical truths'; instead, each will proceed on the basis of trial and error. Periodic elections will ensure that the failures of one competing ideology can be replaced by another through representative democracy.[23]

In Britain, there has never been a period of one-party rule in the sense that rule is exclusive to one party. The sort of democracy we have preferred is one that involves debate, compromise, discussion and a rationality in decision-making. Even in the Labour landslide in 1945 there was a considerable Conservative presence in the House of Commons, and when Margaret Thatcher commanded all she surveyed after the 1983 general election, in which Labour lost badly, Labour still had 217 MPs. A liberal democracy acknowledges that there are divisions within society and the people do not, and cannot, speak with one voice. Traditionally, political parties competing for power have accepted the need to defend constitutionalism, uphold the rule of law and protect minority rights. There has always been an unspoken acceptance of the ground rules.

This liberal democracy consists of two elements: the first is the democratic element, which are the institutions that translate popular expressed views through democratic elections into public policy. This element is the government and the civil service. The second element is the liberal element, the institutions that protect the rule of law and guarantee the basic rights of citizens. These are Parliament and the judiciary. Underpinning both elements should be a vibrant civil society which has faith and trust in the process of representative democracy. A vibrant civil society is governed by periodic elections and by putting faith in the institutions which give expression to the views of the electorate.[24]

If this cohesive and mostly prosperous civil society satisfies the ambitions of most of the citizenry then, generally, the institutional bedrock of that society will not be challenged. One of the reasons why populism is gaining ground is that the 'arrogant liberals' have not responded quickly enough to the global forces which threaten the living standards of many. If, at the same time, the 'establishment' has been asleep on the job when it comes to defending important constitutional arrangements, then the mood is right for the jibes and insults of the populists.

There is more than a grain of truth in the assertion made by Anthony Pagden that the conclusions of the Enlightenment are 'accepted by most intelligent people in the West'.[25] But that is precisely the problem. For populists, the 'intelligent' people are the elite who do not understand the common culture. There is little doubt that the elites in Britain do embrace Enlightenment values. It is also true that elements of the 'enlightened' establishment in Parliament, the City and the civil service supported Remain in the referendum. Was the referendum result, therefore, a victory for populism, or was it merely a difference of opinion among sections of the population about Britain's future trading relations with Europe?

Nigel Farage appeared to see the EU referendum as a pivotal and important moment. At the start of the campaign in 2016 he said, 'It is the establishment, it is the wealthy, it is the multinationals, it is the big banks, it is those whose lives have done really well in the last few years who are supporting remaining and against it is the people.' Ten days into the campaign he said, 'This is our chance to get back at a political class that has given away everything this nation has ever fought for and everything we want to hand on to our children and grandchildren.'[26]

In the unfolding events after the referendum result, it became clear that the decision by the British people to leave the EU was every bit as pivotal as Farage had predicted. He had wanted the referendum to be the opportunity for the people to get their own back at a political class that had ruled over them for so long. Farage had been banging away at the vertical wall which separated the people on one side from the political elites on the other for years. Now the cracks in the wall were becoming large enough for the people to cross over to the other side. The referendum result was not just a decision about the nation's trading arrangements, free movement of people and the authority of the European Court of Justice. It was a decision that smashed open the edifice of Britain's entire constitutional structure. First to fall was a front-ranking elitist, David Cameron, the Prime Minister. Next in line was the clash between the will of the executive and the supremacy of Parliament. Third in line was the demeaning of the judges by the tabloid press and a coterie of politicians in Parliament. Finally, heads rolled when twenty-one Conservative MPs had the whip withdrawn and their careers cut short. Many of them left public life for good.

Some will say that Farage's remarks should not be taken literally. There is not really a dividing wall between the 'people' and the 'elites'. That is a crude simplification and all Farage was doing was speaking for effect. But speaking for effect and saying things you do not really mean is one of populism's most corrosive tactics. By breaking conventional norms of political dialogue, populists attract condemnation from the political establishment. Populists thrive on condemnation, however, as it reinforces the idea that they really do want a break from the status quo. There is a performative aspect to populism wherein the performance is more important than the content.[27] When Boris Johnson was Foreign Secretary, he also had a column in the *Daily Telegraph*. In September 2017, he suggested in the newspaper that the United Kingdom should not pay the EU any money for leaving the single market. This was not government policy and his column had undermined Theresa May's negotiation tactics. Instead of sacking her Foreign Secretary, May reacted by saying that it was just 'Boris being Boris'. This is a revealing remark. Boris the serious Foreign Secretary was putting on a performance of being Boris the journalist who wrote a popular newspaper column. Breaking the rules, making exaggerated claims and committing gaffes is part of the appeal of such politicians. It draws attention to themselves.

If you make a gaffe, or weave a lie into your narrative, then it does not really matter. You are attracting attention and making a point in the way in which you choose to make it, regardless of whether it is true. When the *Daily Express* splashed a banner headline at the start of the referendum campaign which read: 'Major leak from Brussels reveals NHS will be "KILLED OFF" if Britain remains in the EU', it was a total lie, but nobody cared very much. It was part of the populist method.[28]

The language that populists use is important. It is capable of stoking anxiety and corroding trust and at populism's heart is the appeal to emotion, not to facts. When the businessman Arron Banks, who is reputed to have donated £8.4 million to the organisation Leave.EU in the 2016 referendum campaign, was asked why his side had won, his answer was: 'The Remain campaign featured fact, fact, fact, fact. It just doesn't work. You have got to connect with people emotionally.'[29] Banks made a serious and important point. Our digital culture is full of rumour, fantasy, guesswork, fake news and conjecture, which crowds out the space of cool, objective assessments. This makes it more difficult for facts to dominate a political debate. Before populism took hold, a veneration of facts had once been so strong that fact-checking was a necessity for any journalist writing a story. Populist culture has changed this. Instead of a reverence being accorded to facts and a respect given to institutions that thrive upon them, there is a scepticism about facts and a reverence given to mantra. 'Brexit Means Brexit', 'Take Back Control', 'Get Brexit Done' and 'Oven-Ready Deal' are chants expressing loyalty to a belief, not statements that bear any relation to fact. Yet it is the mantra which has become the received fact. The mantra is the space between politics and media where political statements become a ritualised performance, played over and over again in the media and online.

These cultural changes which are taking over from Enlightenment values convert age-old institutions such as the print media, the civil service, the diplomatic corps and the courtrooms of law into bodies of suspicion that may not be trusted. By contrast, the mantra and performance of the populist must be trusted because it is a trust which comes from the people.

The two bedrocks of Enlightenment culture, facts and truth, sit uneasily on the shoulders of populists. In the United States the populist rhetoric of President Trump represents a trend where there is increasing disagreement about what a 'fact' actually is. One academic institution in America has found it necessary to write a study devoted to *Truth Decay*.[30] The conclusions are that the declining status of truth arises largely from the volume of information on the internet, which permits a person to choose his or her facts in order to bolster a preconceived opinion. These are the developments which are capable of persuading people that mantras are facts. This is dangerous. When there is a continuing refrain that the people are being short-changed by remote elites, then the people are deemed to speak with one voice. This message drowns out the natural tensions and clashes of beliefs and values, which are essential to a mature democracy upheld by law. A mantra has connotations which do not admit of dissent. There is a crude majoritarianism about populism which puts pressure on individual rights.

Populism is beguiling because it promotes the idea that elites and existing institutions have been responsible for the instabilities in society. If only we could hark back to a time when conformity shrouded tensions, all would be well. In a recent book, *Cultural Backlash*, two American scholars have observed that populist concerns about security over instability increase fears about immigration and terrorism; the populist desire to preserve conventional traditions and ways of life enhances conformity; and the charisma of populist strong leadership encourages obedience to authority.[31] Populism therefore stokes anxiety, corrodes mutual tolerance and poisons the reservoir of social trust. The depressing conclusion is that liberal values which underpin the rule of law are threatened by populism.

When all the political, social and cultural features of populism are put together, it does appear that Farage really did intend for the referendum to be a pivotal moment. He wanted the result to be interpreted as a victory for the people and a defeat for the norms and customs of our Constitution. While Farage has never said so directly, he intended the referendum to be a test of how durable the elements of Britain's unwritten constitution actually were. We must remind ourselves of what Farage was challenging.

WHY TRUST IN LAW MATTERS

Since the constitutional settlement in the late seventeenth century, in the United Kingdom it has become a way of life that a representative Parliament makes our laws and the judges in the courts protect individual rights. The rule of law exists to subordinate naked power and promote civil order. It is the central legitimating feature of organised public life and a supreme constitutional principle.[32] Mr. Farage has never directly attacked the rule of law or Britain's fundamental constitutional principles. Populists do not challenge the essential meaning that is contained in the words 'rule of law'. Populists take aim at the tenets, norms, precedents and assumptions implicit in the words 'rule of law'. The constitutional theorist Geoffrey Marshall has pointed out that it is only an undisputed convention that Parliament in the United Kingdom will not use its undoubted power in an oppressive or tyrannical way.[33] Populists are capable of disputing this convention. More fundamentally, within the common law of England and Wales (and, separately, Scotland) the rule of law means that each individual before the courts has equal value. Both law and democracy value everyone equally even if the majority does not.[34] The rule of law means that the will of the majority cannot prevail if it is inconsistent with the equal rights of minorities.[35] For the past forty years it has become accepted by nations that call themselves liberal democracies that the rule of law demands standards of pluralism, tolerance and broad-mindedness. These are the standards applied by judges when deciding the cases coming before them.[36]

When populists take aim at pluralism, tolerance and broad-mindedness, they necessarily undermine the rule of law and the judiciary which upholds it. The independence of judges is a fundamental component of our liberal democracy. Judges applying the law provide a brake or a restraint on the exercise of power by the ruling executive. This, if you like, is the procedural importance of the rule of law in a democracy, but the law also contains a substantive element comprising values, equal treatment, protection of minorities and tolerance. The rule of law made by judges has been likened to an exercise over time where several authors take it in turns to write chapters in a book. Chapters in the past are taken forward by others in the future. The rule of law has two aspects: the formal aspect, which is a set of rules, or rule *by* law coupled with sanctions if the law is not obeyed; and a substantive aspect, a set of laws that allow an individual to live in dignity and enjoy personal liberty.[37]

Everyone can understand the rule of law in its formal sense. It is the rule that prohibits conduct which is criminal; enables commerce to flourish; punishes wrongdoers; provides remedies if the law is misused; and protects society from harm. Law in its substantive sense is more difficult to explain. Substantive law is law in its relationship with society; the 'normative umbrella' under which the law operates. This expression was coined by an Israeli judge, Chief Justice Aharon Barak, who was President of the Israel Supreme Court between 1995 and 2006, but it applies equally to all nations calling themselves liberal democracies. The law must exist under that umbrella so that the values of tolerance for the beliefs of others are preserved but also tolerance for intolerance can flourish. The normative umbrella gives the law a tool for balancing and recognising social goals when they are in conflict. It also expects that good faith will inform the decision of any judge who has to balance the needs of the individual with those of society. The normative umbrella provides the context for reasonableness, using impartial, objective reason to decide cases.

The substantive values the law provides to judges when deciding individual cases are a bedrock of liberal democracies, but they are inconsistent with a democracy that takes its instructions from the people. In these democracies the priorities of the majority should always prevail even if they conflict with those in the minority. Such democracies have been called 'hierarchical democracies', as they allow popularly elected leaders to enact the will of the people as they interpret it, without having to make allowances for the rights and interests of obstinate minorities. What sets these democracies apart from traditional liberal democracies is a lack of respect for individual rights and independent institutions.[38]

There is, therefore, a fundamental feature about the rule of law which is in conflict with populism. Populists have come to resent and fear the power of the rule of law within our liberal democracy. Populist rhetoric silences the values of tolerance and broad-mindedness and raises the volume on the challenge law poses to their own political authority. This is not always obvious, as the distinction between liberal and illiberal or hierarchical democracies is often a narrow one. Populists have seized upon a trend which has been evident for nearly twenty years that allows politicians to criticise the motivations, impartiality and intelligence of judges with impunity. These attacks have gone far beyond acceptable discourse which should exist in a liberal democracy. Judges, like everybody else, are not perfect and mistakes are sometimes made. But all decisions by judges which involve points of law may be appealed. Most of the obvious mistakes by individual judges can be corrected on appeal but there remains a void of misunderstanding and confusion about the role of judges in upholding the rule of law. In Britain, the reliance on norms and customs for applying constitutional law and respecting the separation of powers makes our country vulnerable to damaging comments by politicians.

An example of such a misunderstanding occurred in the United Kingdom in 2002 when the government tried to reduce the number of claims for income support made by asylum seekers on or after their arrival in Britain. Parliament passed legislation permitting the Home Secretary's officials to refuse income support for an asylum seeker if the official was not satisfied that the claim for asylum was made as soon as practicable after the person's arrival in the United Kingdom. Parliament had in mind the scenario of an illegal entrant to the country who had the means to support themselves claiming income support much later on, or a person not seeking support because they were not a genuine asylum seeker in the first place. When a High Court judge ruled that the procedures adopted by the Home Secretary's officials for implementing Parliament's intentions were unfair, the Home Secretary David Blunkett said that there was widespread abuse of the system and all he was trying to do was reduce unfounded claims. He went on: 'Frankly, I'm personally fed up with having to deal with a situation where Parliament debates issues and the judges then overturn them.' He announced his intention of appealing the decision.[39] A week later, before his appeal (which was eventually unsuccessful) had been heard, he wrote an article for the *News of the World* declaiming, 'It's time for judges to learn their place.'[40] Here, Blunkett combined misunderstanding with populist mis-statement. The judge was not overturning the debate in Parliament, nor was he stepping beyond his judicial role to engage in the merits of Parliament's intentions. The judge made a ruling on the fairness of the procedure adopted by officials for refusing a claim for income support on the facts of the case put before him; he was not overturning Parliament.

The rule of law means the law applies equally to everybody and public powers must be exercised fairly and in good faith. The judge had been faced with a real case of an individual who claimed not to have been treated equally by an executive official who had not exercised public powers in good faith. The rule of law exists in the real world of people's lives, not in abstract theory. The Court of Appeal upheld the judge's ruling on the grounds that the official deciding the claim had not treated the applicant fairly. The implementation of government policy, decided by Parliament, requires a corps of officials, usually executive officers within the civil service, to give effect to Parliament's intentions. In the field of immigration and asylum where there are potentially a huge number of cases to be processed and considered, the executive officers need guidance as to the considerations they should take into account before reaching a decision. There is a rule of law that where Parliament confers an administrative power to officials there is a presumption that the power will be exercised fairly, in the context and circumstances of the particular facts. All that had occurred in this case was that the process adopted by the officials to refuse this applicant's claim had not been fair.[41]

By commenting so publicly in a case where David Blunkett's own appeal was pending, the Home Secretary was treading on dangerous ground. The foundation of judicial independence depends on the existence of legal arrangements that guarantee it, arrangements that are achieved in practice by public confidence in the judiciary.[42] Blunkett, as Home Secretary, was part of the arrangements that guarantee judicial independence. As a prominent politician who was often interviewed in the media, he should have been a guarantor of judicial independence. By choosing to comment that the judiciary had 'overturned' Parliament on a subject as sensitive as immigration he was undermining, not upholding, the rule of law.

A similar personal attack by a Home Secretary on the integrity of an individual judge occurred three years later when Dr John Reid was Home Secretary. A Senior Circuit judge, John Griffith Williams, had passed a life sentence on a paedophile and specified that he could not be considered for release until the Parole Board had decided that he was no longer a risk to the public. In accordance with a formula contained in an Act of Parliament the judge specified that the Parole Board could not consider the defendant's case until he had served a period of five years and 108 days in prison. The *Daily Express* excoriated the judge in pure populist language, describing him as 'deluded, out-of-touch and frankly deranged ... combining arrogance with downright wickedness' and adding that the legal system had lost touch with public opinion.[43] This extravagant language from a newspaper might have been shrugged off, but on this occasion Dr Reid had stated publicly that the sentence was unduly lenient and did not reflect the seriousness of the crime. There was, in law, a safety valve for the venting of public opinion if an individual judge was deranged or completely wrong. The Attorney General could take the case to the Court of Appeal on the grounds that the sentence was unduly lenient. The Attorney General did not refer this case to the Appeal Court with a view to the sentence being increased. The sentencing judge had done precisely what Parliament had stipulated that he should do in the case of a serious sexual offender.

Senior politicians, with an eye to public opinion, have also attacked the judiciary in general, without giving any examples and making it much more difficult for there to be a response from the Lord Chancellor, whose job it is (or should be) to defend the independence of the judiciary. In October 2013, when moving the second reading of her Immigration Bill, the Home Secretary Theresa May said:

> Some judges have still chosen to ignore the will of Parliament and go on putting the law on the side of foreign criminals instead of the public. I am sending a very clear message to those judges: Parliament wants a law on the people's side, the public want a law on the people's side, and this Government will put the law on the people's side once and for all. This Bill will require the courts to put the public interest at the heart of their decisions.[44]

Here, the Home Secretary appears to believe that the rule of law is like some piece of modelling clay, which can be moulded into any desired shape by people who call themselves judges who are biased in favour of criminals; they should be proper democrats and follow the will of Parliament. Mrs May was making a populist generalisation, and, as with all populist generalisations, the accusation is vague, unspecific and garnished with the spittle of prejudice. It is impossible to engage in a reasonable debate at this level because the facts are not established. What was the case? Who were the judges? What will of Parliament was ignored? What law was it that permitted judges to put it on the side of 'foreign' criminals? What, anyway, is 'the people's side'? Populists speak in generalisations because it provides them with a shield against contradiction; judges have to make findings that are carefully grounded in specific facts, justified point by point in a judgment which can be challenged point by point on appeal.

The references to 'the people' by Mrs May as a generic all-embracing term of art is a populist tactic and, inferentially, it becomes a word to convey an exclusion of minorities. The essence of the populist appeal is an appeal to people to restore their sense of belonging, the bonds of loyalty and community that had existed in a past time. It is therefore a way of thinking about politics; a style rather than an ideology.

CONCLUSION

Little by little politicians have altered the tenor of political dialogue. The use of populist language by senior politicians in power had begun in the mid-1990s. Populism rejects a cultural tradition that feelings and emotion cannot speak for themselves on the grounds that emotion can lead the human brain astray. There is a tradition in European and British culture that emotions must be checked empirically to ensure that they are factually sound on the premise that desires and feelings may produce hasty but wrong results. This tradition has contributed to the existence of elites, who are so despised by populists. Elites are supposed to use language neutrally and to base their decisions only on facts. Elites, such as the impartial civil servant or judge, must keep emotion at bay. As the sociologist

William Davies has commented, 'The special status granted to judges, civil servants and scientists is viewed as illegitimate.'[45]

This observation should ring alarm bells in the minds of all who fear the rise of populism. Diplomats, the civil service and the judiciary are parts of the fabric of any functioning nation state. Ambassadors and permanent secretaries provide continuity in the nation's affairs by giving impartial advice. This is essential for a functioning liberal democracy. The importance of an impartial civil service to the functioning of a liberal democracy cannot be over-stated. It provides the ballast in our constitutional arrangements and balance and permanence when, in politics, there is often volatility.[46] Populism threatens this principle, as the following example amply demonstrates.

In July 2019, a prominent public servant, Sir Kim Darroch, resigned his post as United Kingdom ambassador to the United States. He had been hounded from office by populism. The situation which forced him to resign began in 2016 when President Trump tweeted that Nigel Farage should replace Sir Kim as UK ambassador. Naturally, there was no vacancy and Theresa May, who was Prime Minister at the time, made this clear. Unfortunately, Sir Kim's confidential cables to the British government about Anglo-American relations were leaked to the press. The British ambassador had been uncomplimentary about Trump, describing him as 'inept' and 'insecure'.[47] After the leak, Nigel Farage condemned Sir Kim as being unsuitable to be ambassador. President Trump then issued, effectively, an ultimatum, stating that while the UK ambassador remained in post his administration would not deal with him.

These events occurred during the Conservative Party leader-ship campaign and Boris Johnson refused to say whether Sir Kim would remain in the post if he became Prime Minister.[48] Johnson's silence prompted three former Cabinet Secretaries to point out that civil servants who gave robust, impartial advice were essential to dependable public service and in return such servants should be accorded respect by elected politicians.[49] A former head of the Foreign Office, Lord Ricketts, said that Sir Kim had been taken out by an act of 'political sabotage'.[50]

Johnson's failure to support a public servant of distinction was in sharp contrast to his public endorsement of his special adviser, Dominic Cummings, during the coronavirus pandemic in the spring and early summer of 2020. In late March and early April 2020, drastic measures were needed to control the spread of a disease that was killing British citizens in their thousands and threatening to overwhelm the ability of hospitals to treat patients with the virus. The message was clear: 'Stay at Home, Protect the NHS and Save Lives'. In late March 2020, Boris Johnson sent a letter to every household: 'We are giving one simple instruction. You must stay at home.' This instruction was repeated over and over again on television by the Prime Minister and other senior ministers, some of whom, Johnson included, had actually succumbed to the disease. The government had introduced emergency powers which included a legal regulation that no person may leave the place where they are living without reasonable excuse. At the height of the pandemic, when the entire country was in self-imposed lockdown and shops, businesses and schools were closed, Cummings left his London house with his wife and child and made a 260-mile journey to Durham to take up residence at his parents' farm. At the time, he believed both he and his wife might have contracted the virus. During his stay, after recovering from the effects of the virus, he made a sixty-mile round-trip car journey with his wife and child to a beauty spot. These activities had been discovered purely by chance when a member of the public spotted him walking with his family at the location. The Prime Minister had not been told that his special adviser had left his London home in what was, in the opinion of almost the entire press, many Members of Parliament and a majority of the public, a clear breach of government instructions and the law of the land.

Plainly, the Prime Minister had to act. The public were indignant. While they had obeyed government guidance and stayed at home, sacrificing time with grandchildren, friends and loved ones, a privileged member of Johnson's inner circle had, it seemed, ignored the very guidance that Downing Street insisted applied to everybody. Calls for Cummings to resign or be sacked filled the inboxes of Conservative MPs. Yet, unlike his attitude towards Sir Kim Darroch, whose only offence was to give a candid assessment of the abilities and character of President Trump, Johnson stoutly defended his personal chief adviser. Speaking on television, Johnson read from a prepared text: Dominic Cummings, he said, had acted 'responsibly, legally and with integrity'. His words provided Cummings with his survival kit. Without them he would have either broken the law he, himself, had helped to write or he would have broken the civil service code to which he was bound. He would have had to resign or be sacked.

The nation was dumbfounded. Cummings appeared to have no excuse for his behaviour, let alone a reasonable one. Like Darroch, Cummings was a public servant, paid by the taxpayer. In Cummings's case, he was subject to the code of conduct applicable to civil servants, with the exception of political impartiality. As a political adviser, Cummings was employed to offer political advice, but in other respects he was bound by the high standards applicable to all civil servants.

There is a delightful irony about the Cummings affair and the Prime Minister's response to it. Covid-19 is a highly contagious virus, easily transmitted from person to person and is liable to kill anyone infected by it. The only way to keep the disease at bay is for the population as a whole to 'take control' of the situation and self-isolate. The exercise of people power at such a time of emergency necessarily involves community solidarity and the exercise of individual responsibility where the privileges of the elite are irrelevant. Everybody must act together, irrespective of status. The people were in control of the pandemic by obeying government instructions. Yet, it was Cummings, who has expressed a contempt for the 'hollow men' of the civil service elite, who acted as if he were in a privileged class.[51] It was Cummings who had coined the phrase 'Take Back Control' in a populist appeal to voters in the 2016 referendum. It was Cummings who broke the spirit, if not the letter, of his own government's guidance and it was Cummings who steadfastly refused to apologise or offer his resignation afterwards. One informed commentator has said that Cummings is a man who has contempt for conventional rules of political engagement and the 'petty codes that apply to other people'.[52]

Contrasting the way in which Johnson dealt with an ambassador to the United States and his personal political adviser within Downing Street is symptomatic of a wider malaise. In Johnson's mind, it was more important to protect at almost any cost a personal adviser who was helping him shore up power in Downing Street than it was to preserve the career of a distinguished diplomat abroad.[53]

From across the Atlantic, two American academics have observed with sadness that Britain is discarding its traditional consensus of entrenched political norms and the rule of law through an independent judiciary, professionalism in the public sector and stable majority governments counterbalanced by the protection of minority rights.[54] Britain's traditional pragmatism of tolerance, democracy and decency are being cast aside. It should have come as no surprise that in November 2019 Boris Johnson felt able to announce that his party would now look at the relationship between the government, Parliament and the courts.[55]

By openly calling into question the legal arrangements which guarantee our precious liberties, Johnson was revealing his populist political instincts. There is an eerie confidence about a politician who can say that he no longer has respect for entrenched political norms. Johnson's behaviour during the Darroch controversy and his reaction to the Supreme Court ruling in September 2019 about his unlawful prorogation of Parliament give clues to the populist direction in which he is taking his government. The prorogation decision will be discussed fully in Chapter 4.

Populists feel that they have a mandate to ignore old values and reign in those centres of power beyond the echo chamber of their mantras and rhetoric. This is beginning to happen in the plans that Johnson's adviser, Dominic Cummings, has for the reform of the civil service. Populism is arriving within the corridors of power of the United Kingdom and we need to understand what, if anything, we can do to stop it.

CHAPTER 2

THE NOT SO GOOD OLD DAYS: POWER, THE POLICE AND THE LAW

W hen we say there must be public confidence in the adminis- tration of justice and trust in the existence of impartial and incorruptible judges, we should be stating the obvious. However, on closer examination this statement is not quite as obvious as it first might seem. Trust in the administration of justice breaks down if those administering it appear to be too powerful and are exceed- ing the boundaries of impartiality we have come to expect of them. Power and trust therefore go together. This is particularly impor- tant in the case of powers we entrust to the police.

This chapter concentrates on trust in the police, which is essential if their work is to command public respect. We trust in return for somebody else being trustworthy; having confidence in our trust being borne out. By definition we cannot put our trust in the un- known, only faith or belief.[1] 'Trust is an attachment to a person, body of persons or institution, based on the well-founded but not certain expectation that they will act for my good, or the expectation, based on good but less than perfect evidence, that events will turn out in a way not harmful to me.'[2] There is an element of risk in placing trust in somebody, but usually by taking the risk we have weighed up the pros and cons of doing so. Our expectations should be well-founded or evidence-based. Trust is confidence in one's expectations.[3]

When it comes to trust in the police, some lessons from history are revealing. In the past we tended to have an idealised vision of our police force. They were deemed to be conscientious, self-controlled and classless. They could rise from the position of a humble constable to superintendent by dint of devotion to duty, exhibiting 'impartial solemnity and clockwork regularity'.[4] These are the visible police, the kind of constable who helps your daughter across the road to school, the sympathetic detective who visits your home after a burglary or the brave traffic officers who help the injured after a road accident. The invisible police used to be those who work inside police stations, interrogating suspects.

Until 1985 the only people who ever set foot inside a police station were the police themselves or the villains who were arrested and brought there. Once a suspect had been arrested, the police were largely masters in their own house when it came to interrogation and questioning. Often convictions were obtained in criminal trials because a suspect had provided a full confession to the crime they were alleged to have committed. However, the process of obtaining this confession, the interview under caution, was done entirely in secret and based on trust. The police were a trusted part of the community. Judges, lawyers and the public generally placed trust in the police not to invent a confession or extract one by using disreputable behaviour.

Yet, there was a certain contradiction in this faith in integrity. The wise and learned judge Lord Devlin, who wrote copiously about the criminal process, frankly acknowledged that, in the privacy of the police station, the police had a 'tendency to press interrogation too hard against a man they believed to be guilty'.[5] Devlin defended these methods on utilitarian grounds as the police would often know that the suspect had similar previous convictions to the offence under investigation and, as a result, would be less fair and compassionate than they should be in the interrogation process. If the police were constantly confronted by 'pestilential crime' then the results obtained by interrogation generally benefited society.[6]

The legal establishment was far too easily persuaded that this utilitarian argument should prevail at all costs. This trust, sadly, often betrayed those who were charged and brought to trial. This was the misplaced trust by lawyers and judges in the process of criminal justice which, in their view, must not be allowed to fail. There was an assumption that if such a system had survived the tests of time, it could not fail. If it could not fail, it could not be seen to fail. The alternative was that the whole edifice on which criminal justice rested would start to collapse and this could not be allowed to happen. Nearly all the cases described in this chapter were subjected to scrutiny by independent panels and, with the exception of two, no faults were found in the justice system which required any changes or improvements.

Devlin's utilitarian argument might be justified if the suspect from which the confession was extracted was indeed guilty of the offence under investigation. The real-life stories in this chapter are chosen because they demonstrate another form of trust: the trust by the legal establishment in a system which betrayed those who were charged and brought to trial. Until the early 1980s the whole process of criminal justice was immune to any criticism from within and the incorruptible judges themselves could not be criticised. When, after his death, Lord Goddard's unfair and biased handling of the Derek Bentley case, which is discussed later, was commented upon, there was uproar within the legal establishment.

This chapter highlights the necessity of having in place clear legal rules to govern the investigation of crime and the questioning of suspects and for the rule of law to replace unregulated trust. The intervention of law into police conduct was not achieved until the Police and Criminal Evidence Act 1984 came into force. Later, spurred on by the judiciary, the Criminal Procedure and Investigations Act 1996 set down the need for consistent rules of disclosure of material which might assist the defence of a suspect. There was a realisation by senior judges and politicians that the rule of law should replace internal rules and regulations, custom and practice. This change of direction involved courage and foresight and was a sharp reminder of the central place of the rule of law in the life of the nation.

It is necessary to understand how this evolution happened; how our society changed from the time when the police represented the law to the new era when the police could only function under the rule of law. We need to know this to appreciate the full nature of the threat to the rule of law today. The change occurred only because the judiciary came clean and apologised publicly for how bad ingrained practices had become and politicians ensured that change happened. Roy Jenkins, Merlyn Rees, Douglas Hurd and William Whitelaw were Home Secretaries of a different hew from David Blunkett, Michael Howard, John Reid and Theresa May. However, their differences were not based on the party-political spectrum; their differences were between those who stuck fast to liberalism and those who veered towards populism.

THE CASES OF EVANS AND CHRISTIE

One of the themes of this book which will be developed in later chapters is that those Home Secretaries who were not liberal have wanted to follow and reflect public opinion, whereas those who were liberal have been ahead of it. The stories in this chapter, which begin in 1950, only reached their conclusion many years later when uncorrected miscarriages of justice were finally put right. The story of how they were put right illustrates how important it is for the legal establishment not to be a slave either to public opinion or to a culture of complacency within the executive. The real-life events which led to the rule of law being given a central place in the investigation of crime begin with the case of Timothy Evans and John Christie.

John Reginald Christie was convicted and sentenced to death for the murder of his wife, Ethel, in March 1953, but he was, in reality, a mass-murderer. He had strangled an Austrian munitions worker in 1943 and gassed another woman to death in 1944. He buried their bodies in the garden of 10 Rillington Place in the Bayswater district of London, premises he shared with Timothy and Beryl Evans, a young couple who had a daughter, Geraldine. After killing his wife and three further women in late 1952 and early 1953, he roamed around London as a vagrant before he was arrested. The macabre and sickening details of Christie's crimes during the trial at the Old Bailey, which held the nation in thrall, revealed he had confessed to the police that he had also strangled and gassed Beryl Evans in 1949. Her body had been placed in the disused washhouse in the garden of Rillington Place. Around the same time, he strangled Geraldine with a tie and her body was placed next to her mother's, concealed behind some timbers in the washhouse. Three years before these gruesome facts came to light, Evans had stood trial in the same courtroom as Christie and had been convicted of Geraldine's murder. The only reason that he was convicted of this murder was because the Crown argued that Evans had killed his own wife. It followed, said the Crown, that whoever had killed Beryl had also murdered her daughter, and that person was Timothy Evans. It was

Beryl's second pregnancy that set in train the terrible sequence of events that put Timothy Evans in the dock in January 1950.

Beryl had told her neighbour Christie that she had become pregnant and that she wanted an abortion. As Christie later confessed, he invited Beryl to his flat after telling her that he could abort the foetus and then gassed and strangled her. When Evans came home, he told him, 'It's bad news. It didn't work.' There then remained the problem of disposing of Beryl's body. Evans helped Christie carry his wife's corpse downstairs but then, in shock and panic, and on Christie's advice, he left London for Merthyr Tydfil in Wales, to his family home. Christie had said he could find foster parents for his young child, Geraldine. When Evans left, Christie put the bodies of Beryl and Geraldine in the disused washhouse in the garden at 10 Rillington Place. Unknown to Christie, Evans surrendered himself to Merthyr Tydfil Police Station and, in a bizarre lie, confessed to putting Beryl's body in a drain outside Rillington Place. This was later revealed as being untrue as it took three police officers to remove the manhole cover and there was no body in the drain. When confronted with this falsehood, Evans's response was: 'I said it to protect a man called Christie.' He then said he was willing to put his account in writing and dictated his version of events about being told about the failed abortion. Evans was illiterate and could not write the statement for himself. The statement had to be taken twice; in the first instance he created a lie about obtaining abortion tablets himself, but this was then corrected.[7]

Meanwhile, back in Rillington Place, the bodies of Beryl and Geraldine were found by the police. Christie had to give an explanation, given his ground-floor flat was immediately next to the washhouse. Christie's account, which the police found entirely plausible, was this: he and his wife had heard a very loud thud coming from upstairs in the middle of the night, followed by the sound of movement. Christie then said he never saw Beryl and Geraldine again after this point but added that when Evans returned from work the next day, Evans said that Beryl and Geraldine had gone away to Bristol for a holiday. Christie adamantly denied being an abortionist and instead turned the tables on Evans, describing him as a liar and, to boot, somebody who beat his wife. There was a grain of truth in this. Evans had lied to the police at Merthyr Tydfil and there were undoubtedly some incidents of marital strife in the Evanses' relationship.

From this moment on, the minds of the investigators were made up. Christie, a First World War veteran and former volunteer special constable, was a reliable witness, and the illiterate heavy drinker and fantasist in custody in Merthyr Tydfil was not. The Notting Hill police immediately arranged for Evans to be brought from Wales to London for questioning. Within a few minutes of his arrival at Notting Hill Police Station, Evans had made a full confession to murdering both his wife and his daughter.

This confession, which sent Evans to the gallows, was suspicious. On his arrival at the police station he was taken straight into the charge room, where he was confronted with two piles of clothing. On top of Beryl's pile of clothes were the blanket, tablecloth and cord in which her body had been parcelled up, and on top of Geraldine's clothes was the tie, still knotted, which had been used to strangle her. Although obviously stunned by the sight of the clothing and the realisation that his daughter was dead, Evans then made an unprompted and spontaneous confession, which began with the words: 'She was incurring one debt after another and I could not stand it any longer, so I strangled her with a piece of rope and took her down to the flat below [which was empty] the same

39

night.' This was language redolent of police-speak, not of an illiterate and frightened suspect. He went on to say that two days later he used his own tie to throttle his daughter to death, whereupon he put her infant body next to her mother behind the timbers in the washhouse. Evans made a second, much longer statement in which he explained, no doubt to the satisfaction of the police, why he happened to have a rope in his flat with which to strangle his wife: 'I had brought it up from the van and it was on the chair.' There was something rather unreal in both the circumstances of the confession itself and the fact that Evans was apparently content to divulge his own guilt without any prompting by the police. Evans's version of events, given at his trial, was that he was interrogated for so long and with such intensity that he feared he would be beaten up if he did not confess.

It is now understood how and why false confessions can be made: the suspect may be a fantasist; there may be coerced compliance, where the stress of confinement induces the suspect to say things to bring police questioning to an end; or there may come a time, after intense interrogation, that the suspect comes to believe, genuinely, in his own guilt.[8] There were also inconsistencies about the timing of Evans's confession, which according to police evidence took seventy-five minutes and was concluded at 11.15 p.m. However, a newspaper reporter on the *News Chronicle* was told at 3 a.m. the following day that the suspect was being questioned 'earlier today'. Of course, this discrepancy could not be resolved as there was no independent witness at the police station, nor any satisfactory independent method of recording the timings of important events. Nonetheless, with John and Ethel Christie as witnesses for the prosecution and Evans's signed confession in their hands, the prosecution case at Evans's trial was formidable.

However, there was a serious obstacle to the prosecution case. There had, by chance, been workmen in 10 Rillington Place around the time of the murders, who made statements about their activities which were documented in their worksheets. These demonstrated that Evans had apparently confessed to placing the bodies in the washhouse before the workmen had placed the timbers there. This important piece of the jigsaw had been withheld from the defence at Evans's trial and the workmen were not called by the prosecution. This, in itself, would have been enough to allow Evans's conviction to be quashed on appeal if the trial had taken place in a modern court, but in 1950 it was assumed that the defendant's rights were sufficiently protected by the rule that the prosecution had to prove the defendant was guilty; the defendant did not have to prove his innocence.

Although it was the prosecution case that Evans had strangled both his wife and his daughter, the Crown put Evans on trial for the murder of Geraldine only. At this time a person could not be tried for two murders on the same occasion. However, the jury were allowed to hear all about the details surrounding Beryl's death in deciding whether Evans had murdered his daughter. Evans had retracted his Notting Hill confession to his solicitor as soon as he saw him and he maintained his denial of murder until the very day he was executed in March 1950. But Christie, supported by his wife, was a convincing witness and Evans struggled to provide a motive for Christie killing Beryl during the abortion attempt and explaining why he had apparently confessed to a murder that he had not committed. However, the conviction of Evans left a nasty taste in the mouth of most impartial observers once Christie's proclivities for murdering women became known three years later.

Could it really be possible that two men, living in the same building, would choose to murder women by strangulation in the same place quite independently of each other? And, why, if Evans was ignorant of Christie's proclivities, should he choose to blame Christie, rather than anybody else, for murder unless it was true? It was a big risk to take since, in January 1950, Christie was the prosecution's star witness and an apparently respectable man. By 1953, the miscarriage of justice which had sent Timothy Evans to his death seemed to be staring the authorities in the face.

The problem lay in recognising that vista. At the time there was a culture of benign complacency within the Home Office, the judiciary and in sections of the political establishment. They believed that the English judicial system could do no wrong and that the police were incapable of obtaining a false confession. In 1950, the punishment for murder was death, but the death penalty could only be justified if the judicial system hanged only the guilty and did not execute the innocent. Parliament and the judiciary had to provide a justification for capital punishment by maintaining that miscarriages of justice in capital cases did not occur. The Home Secretary at the time of Christie's conviction was David Maxwell Fyfe QC. He not only believed in the death penalty; he also believed that a miscarriage of justice in a murder case was impossible. In a debate on capital punishment in 1948, he told the House of Commons:

> As a realist I do not believe that the chances of error in a murder case, with these various instruments of the State present, constitute a factor which we must consider, any more than we must consider the danger of death in crossing a street ... it is impossible for anyone who views and examines fairly the facts of any murder case of which he has knowledge to say that such a miscarriage of justice has taken place.[9]

There was an unwillingness among judges, politicians and civil servants to recognise and remedy injustices within the system. Institutions responsible for justice closed ranks and protected themselves against criticism from outside their own cloistered environment from 1950 until at least 1982.

At Christie's trial (during which he put forward a defence of insanity), he admitted strangling Beryl Evans but denied the murder of Geraldine. Even the complacent government of the day was forced to bow to pressure and held an urgent inquiry into whether Evans had been the victim of a miscarriage of justice. The man appointed for this task was a QC called John Scott Henderson. He concluded 'with overwhelming cogency' the reassuring fact that Evans was, beyond reasonable doubt, guilty as charged. How overwhelmingly cogent Scott Henderson's mind was when writing his report can be gleaned from his own summary of the task he had to perform:

> The crucial question which I have asked myself during my investigation is: Is there any doubt that Evans murdered his wife? Putting the question in the converse way, I have considered whether there is any possibility that Christie murdered Mrs Evans. But a negative answer to that last question does not necessarily mean that the answer to the first question is 'no'. On the other hand I cannot be satisfied that the answer to the first question is 'no' unless I am also satisfied that the answer to the second question is that there is no possibility that Christie murdered Mrs Evans.[10]

In order to produce a conclusion that would satisfy the Home Secretary, Scott Henderson had to tie himself in knots – and require his readers to scratch their heads in puzzlement as they read this paragraph. Nonetheless, Scott Henderson had no qualms in deciding, to his complete satisfaction, that Christie's true confession during his trial that he had killed Beryl was false and Evans's false confession, retracted at trial, that he had killed Beryl, was true.

Despite the evident shortcomings of the Scott Henderson report, it was accepted with relief by the government of the day and, more importantly, the civil service. The image in which all senior civil servants were moulded in the period between 1953 and 1966 was one of calm rationality and the drafting skills of each succeeding senior member was cloned to repeat the conclusions that had been reached by their predecessors. Therefore, as James Chuter Ede, the former Home Secretary, had signed Evans's death warrant and ordered that 'the law must take its course' in March 1950, civil servants who came along later became clones of a former colleague who had placed Evans's papers before Chuter Ede.[11]

A senior civil servant confidently asserted that there could not have been a miscarriage of justice because 'it is not a proper use of the term "miscarriage of justice" to say that, if all the facts about Christie had been known when Evans was tried, he would have been acquitted'. With a logic that only a loyal public servant is capable of mustering, this argument is justified on the grounds that even if Evans was shown not to have murdered his wife, that would not mean that Evans had been wrongly hanged because he was only hanged for the murder of his child.[12] David Maxwell Fyfe, as Home Secretary, would have been as comforted by this observation as he was, no doubt, by the further ingenious argument that was made. The civil servant maintained that as there was a proven gap in Christie's murders between 1943 and 1944, when he strangled two women, and 1952, when he strangled his wife, 'an isolated outburst in 1949 does not seem very likely'.

This benign confidence that the process of criminal law was infallible and that innocent men were simply not sent to their deaths in Britain was, fortunately, not shared by all. Ludovic Kennedy had demolished the case mounted against Evans in his book *10 Rillington Place* and Lord Birkett, a former barrister of distinction and later a Law Lord, distilled the issue into one simple sentence: 'If the facts, as they are now known, had been known in 1950, no jury could possibly have said the case against Evans had been proved beyond reasonable doubt.'[13] It is one thing to make a point of such cogency in a newspaper; it is quite another to get something done about it. The rehabilitation of the reputation of Timothy Evans lay in the hands of the civil service.

In the late 1950s the permanent secretary at the Home Office was the redoubtable Sir Charles Cunningham, a man who was respected and feared in equal measure. He had to ascertain whether Ludovic Kennedy's thesis merited serious attention by the department and, if so, whether it was constitutionally possible for Evans to be posthumously pardoned. In Home Office precedent this would be a free pardon and this could only be granted if innocence was established; it was not enough simply to cast doubt on the correctness of the conviction. The permanent secretary accepted the verdict might have been different had the jury known about Christie's murders but stated that 'there was no case on record of a free pardon being granted posthumously and the view has been taken that a free pardon cannot be granted to a dead man.'[14] The Home Secretary, R. A. Butler, was mightily relieved, as he later told Parliament, to receive this advice from Cunningham. His department was in the clear; Evans's conviction was sound and even if it was deemed not to be, he was dead. A free pardon was simply out of the question.

The stonewalling by the Home Office continued when the MP Frank Soskice QC and others raised Evans's case again from the opposition benches in 1962 and pressed for another inquiry. When the Labour Party won the 1964 general election and Frank Soskice became Home Secretary, it seemed, at last, that an inquiry would take place. To the surprise of Parliament, Soskice declined to order an inquiry, saying that 'it would be kinder not to express views one way or another as to whether this unfortunate man was guilty or not guilty'.[15] In other words: 'Let sleeping dogs lie. My permanent secretary, Sir George Cunningham, does not want an inquiry.' Antony Jay, creator of the hilarious television series *Yes, Minister*, thought that there must be some mysterious inverted alchemy that transmuted gold into base metal within the corridors of power.[16] In fact, the truth is much simpler. Home Office advice to ministers was based on precedent, not on imagination, and senior civil servants were loyal to their predecessors as part of an entire legal institutional culture which included judges and the police. It was this solid phalanx which stuck together to protect their own institutions and the other pillars holding up the system. Each depended on the other. If one was to break ranks, inevitably another would suffer. The police had investigated Evans and produced his confession as evidence; the judicial system had tried and convicted Evans; and the legal profession, in the person of Scott Henderson, had given a clean bill of health to the trial process and to the role of the police. All respective entities had survived intact. It was only the Prime Minister, Harold Wilson, whose political antennae were acute, who saw that the emperor, in the guise of the justice system, was, on this occasion, bereft of clothes. He persuaded Soskice, whom he later sacked, not to stand in the way of another inquiry. This time, Mr Justice Brabin, a genial judge of the High Court, was given the time and resources to conduct a proper inquiry. When the report was published in October 1966, it contained a conclusion that nobody had ever before thought remotely possible. He concluded that it was more probable than not that Evans had killed Beryl, but equally more probable than not that he had *not* killed Geraldine, the murder which sent him to his death.[17]

In an effort to please everybody, Brabin had pleased nobody. The contradictions in Brabin's new reasoning were obvious. At the trial in 1950, the prosecution had said Evans killed Geraldine *because* he had also killed Beryl. According to Brabin, Evans, who was ignorant of Christie's methods of using the house or garden to hide his victims, had done exactly the same thing by concealing his wife in the washhouse. But if he murdered Beryl and left Geraldine at home when he went to Wales, why didn't Christie go to the police or at least alert somebody? By an extraordinary tour de force, Brabin had arrived at a version of events that made Evans both guilty and not guilty.

In December 1965, Roy Jenkins had succeeded Soskice as Home Secretary and he soon had a new permanent secretary, Sir Philip Allen. Each of the two men read the Brabin report with care. With the kind of masterly understatement only the British civil service is capable of, Allen reported to Jenkins: 'I find the crucial part of the report less clear than I would have wished.' He pointed out that 'on the question whether, if all the facts had been known, Evans ought to have been convicted, we are not really further advanced from the position as at the end of 1961'. Unhappily, Allen had to advise Jenkins that Brabin's conclusion that Evans probably did not kill Geraldine was not good enough for a free pardon.[18]

Jenkins overrode the advice of his senior officials with sharp arguments. If Evans were still alive, he, as Home Secretary, would order his immediate release from prison and Evans ought not to be in a worse position because he had been executed. After a quick telephone call to the Attorney General he received the response there would be no legal objection to a posthumous pardon. Evans was pardoned in 1966, but the pardon only expunged his conviction from his record; this was not the same as quashing the conviction, which can only be done by the Court of Appeal. It took another thirty-eight years for the High Court of England and Wales to ac-knowledge, in 2004, that the case of Timothy Evans was one of the most notorious, if not *the* most notorious, miscarriages of justice in British legal history.[19]

There are a number of lessons to be learned from the tragedy of the Evans case. Capital punishment enjoyed widespread popular support in the early 1950s and continued to do so until a campaign – led mainly by writers and journalists – succeeded in persuading parliamentarians to defy public opinion and to abolish it. It was abolished in the face of a majoritarian preference. Secondly, the case demonstrated that there was a complete lack of objectivity in evaluating the criminal investigation and trial process. There was an assumption that both were fit for purpose and this also chimed with public opinion at the time. The police were admired, the judi-ciary were respected and the death penalty was popular.

THE CASE OF DEREK BENTLEY AND CHRISTOPHER CRAIG

Two years after Evans's execution and six weeks before Christie murdered his wife, two young criminals broke into a confectionery warehouse in Croydon. The intruders were Christopher Craig, aged sixteen, and Derek Bentley, aged nineteen.[20] Craig had a revolver with a shortened barrel in his pocket and Bentley had a knuckleduster. Although Craig was only sixteen years of age,

THE NOT SO GOOD OLD DAYS

he had fully developed mental faculties and was accumulating a criminal record. Bentley, on the other hand, was deemed to be 'borderline feeble-minded' and had an IQ of sixty-six. By the time the police arrived, the boy and the young man were on the roof of the warehouse. Realising that they were cornered, Craig shouted, 'If you want us, fucking well come and get us.' One policeman shouted to Craig, 'Hand over the gun, lad,' while another made a grab for Bentley, who broke away from the policeman's grasp and shouted to Craig, 'Let him have it, Chris.' There was then a flash and a loud sound. One of the officers trying to arrest the pair, PC Sidney Miles, was shot dead in the execution of his duty. It was a shocking event and few sympathised with Craig or Bentley, who had gone to the warehouse intending to break in. They were tearaways who deserved all they got.

There were, however, considerable legal and ethical issues surrounding the case. Craig, who had the gun in his possession and who deliberately fired at the policeman, was too young to hang for murder. His co-defendant, Bentley, on the other hand, was of an age to be executed, but only if he was, in the eyes of the law, an accomplice to murder by encouraging Craig to pull the trigger. The case called for careful handling by the trial judge, especially as there was a public clamour for justice to be done for the family of the murdered police officer. Did Bentley know Craig had a gun? Did he contemplate someone being killed or seriously injured if they were caught at the warehouse? What exactly did he mean when he shouted, 'Let him have it, Chris' when the pair were in the course of being arrested? Were the words an encouragement to shoot or a request to hand over the gun?

Unusually for a murder trial at the Old Bailey, the case was tried by the Lord Chief Justice, Rayner Goddard. Despite his eminence and intellect, the trial was a travesty of justice. Goddard displayed bias and an obvious hostility to Bentley and the credibility of his defence. He gave legal directions to the jury which were defective, confusing and legally inaccurate. In the words of Lord Bingham, Goddard's successor as Lord Chief Justice, Bentley was denied a fair trial, 'the birth-right of every British citizen'.[21] The jury took little over an hour to find Bentley guilty of murder and he was executed in January 1953.

As with the case of Timothy Evans, the events following the trial demonstrated how fragile the application of the rule of law was when applied to criminal trials in the 1950s. At Bentley's trial the jury had urged mercy when returning their verdict. This was a signal that, in their opinion, the Home Secretary should recommend to the Queen that the sentence of death be commuted to life imprisonment. This was particularly apt as Craig, the more culpable of the two defendants, could not suffer capital punishment. He was released from detention after serving ten years in confinement. Bentley might have lived to serve a life sentence as well had David Maxwell Fyfe (who believed the English trial process was infallible in murder cases and who welcomed the Scott Henderson report in 1953 on the Christie and Evans's cases as a vindication of this view) recommended it. It was hardly surprising, given Maxwell Fyfe's well-known views, that he refused to interfere in 'the due process of law'.[22] It now fell to the civil servants at the Home Office, Sir George Cunningham's department, to decide on the Bentley family's appeal for a Queen's pardon.

The Criminal Justice Department in those days consisted of about 100 civil servants who dealt only with 'prerogative work', complaints that an injustice had been done in a criminal case. Despite the apparent expertise of these officials, none of them thought to raise the Bentley case with a minister of the Crown. It was not until 1993 that Derek Bentley was pardoned, on the grounds that he should not have been hanged. His conviction was not overturned until 1998.

The smugness of the establishment in the Evans and Bentley cases was matched only by the obsequious deference accorded to Lord Chief Justice Goddard. When John Parris, the barrister who represented Craig, voiced the opinion that it was by no means the unanimous view of lawyers that Goddard was courteous, fair and impartial, he was suspended from practice for four months. On Goddard's death in 1971, the *Times* journalist Bernard Levin described Goddard's conduct at the Bentley trial as being unjudicial, vindictive and crudely emotional (which was absolutely true, as Lord Bingham acknowledged in 1998 when he quashed the conviction). For his pains on pointing this out Levin was vilified and abused by lawyers and judges and blackballed from membership of the Garrick Club, a favourite venue among male lawyers.[23] The perspicacity of Levin in pricking the bubble of the arrogance and complacency of lawyers in the years between 1950 and 1971 was recognised only much later. Writing in 2004, David Pannick QC expressed the view that Levin had helped remove some of the layers of deference and self-satisfaction that had slowed down legal reforms during this era.[24]

THE CASE OF HAROLD CHALLENOR

While the bodies of Timothy Evans and Derek Bentley lay in the unconsecrated ground of prison yards, police constable Harold Challenor was on the beat in south London. He was an officer of exceptional ability, according to David Ascoli, who is a historian of the Metropolitan Police.[25] This was demonstrated by the fact that he had arrested more suspects who walked the streets of Mitcham than his colleagues. Most of these arrests were made for the now discredited offence of 'sus', which has since been abolished.[26] In those days anybody could be arrested for this catch-all offence, dating from 1824 when Georgian society wanted to clear undesirables from the streets away from the nobility. All it involved was for a diligent police officer to catch somebody loitering with intent to commit an arrestable offence. As the necessary ingredient of an intention to commit an offence usually came from the mouth of the suspect himself, it was not difficult to make an arrest if the suspect was 'verballed'. A 'verbal' consisted of an unequivocal oral admission of guilt made to a police officer on the street, which, later on, the police officer transcribed into his notebook. It is called a 'verbal' if the suspect later denies making the incriminating remark. Later in his career, Harold Challenor acquired a reputation for 'verballing'. Whether in the early 1950s Challenor engaged in verballing or whether he was simply the most diligent police constable in Mitcham cannot be known for certain. What was certain was that he had a rather eccentric and bizarre demeanour. He invariably called everybody, whether his police superiors or the thieves he arrested, 'my old darling' or 'my old beauty'.

A veteran of the parachute regiment in the Second World War and decorated for bravery, Challenor was a tall, imposing figure who had been an amateur boxer. He had been promoted to the Flying Squad in 1958 which was a specialist unit within the Metropolitan Police and consisted of exclusively plainclothes officers who were often armed and were prepared to use unorthodox tactics to catch criminals. The character of the squad was immortalised by John Thaw and Dennis Waterman in the television series *The Sweeney*. Challenor was only slightly different in that he was always smartly turned out in a blue suit, trilby hat and highly polished shoes. He stated that his mission in life was to 'frighten the criminal underworld into submission' and to eradicate crime wherever he found it.[27] Sometimes, he carried this to extreme lengths. On one occasion he was part of a team keeping a gang of suspected robbers under observation at Liverpool Street station. Contrary to instructions, Challenor strolled up to one of the suspects, felled him to the floor with a commando chop to the throat and then sat on top of him, saying, 'You are nicked, my old darling. My boss will tell you that formally in a minute.' A passing member of the public was so alarmed by what he saw that he reported to a uniformed officer that he had just witnessed a mugging.[28] Despite this gross misconduct, Challenor was not disciplined nor taken off plain-clothes duties. On the contrary, his career prospered. At that time, the police were society's police and whatever they said or did was beyond reproach or question.[29]

In July 1962, Challenor, now a detective sergeant, was posted to West End Central Police Station in Mayfair. He was acquiring a reputation for disreputable behaviour. In August 1962, at a time when there were no betting shops and gambling was a clandestine activity, he had almost certainly planted some detonators on a bookie's runner who worked in the West End clubs.

Society in the early 1960s was becoming more politically aware and people were taking a less censorious view of sex than the law of the land wanted to uphold. The Campaign for Nuclear Disarmament organised annual marches from Aldermaston to protest about nuclear weapons and D. H. Lawrence's explicit descriptions of sexual love across class barriers in *Lady Chatterley's Lover* survived condemnation on the grounds of obscenity by a jury at the Old Bailey in 1960. Only three years earlier the British Medical

Council had pompously declared that 'the proper use of sex, the primary purpose of which is creative, is related to the individual's responsibility to himself and the nation'.[30] In politics as well as sex, British people were expressing themselves as they chose to and did not care much whether their desires chimed in with a responsibility to nationhood. Challenor's biographer was wrong to say that when political protests took place, 'often the reason behind a demonstration was spurious ... many of those who took part had little or no idea what it was they were protesting about'.[31] The early 1960s, when the government of Harold Macmillan was dying on its feet, was a politically energised period and most people who attended demonstrations knew exactly what they were protesting about.

This is the background to an incident which came to define the moment when public trust in the police began to crumble.[32] The incident occurred in the streets around Claridge's Hotel in the heart of Mayfair. A left-wing politician in Greece, named Grigoris Lambrakis, had been assassinated in broad daylight in Thessaloniki by two far-right extremists in May 1963. His funeral became a mass demonstration and led to the resignation of the Greek Prime Minister. The murder of Lambrakis was headline news throughout the world and appalled left-leaning students and others. By coincidence, Queen Frederika of Greece had been invited for a state visit to Britain. She and her husband arrived in London in July 1963 and they stayed at Claridge's Hotel. A rally to protest against Lambrakis's assassination was held in Trafalgar Square on 11 July, followed by a march to Claridge's.

Donald Rooum, an artist and lecturer, was one of many demonstrators who joined the march. He carried a banner bearing the words 'Lambrakis RIP'. Four plainclothes police officers snatched the banner from him and Challenor said, 'You are fucking nicked, my old beauty.' When he was at Vine Street Police Station, Rooum was repeatedly assaulted by Challenor before a brick wrapped in newspaper was produced from Challenor's own pocket and presented to Rooum with the words, 'There you are, my old beauty. Carrying an offensive weapon. You can get two years for that.'

By merciful chance, two juveniles called Gregory Ede and George Hill had been separately arrested by two of Challenor's aides, young police constables, assigned to assist plainclothes detectives and were under Challenor's personal supervision. Their notebooks were later written up and stated that each of the juveniles had also been carrying a brick. In the charge room at Vine Street, pieces of brick were presented to them with the words 'a present from Uncle Harry', in reference to Challenor. There was something of a rumpus in the police station on the evening of the demonstration and Challenor was observed walking about opening and closing his fists like an uncoiled spring. In this general confusion Rooum was mistakenly held in custody overnight and therefore on the following morning, when he was granted bail, he was wearing the same jacket that had, according to Challenor, contained a brick when he was arrested. Rooum had the presence of mind to engage the services of a solicitor and a scientist. When his case came on for trial at Marlborough Street magistrates' court, the defence were ready to confront Challenor. Challenor approached the witness box, his suit nicely pressed, and took the oath in a confident, booming voice. He then gave his account of events, which now included Rooum's 'verbal': 'I will throw my stone, not in revenge, but as a demonstration of my ideals.' For Challenor, this case was probably no more than routine. However, it was to bring his career to an end and tarnish the reputation of the police for generations.

Rooum was represented by Michael Sherrard, a barrister of some skill. The defence scientist told the court that the brick, an exhibit in the case, could not possibly have been in Rooum's pocket as there would have been traces of brick dust left behind, and there were none. The size of the brick would have caused scratching and tearing of the lining and there was none. The *coup de grâce* was the presentation of the pieces of brick, which were alleged to have been found quite independently in possession of the two juvenile defendants, to the magistrate. When they were presented alongside Rooum's brick they fitted together perfectly into one single brick, with the manufacturer's name clearly visible across all three pieces. Challenor had admitted his aides had been involved in the arrest of Hill and Ede. His explanation for the pieces of brick being three parts of one single brick was that the juveniles and Rooum must have known each other and shared a brick. This was remarkable considering the huge numbers of demonstrators outside Claridge's, and a coincidence that Challenor's aides should have arrested, independently, two people who had happened to have shared a brick with the person Challenor had personally arrested. It was Challenor's last desperate throw of his rapidly diminishing store of dice. When the juveniles' case came on for trial in the Juvenile Court, Challenor was nowhere to be seen. He was 'off sick'. The prosecution offered no evidence.

It did not take long for the press to take an interest in what became known as the 'brick' cases. As a result, other people came forward to make allegations that they had also suffered at Challenor's hands. A bandwagon was staring to roll and questions were raised in Parliament. There was an internal investigation conducted by Chief Superintendent John Du Rose of Scotland Yard, who submitted a report to the Director of Public Prosecutions. Challenor and his aides were prosecuted for perverting the course of justice in relation to the 'brick' cases. But Challenor never stood trial. In March 1964, two doctors certified that he was suffering from paranoid schizophrenia and therefore was medically unfit to stand trial. He was committed to a mental hospital. The trial continued against the aides and they went to prison. At the end of the trial, the judge stated that he was gravely disturbed that Challenor had been apparently fit to carry on his duties in July 1963, as the doctors had concluded that he had been mentally unbalanced for some time. He wanted further enquiries to be made.

Once again, it was Sir George Cunningham, the permanent secretary at the Home Office who had resisted for so long a free pardon for Timothy Evans, who rose to the task. He tendered the advice which led to the Home Secretary setting up an inquiry.[33] The following day the Home Secretary introduced Harold Challenor to the House of Commons as a man 'who, by excessive devotion to duty and overwork in the police service, appears to have precipitated a mental breakdown'.[34] He gave a free pardon to all those who had been involved in the 'brick' offences on 11 July 1964 and set up a full inquiry under the Police Act 1964, which had only just come into force. There was no precedent as to how the inquiry should be conducted. The terms of reference were to investigate how it was possible for Challenor to have continued to work when he appeared to be mentally affected by overwork.

Henry Brooke, the Home Secretary, appointed Arthur James QC, a popular and successful barrister who had recently prosecuted the 'great train robbers', to conduct the inquiry. James interpreted these terms to use all the powers the law gave him to compel a huge number of witnesses to appear before him. In all, 137 witnesses gave evidence, no fewer than forty-three of whom were police officers who could cast light on Challenor's behaviour. It was a huge inquiry which lasted forty-five days. The absent Challenor was represented by the doyen of the bar at the time, James Comyn QC, whose silken tones were much in demand by litigants in the criminal, civil and divorce courts. The Metropolitan Police were represented by Geoffrey Lane QC, a formidable cross-examiner who went on to become Lord Chief Justice.

James wanted everybody to give their accounts, including Donald Rooum, who had been acquitted by the court, but in the inquiry Rooum was treated as a prosecution witness against Challenor and was subjected to heavy questioning by Mr Lane QC and other barristers representing police interests. It took a little over a year, from the date of his appointment to the publication of his conclusions, for James to complete his inquiry.

There were one or two interesting revelations about the 'brick' cases in James's conclusions. For example, on the day before the Claridge's demonstration, Challenor had produced a brick at a police briefing at Vine Street Police Station and told his aides that 'we must do something to stop bricks being thrown at royalty'.[35] After Rooum's arrest Challenor was excited and boisterous and this was explicable, according to James, because Challenor had not kept in check his ready wit and boisterous nature. He accepted that Rooum had been assaulted by Challenor, although stated that the number of occasions that he was assaulted was exaggerated. James could barely disguise his contempt for Donald Rooum:

> By the time of the inquiry he was well versed in his evidence and his apparent enjoyment in the giving of evidence detracted from its objectivity and the weight to be given to it. He gave his occupation as a cartoonist, teacher and typographer but in a statement dated 20 November 1963 he said he was an anarchist

and a member of the National Council for Civil Liberties. His evidence and demeanour at the inquiry confirmed this.[36]

The passage is revealing. Rooum was, indeed, well versed in his evidence. In addition to his own court case, he had assisted the Du Rose investigation and an investigation conducted by Norman Goodchild, Chief Constable of Wolverhampton, into issues of corruption surrounding Challenor. No evidence of corruption by Challenor was found, but Goodchild had submitted a report running to fifteen volumes to the Commissioner of the Metropolitan Police in March 1965, dealing with many failings, as he saw them, in the practices adopted in London in respect of arrest, charging and recording of evidence.[37] Rooum had given his account three times before testifying at the James Inquiry. There is nothing inconsistent with having an occupation of a cartoonist and also being a member of a voluntary organisation (the National Council for Civil Liberties). But it is in the final sentence that the preconceived opinions of James are exposed. He clearly had a jaundiced view of members of the National Council for Civil Liberties and this may explain why he took such a favourable view of police evidence in the inquiry.

The barrister representing the National Council for Civil Liberties had argued there was a culture and an atmosphere at Vine Street Police Station whereby Challenor could use violence, show disrespect to persons in custody and fabricate evidence without exciting attention. James rejected this contention as being a reason for Challenor's mental illness going undetected. No evidence justifying Challenor's suspension from duty existed, James concluded, until early September 1963, even though he had, in fact, been medically incapable of being a detective sergeant for a considerable time and had assaulted suspects that he had arrested. James invariably accepted police evidence wherever it conflicted with testimony from those who had complained about Challenor's behaviour towards them. The inquiry's conclusions have been severely criticised. The criminal academic Paul O'Higgins commented, 'One wonders why in almost every single case Mr James chooses to believe the evidence most favourable to the police … Reports of this kind contribute neither to improved police efficiency nor to improved relations between police and public.'[38] Critically, James had not attributed responsibility to anybody for the state of affairs that allowed Challenor to behave as he did.

On the one hand, the Home Office had granted free pardons and paid compensation to those who had been wrongly convicted; on the other, James failed to explain – and seemed uninterested in trying to explain – how the police service as a whole allowed such miscarriages of justice to occur. Mary Grigg, who brought the Challenor affair to public attention, has stated that 'to ask who was responsible for Challenor's misconduct is like casting a stone into a pond and watching the ripples move outwards in ever-growing circles … There was a failure of the complete system, but the system was not supposed to fail.'[39]

The Challenor affair is now a part of history and largely forgotten. The Commissioner of the Metropolitan Police, Sir Joseph Simpson, received the Goodchild report with ill-grace. He criticised the Chief Constable of Wolverhampton for being misleading and for failing to understand the special difficulties of policing the capital city. Goodchild had identified a culture in London, emanating from officers close to Challenor, that unorthodox methods were sometimes justified in fighting 'dirty crime'. Simpson commented, 'Circumstances can arise in which unorthodox methods can be justified in bringing criminals to justice ... Officers taking such action are normally protected by the common sense of the courts.' The Commissioner dismissed Goodchild's recommendation that suspects should be asked to sign an officer's notebook if a 'verbal' was to be used in evidence and stated that the 'rule book of good practice' was perfectly sufficient to ensure suspects were not 'verballed'.[40] Coming from the Commissioner of the Metropolitan Police, this was an extraordinary statement. It excused 'unorthodox' methods, meaning those contrary to good practice; justified 'verballing'; and praised the common sense of judges not to press for laws to control police behaviour. He went further in his annual report of 1965 and argued that to put police conduct under the microscope meant that police officers would be deprived of rights enjoyed by ordinary citizens.[41]

The Commissioner's faith in the 'common sense of the courts' was, in reality, a faith in the judiciary to support the police in 'bringing criminals to justice'. As Helena Kennedy QC has observed, there was a culture in which the judiciary simply failed to admit there could possibly be unacceptable police practices in the questioning of suspects under interrogation. Judges saw their role as protectors of good order against anarchy 'even as joined with the police in the battle against crime'.[42] Yet, it was the 'Judges' Rules' that were supposed to protect suspects from bad behaviour by the police.

Originally formulated in 1912, and supplemented in 1947 by the Lord Chief Justice, the 'Judges' Rules' were, in effect, a drill manual of processes that should be followed when a suspect is under interrogation at a police station. They were not enshrined in law and a suspect's confession could be admitted in evidence at his trial even if the process in the drill manual was not followed. If a suspect was subjected to violence, or confessions were written out in advance and offered to the suspect for signature, then under the common law the confession should not be placed before the jury. The problem for defence lawyers was in presenting credible evidence that such corrupt practices had occurred. The judge would have to decide, in the absence of the jury, whether the disputed confession could be used as evidence. Invariably, the judge would accept the account of the police officer, rather than the accused, about the circumstances in which a disputed confession came to be made. There was no appetite for reform in either police practice or the criminal trial process in the 1960s and 1970s. Everything went on as before as if Challenor had never existed. After three years as an in-patient at the Netherne Hospital, the medically retired Harold Challenor was released. He never stood trial and led an uneventful life before retiring, with his wife Doris, to live in Devon. He died in 2008.

The lessons learned from the Challenor affair were clear. Not only was there nothing worthy of criticism in the methods of the Metropolitan Police, but it was dangerously radical and rather unseemly to suggest otherwise. It was not only the judges, the Commissioner and an independent chair of an inquiry who supported, on utilitarian grounds, the work of the police in fighting crime; there was no appetite for change among the public either. Crude majority preference had come to the rescue of Harold Challenor. It did not occur to anybody that a greater role for the law in providing a strong judicial oversight over police work would be a solution to what was becoming a scandalous state of affairs.

THE IRISH CASES

The new era of the 1970s bore the hallmark of bombs and Ireland. By March 1973, the Provisional IRA were planting bombs all over mainland Britain. On 8 March 1973, one person was killed and 200 people injured when a giant bomb exploded outside the Old Bailey in the City of London. By the summer of 1973, incendiary bombs were planted in Birmingham shops. In February 1974, a coach carrying soldiers and their families was bombed on the M62, causing twelve deaths and numerous injuries. Judith Ward, an IRA 'groupie' who hung around in Dundalk pubs and claimed, falsely, to have married an IRA activist, was arrested and convicted of mass murder later the same year. She was something of a fantasist and her medical report, which was written while she was on remand, described her as being an unreliable person. Her barrister described her as a 'female Walter Mitty' character.[43]

In October 1974, two public houses in Guildford frequented by British soldiers were bombed, followed shortly afterwards by a bomb being thrown into a pub near the Woolwich barracks in south-east London. Five people were killed and sixty-five injured in the Guildford bombings, while two people were killed and thirty-five injured in Woolwich. Two IRA activists were arrested trying to plant a bomb in a Bristol factory and an IRA operative called James McDade had blown himself up while trying to plant a bomb in the telephone exchange in Coventry. England was in a state of panic.

In the year 1974 there was, on average, one IRA bomb, successful or otherwise, planted in Britain every three days. Bombs in pillar boxes or minor explosions at a public school, clubs in St James's in London or restaurants and railway stations hardly received a mention in news bulletins unless there were fatalities.

In the midst of this sustained campaign, on 21 November 1974, an event of extreme barbarity occurred. Two public houses in central Birmingham, the Mulberry Bush and the Tavern in the Town, each packed with revellers, were shattered by massive explosions.

Twenty-one innocent people died and 182 were injured.[44] It was the biggest murder in British history and led to a trial known now as the trial of the Birmingham Six. Five Irishmen were detained on their way to Belfast, having boarded a train to Heysham from Birmingham to catch a ferry. A sixth man was arrested later in Birmingham. At a police station in Lancashire, a scientist called Frank Skuse did a test which revealed the presence of nitroglycerine on two of the detained men. This in itself was not conclusive proof of an association with the bombs, as a positive test for nitroglycerine could occur following contact with lacquers, varnishes or paints. What was thoroughly incriminating were the confessions the police produced in evidence at the trial. The defence case was that while in custody in Birmingham the defendants were deprived of sleep and subjected to mock executions in addition to being physically assaulted.

Both the prosecution and the defence relied on the evidence of prison and medical officers at Winson Green Prison, where the six were taken after being charged. One of the six had four upper teeth missing, a black eye and cuts to his nose and elbow; another had cuts on his face and bruising on his chest and loin; a third had two black eyes, cuts on his face and bruises on his chest and shoulder; a fourth had bruises on his head, eyebrow and ribs; a fifth had bruising to both arms, chest and ear; and the sixth had a black eye and bruises to the hip and upper arm. The question, which was to loom large in later events, was how did these injuries happen? Were they caused during interrogation, before their arrival at the prison, or had they been caused by prison officers at Winson Green? Or, as the six maintained, had they been assaulted by both the police and prison officers? Although this question featured in the trial, it was the confession evidence which persuaded the jury to convict all six of mass murder.

As the Birmingham Six began their life sentences, another bomb trial was getting underway at the Old Bailey. In late November 1974, a man called Paul Hill who had had some IRA involvement in Belfast was arrested in connection with the bombing of the Horse and Groom and Seven Stars pubs in Guildford on 5 October, when five people had been killed. One of Hill's old school friends from Belfast was a man called Gerry Conlon, whom Hill had implicated in his confession. Conlon's aunt was Annie Maguire, who, Hill alleged, had taught him how to make bombs. Conlon told police that he knew Hill was a 'provo' (a member of the Provisional IRA) and he also implicated a man called Patrick (Paddy) Armstrong in another bombing incident in Woolwich when a bomb had been thrown through the window of the King's Arms pub and two people were killed.

Patrick Armstrong lived in a squat in Kilburn with his girlfriend, Carole Richardson. He was a burglar and worked occasionally in pubs. She was an eighteen-year-old drug addict who was probably withdrawing from the effects of barbiturates when she made a series of confusing and contradictory statements to police, including an admission that she and her boyfriend had gone to Guildford to plant a bomb. Conlon's aunt, Annie Maguire, lived with her husband Patrick (Paddy) and their sons Vincent and Patrick in Kilburn, north-west London. When Surrey police arrived at her flat, Giuseppe Conlon was there; he was Gerry Conlon's uncle and Annie's brother-in-law and had come over from Belfast to try to get legal representation for his nephew in the Guildford bombings trial. He was arrested, as were Annie's two teenage sons, who returned home to find two family friends, Sean Smith and Patrick O'Neill, were in the flat, in addition to police officers. Everybody was arrested and they became known as the 'Maguire Seven'.[45]

The case against all seven people arrested at Annie Maguire's flat depended on one pair of plastic gloves and nail scrapings taken from the fingers of the suspects. Annie Maguire's washing-up gloves and the nail scrapings from the other suspects were tested at the Royal Armament Research and Development Establishment and a scientist found, in a thin layer chromatograpahy test (TLC), that the gloves and scrapings were positive for nitroglycerine. The prosecution argued that the pub bombs in Guildford were a nitroglycerine-based explosive and that the Maguire family had hastily got rid of their bomb-making equipment when they learned of Gerry Conlon's arrest. But the TLC test was not specific for nitroglycerine and there was another explosive, pentaerythritol tetranitrate, which also created a positive result. Did the defence team of the Maguire Seven want the jury to know this, the judge asked? Not surprisingly, the defence backed down. The Maguire Seven were convicted for the possession of explosives and given lengthy sentences of imprisonment.

Although Judith Ward, the Birmingham Six, the Guildford Four and the Maguire Seven were behind bars, there was no let-up in IRA bombings and no apparent breakthrough to catching the bombers. The author and editor of the *Guinness Book of Records*, Ross McWhirter, had offered a reward of £50,000 (nearly half a million pounds in today's money) for information leading to their apprehension. Nobody came forward to claim the reward, but a number of years later an IRA operative called Brendan Dowd, who was serving a life sentence for an IRA shooting in Liverpool, volunteered to receive a visit from Alastair Logan, the solicitor for the Maguires. This proved to be a turning point. Dowd was a former member of the Balcombe Street Gang, a group of dedicated and extremely dangerous members of an active service unit of the Provisional IRA. He confessed to Logan that he had participated in the

Woolwich pub bombing with two members of the Balcombe gang, Henry Duggan and Edward Butler. In December 1975, that gang had been pursued by police after a drive-by shooting into a West End restaurant and were arrested after a siege in Balcombe Street in Marylebone, west London. They were sent to prison for committing over seventy separate bombing incidents.

During their trial in early 1977, the Balcombe Street Gang admitted, through their lawyers, to taking part in the Woolwich pub bombing and one member admitted to also being part of the team that bombed the Guildford pubs. Dowd's confession tallied with the Balcombe account. During questioning, the gang said that as far as they knew Paul Hill and Paddy Armstrong were not members of the Provisional IRA. Cracks were beginning to appear in the previously impregnable edifice of the prosecution case against the Guildford Four.

Once the Balcombe Street Gang had been arrested, IRA bombings on mainland Britain began to peter out. Life for ordinary people began to resume normality. Seventeen people were serving long sentences as a result of the Birmingham, Guildford and Woolwich bombings, and IRA activists who never disputed their guilt were also behind bars. The case of the Birmingham Six, however, was far from over. The Assistant Chief Constable of Lincolnshire begun an inquiry relating to mistreatment of the Birmingham Six at Winson Green Prison when these allegations had become the subject of gossip and speculation in December 1974. His investigation was thorough and he concluded that there was credible evidence that the prisoners had been assaulted on their reception at the prison and while bathing took place. The papers were submitted to the Director of Public Prosecutions. Nothing happened until after the trial and a failed appeal by the members of the Birmingham

Six, but in June 1976 fourteen prison officers were put on trial for assaults occurring at the reception or in the bathroom at Winson Green Prison.

Police officers who had taken the Birmingham Six to the prison were called by the prosecution to say that the prisoners were unscathed on their arrival (with the exception of one of the group, who had a black eye). This injury had, on the prosecution case, occurred accidentally during the journey from Lancashire to Birmingham. The Six gave evidence to say that assaults had occurred at the hands of the police and prison officers. None of the prison officers gave sworn testimony but each made a statement from the dock, which was allowed at that time, denying responsibility. All were acquitted. These verdicts resolved nothing. The jury in the Birmingham Six's criminal trial must have concluded they had not been assaulted during interrogation and their confessions were voluntary, but the jury in the prison officers' case found there was insufficient proof that the Six had been beaten up in prison. The only way out of the impasse seemed to be a civil action. Liability was admitted by the Home Office in respect of misconduct at the prison, but the West Midlands Police argued a civil case against the police was an abuse of the process of the court; the jury in the criminal trial had already exonerated them. Mr Justice Cantley, who later went on to become a household name as the judge in the Jeremy Thorpe trial, dismissed this argument, but Lord Denning, also a household name with something of a reputation for supporting the individual when confronted by state power, agreed with the police. In pronouncing the Birmingham Six's action an abuse of process, he said in November 1980:

> If they won, it would mean that the police were guilty of perjury;
> that they were guilty of violence and threats; that the confessions

were involuntary and improperly admitted in evidence; and that the convictions were erroneous … That was such an appalling vista that every sensible person would say, 'It cannot be right that these actions should go any further.'[46]

These words, which Lord Denning later came to regret, revealed the deep-seated belief among judges and the civil service since the early 1950s that the criminal justice system must not be allowed to fail. Denning could not bring himself to say that the English legal system might contain flaws or that the police might obtain confessions which were not given voluntarily. Such an attitude can be traced back to the Scott Henderson report into the case of Timothy Evans, the refusal of David Maxwell Fyfe to commute Bentley's death sentence and the James Inquiry into the activities of Harold Challenor. Lord Denning's fear was that the dam that secured criminal justice within still waters might burst and reveal the mud and detritus of bad practice that lay beneath. This was too awful to contemplate; it would be, in his words, 'an appalling vista'. The vista of criminal justice, consisting of the honest and trustworthy bobby, the common sense of the English jury and the wisdom of the English judge, should not be allowed to be spoiled by convicted criminals taking a civil action.

This pleasant vista of justice was, however, a figment of Lord Denning's imagination. Another great judge, Lord Devlin, wrote in 1950 about his experience of watching an accused giving an account in the witness box, full of 'voluble incoherences' when the police had asserted that he had provided a 'lucid, well-punctuated flow of a statement' under interrogation after arrest.[47] Lord Devlin understood, completely, that police evidence often strained credulity, but he justified interrogation without independent supervision on the grounds that the ends justified the means. The police were in daily contact with 'pestilential crime' and they had to act as prosecutor and judge, player and umpire. 'The general reputation of the police is good enough for their version of statements [at the police station] to carry great weight.' Here, Devlin is identifying the widespread belief that the police should be supported by juries in their work in protecting the public.

This is a purely utilitarian argument and a jury's faith in the police's reputation is not the same as a jury placing trust in a method of interrogation which was conducted entirely in secret. When it comes to interviews at a police station, something more than reputation is needed for the jury to have faith in the accuracy of the interview. Devlin was right, however, to have identified 'reputation' as an important factor influencing the decisions of a jury where there was a conflict of evidence between the police and a suspect.

Throughout the 1950s and into the 1970s the police were held in high regard by the public, but they were a law unto themselves, entirely unregulated. The public were happy even though few people had any idea how the police operated. Police forces were part of the machinery of the state and enjoyed 'righteousness, power and authority rooted in ritual and tradition – but with the consent of the entire nation'.[48] There was little appetite for opening up the work of the police to public scrutiny and while the probity of the police was engaging journalists, the police's general reputation did not markedly decline.

In 1969, two journalists on *The Times* conducted an in-depth investigation into police corruption within the Metropolitan Police. They found that at least three detectives were taking money in exchange for dropping charges. The detectives in question were charged and successfully prosecuted for corruption at the Old Bailey.[49]

At this time the Criminal Investigation Department in London was described by an honest police officer as 'the most routinely corrupt organisation in London ... a sink of iniquity'.[50] By the time Lord Denning refused to allow the Birmingham Six to sue the West Midlands Police for assault, *The Sweeney* was on national television. The show featured a fictional portrayal of the Flying Squad who were prepared to break the rules and cut corners to nail villains and ran through the 1970s. Four television plays called *Law & Order* by G. F. Newman were also screened in 1978, by which time the image of the contemporary policeman was one 'seemingly more corrupt than the villains they were fitting up'.[51]

Despite these television programmes, faith in the police was not destroyed by the scandals uncovered by the *Times* investigations and subsequent prosecutions of corrupt officers. For the public, the acceptance of police corruption as being endemic was still perhaps a step too far. There was general public support for the police holding the line, especially against the Provisional IRA. The Balcombe Street Gang, the Birmingham Six, the Guildford Four and the Maguire Seven were behind bars, but no sooner had the spate of IRA bombings begun to abate than the Home Secretary had to turn his attention to another disturbing case. In December 1977, a retired High Court judge, Sir Henry Fisher, produced his report on a murder trial which had gone wrong. It was known by all as the Confait case.

THE MAXWELL CONFAIT CASE

Maxwell Confait (or Michelle, as his clients knew him) was a transvestite homosexual prostitute who lived in Doggett Road, Catford. His landlord, a Jamaican man called Winston Goode, lived separately from his wife in a basement room in the same house. In the early hours of 22 April 1972, the fire brigade attended a fire at the house and found the body of Confait, who had been strangled with a piece of flex. Living nearby was Colin Lattimore, an eighteen-year-old youth who had a mental age of eight and an IQ of sixty-six and attended a remedial day centre. During the evenings he often went to the local Salvation Army youth club. He was friendly with a boy called Ronnie Leighton, aged fifteen, and a younger boy called Ahmet Salih. The three boys had started a fire in a nearby storage shed a day or two after the murder and there had also been fires started on the railway embankment which ran along beside Doggett Road.[52]

Lattimore was a prime suspect for the Confait murder when he was arrested on suspicion of arson of the storage shed on 24 April. When interviewed, he admitted entering 27 Doggett Road with Ronnie, whom he accused of strangling Confait shortly after going in. On this account they would have entered the house at approximately 1 a.m. on 22 April. Later, the other boys also made incriminating admissions of complicity in arson and murder.

The boys were not the first suspects. Winston Goode, Confait's landlord, was questioned. Although he was married, he did not sleep with his wife and had admitted to being friends with Confait and to being a bisexual with a liking for dressing in women's clothing. He also admitted to police that he was jealous when Confait had started a relationship with another man. However, there was insufficient evidence to charge Goode and the police were confident that the case was solved when Lattimore made the first confession, in writing, which he signed. The problem for the prosecution was the time of Confait's death. Rigor mortis had set in when the doctor attended the scene early on the morning of 22 April. This pointed to the death having occurred between 8 p.m. and 10 p.m. on Friday

21 April. If this were the case, Lattimore had a cast-iron alibi as he was with dozens of other individuals at the Salvation Army youth club for the whole of that time.

There were other features in the investigation of the case which were disturbing. The house at 27 Doggett Road was quite large. How did the boys know which rooms Confait occupied, and why was there no sign of a struggle when the flex was applied to Confait's throat? Was there a sexual aspect to the killing? Answers to these questions were never sought. Winston Goode committed suicide shortly after the three boys were convicted of murder at the Old Bailey. At their trial, counsel for the prosecution had asked questions of the pathologist for the prosecution to attempt to provide a bigger window for the time of death. The pathologist did not rule out that the death could have occurred at midnight on 22 April.

The local MP, Christopher Price, and the *South London Press* campaigned tirelessly for the case to be reopened. This eventually occurred when Roy Jenkins, in consultation with the Lord Chief Justice, Lord Widgery, referred the case to the Court of Appeal for a second appeal, the first one having failed. In October 1975, all the boys were freed when Lord Justice Scarman and two other judges quashed the convictions. At the hearing, new medical evidence called by the defence placed the time of death between 8 p.m. and 10 p.m. on 21 April, which was the original opinion of the prosecution doctors. This was plainly so inconsistent with Lattimore's confession that his admissions of guilt could not possibly be true.

An inquiry was set up under the chairmanship of Sir Henry Fisher, a retired High Court judge, to report to the Home Secretary on what had gone wrong in the handling of the case. Fisher identified a series of breaches in regulations which the police should have followed when young or 'mentally backward' (a phrase used for people with special educational needs at that time) suspects were under interrogation and noted that there was scant regard for a rule, which was supposed to be observed by the police, that suspects should be told of their rights to consult a solicitor.[53] Once these failures had been identified in a single case, it was imperative that the practices of the entire police service in England and Wales be looked at thoroughly. The most appropriate way for this to be achieved would be by the appointment of a royal commission, and the Home Secretary, Merlyn Rees, appointed one in 1978.

The chairman of the commission was Sir Cyril Philips, an academic historian from Birkenhead. He was director of the School for Oriental and African Studies at the University of London at the time of his appointment and was an outsider, as were the majority of his fellow commissioners. Finally some independent minds that were not imbued with establishment beliefs began to look at the criminal justice system. Their approach was completely new. Philips and his team questioned the validity of many assumptions about the interrogation of suspects by the police which had never been confronted before. The commission did not attempt to resolve or to reconcile two fundamentally different approaches: the utilitarian one, inherited from Jeremy Bentham, that the purpose of criminal investigation was to bring the guilty to justice; and the libertarian one, based on rights-based theory, which gave primacy to the presumption of innocence. Instead, Philips insisted that the real problem was one of public confidence and trust.

Philips proposed a way of restoring public confidence in police methods by recommending there should be standards against which police methods should be judged. He proposed four benchmarks:

- Did they command public confidence?
- Were they fair and open?
- Were standards uniformly applied?
- Were suspects always aware of their rights?

Answering these questions in a way which would make trust in the police transparent required legislation making standards of behaviour mandatory and written in black-letter law. But in order to achieve this objective the layers of ingrained police culture had to be stripped away. Police interviews would have to be recorded on tape, a suspect should have the right to have a solicitor present and 'verbals' by a suspect made away from a police station would not, usually, be admissible in evidence.[54]

THE DAWN OF A NEW ERA

These proposals were accepted by the government of the day, which by this time was a Conservative one, and in 1984 the Police and Criminal Evidence Act, known universally as PACE, was brought into force. Almost at a stroke a new era in the investigation and prosecution of crime was unveiled. The change in culture which the Philips Commission spearheaded coincided with press and media campaigns against police corruption and the work of investigative journalists who were examining the cases of the Birmingham Six, the Guildford Four and the Maguire Seven. The appeals in the Guildford and Woolwich cases were heard first and the suspects were released in October 1989. An independent inquiry into the case had found that the police in Surrey had edited or deleted sections of notes which were produced at the trial as contemporaneous records. There was no escaping the fact that some so-called contemporary notes had been written afterwards.

On the day the Guildford Four were released, a senior retired appeal court judge, Sir John May, was appointed to conduct a full judicial inquiry into the wrongful convictions, but this overlapped with a Royal Commission on Criminal Justice which had been appointed in 1991, under the chairmanship of Viscount Runciman, who, like Philips, was a historian. The May Inquiry had commissioned some independent research into possible sources of nitroglycerine contamination. This, together with other evidence, led the Director of Public Prosecutions to conclude that the convictions of the Maguire Seven were unsafe and their convictions were quashed in June 1991.

The Birmingham Six, however, remained in jail. Their convictions had been upheld in an appeal in 1988 when the Lord Chief Justice, Lord Lane, gave the court's judgment. But two years later, another independent investigation found that the record of interview of at least one of the Six had not been recorded contemporaneously, as the jury had been told. In addition, following Sir John May's research, doubts about the reliability of the scientific evidence in the case became apparent. The Home Secretary referred the case back to the Court of Appeal and the convictions of the Birmingham Six were quashed in 1991. That left Judith Ward.

Judith Ward did not appeal her conviction, but the Home Secretary referred her case to the Court of Appeal as, once again, the discredited Dr Skuse, had provided scientific evidence to the jury, but many more shortcomings in the criminal justice system were revealed when her conviction was quashed in June 1992. Lord Justice Glidewell publicly regretted the miscarriage of justice in her case, noting that one or more members of the West Yorkshire Police, the scientists who gave prosecution testimony, the staff in the office of the Director of Public Prosecutions and counsel had all 'failed in their basic duty to ensure a trial which is fair'.[55]

These stinging comments by a senior judge, apologising, in effect, on behalf of the whole judicial system, were unprecedented and a complete break from the days when the judiciary saw it as their duty to support and defend the system that they were part of. It led to yet more legislation when further investigative duties were placed under the rule of law.[56]

CONCLUSION

A number of lessons can be learned from these cases. First, the rule of law does not exist in a vacuum. It must be administered by human beings who, by their position and rank in society, have a responsibility to obey the rule of law. The senior barristers, John Scott Henderson QC in the Evans and Christie cases and Arthur James QC in the Challenor case, concluded that there was nothing basically wrong with the institutional legal and police culture that they were asked to investigate. The judges, Mr Justice Brabin and Lord Denning (on one significant occasion), were also more interested in preserving a system that was not allowed to fail than in trying to ensure an injustice was avoided. The deep-seated problems of 'bent coppers' and corrupt police officers were not identified in the James Report, even though there was an opportunity to do so, had James chosen to make robust recommendations. It took another seven years for an endemic culture which sapped public trust in the Metropolitan Police to be stamped out when Sir Robert Mark became Commissioner for the metropolis. The miscarriages of justice in the 'Irish cases' took many years to be put right. The rule of law is a fragile concept. In the verdurous garden of the English Constitution, the rule of law is still a weak plant that can be blown over and trampled upon by those charged with administering it. The rule of law needs caring for and nurturing. One nurturing method is for the Home Secretary of the day to appoint a royal commission to investigate weaknesses which come to public attention and ask for improvements to be suggested by an impartial board. This was done by Merlyn Rees (a Labour Home Secretary) in 1978 and by Kenneth Baker (a Conservative one) in 1991.

The recommendations of these commissions did more than party politicians – following election mandates and political pressures – to promote confidence in the rule of law. The innovations described in this chapter would not have happened without objective outsiders looking at criminal justice from a different perspective than the myopia of the legal elite. But politicians no longer seek objective evidence-based advice from academic and lay members of commissions on a regular basis. Since Margaret Thatcher came to power in 1979 there have been only three royal commissions appointed to give advice and recommendations, compared with thirty-four in the period between 1945 and 1979.[57] Home Secretaries of both parties prefer to set their own agenda within their own perceived political interests, appealing to their own voters. This has been one factor which has allowed populism to prosper as the prominence given to objective, evidence-based policy gradually gives way to policy based on party-political considerations.

The second spur to populism has, paradoxically, been a by-product of a much-needed reform. The Runciman Commission had recommended the creation of an independent body to investigate miscarriages of justice and the Criminal Cases Review Commission was set up in 1995. This was a welcome development, as it removed from the Home Office the responsibility of investigating and then referring miscarriage cases to the Court of Appeal when the normal appeal mechanisms had been exhausted. The side effect was that the Home Secretary was relieved of a great responsibility which made the holder of the office a quasi-minister of justice. The former Home Secretary Douglas Hurd explained in his memoirs the burden of considering the case of the Guildford Four: 'I had to consider with as much care and thought as I could where my responsibilities lay ... Men and women were alive and in prison ... The future of the life of human individuals rested on it, as well as the reputation of justice.'[58] Roy Jenkins, the Home Secretary who pardoned Timothy Evans, wrote how a mistake in the Home Office will have a direct impact on an individual, whereas a mistake at the Treasury will only involve a loss of resources.[59] It is no doubt a relief that modern Home Secretaries no longer have these responsibilities, but by losing them they are more free to be overtly political, knowing that they no longer have any role in dealing with miscarriages of justice. This new freedom is also a liberation that provides a window for populism should an incumbent Home Secretary choose to follow that route.

The third factor that has driven the rise of populism is that while trust is an important cultural ingredient in the way society functions, it is not a sufficient ingredient when it comes to criminal justice. Between 1972 and 1975, academics at the LSE conducted a survey into attitudes towards the Metropolitan Police. The survey found that there was a 96 per cent overall satisfaction rating; 93 per cent liked the police and 90 per cent trusted them.[60] If trust were the only measure by which to judge an institution with power to enforce law then there would have been no need for any of the reforms ushered in during the mid-1980s. If 'the will of the people' were the only measure of efficacy then, equally, no reforms would have been introduced. The public believed they were putting their trust in the police to behave honourably in the privacy of the police station in the years prior to 1985, when, in reality, they were placing faith, not trust, in the system. Much of what they believed they were trusting was hidden from scrutiny. Those who did know, or had the opportunity to know by presiding over criminal trials, appeals, inquiries and investigations, refused to believe that the system could fail until the Fisher Report was released at the end of 1977.

The Home Office civil servants and elected politicians similarly gave nourishment to a system that needed a change of diet, rather than further sustenance of the same kind. It was really the painstaking work of campaigning journalists and writers such as Ludovic Kennedy, Chris Mullin and Robert Kee, and politicians like Christopher Price, who uncovered uncomfortable truths about trust and paved the way for the rule of law to take a firm hold on the process of investigating and prosecuting crime and uncovering miscarriages of justice. A similar vigilance is now urgently required, as the new populism is challenging the rule of law in the new ways which will be described in the succeeding chapters.

CHAPTER 3

CLASS, DEFERENCE AND THE RISE OF JUDICIAL POWER

The year after Timothy Evans went to the gallows for a crime that he did not commit, one of the country's most eminent lawyers and public servants delivered the Reith Lectures for the BBC. Viscount Radcliffe was an outstanding lawyer who had been a scholar of distinction at Oxford. He was often asked by the government to chair royal commissions and public inquiries that were especially difficult or sensitive. He was also a Law Lord. His chosen subject for his Reith Lectures was 'The Problem of Power'. Radcliffe pondered on a topic that his fellow brethren on the bench had barely considered worth a passing thought. His thesis was that in medieval England absolute power had never been given to the king in an unqualified form, as the feudal system diffused power with the barons. Why, then, in contemporary post-war Britain did Parliament have the power to give the executive 'safe conduct' through the ordinary law? He warned against an over-powerful Parliament exercising such power that the glories of the common law liberal tradition have shrunk into 'meaningless constitutionalism' asserting that anything is right if it is permitted and nothing is right if it is forbidden.[1]

Radcliffe had no particular solution to this apparently insoluble state of affairs, but his warning about untrammelled power was to surface again many years later. In the meantime, his fellow judges wallowed in their own reflections of prestige with an authority that had been won through years of respect and deference accorded to them by a grateful public.

Lord Greene, a contemporary of Radcliffe's and Master of the Rolls, an ancient term which now means head of civil justice, during and just after the war believed firmly that: 'Parliament should make the law, the executive should administer the law, and the judiciary should interpret and enforce the law ... it is not for the judiciary to decide what is in the public interest nor is the judiciary concerned with policy.'[2] Five years later, Lord Greene's successor, Sir Raymond Evershed, submitted his views to the Lord Chancellor about government proposals to reform the administration of justice:

> It is, I think, clear that the supremacy of the so-called 'rule of law' in our country (which in the last resort may be the best protection against 'authoritarian' systems) is largely bound up with the immense prestige and personal position accorded to the judges ... The protection of the individual and his proprietary or other interests against the state can be easily over-rated.[3]

Evershed explained that the immense prestige of the judges came from the fact that they are picked from a highly reputable but cloistered aristocratic profession and that the judge was in complete control of the trial in both law and fact. He concluded by warning the Lord Chancellor that the government should not be too ambitious in seeking to reform the administration of justice. The personal position and prestige of the judges should not be undermined.

The views of these two senior judges during and just after the Second World War are significant. First, neither envisaged a particular role for judges within the Constitution other than to interpret the will of Parliament. A protection of the individual against the state was, for English judges, unlike their European counterparts, of minor importance. Sir Raymond Evershed was especially proud of the fact that judges had kept out of politics between 1945 and 1951 and had not sabotaged the social welfare state or the designs of the Labour government.[4] Second, Evershed placed great stress on the prestige and status of judges within the Constitution. These views coincided exactly with the opinion of the Lord Chancellor himself. The Lord Chancellor in the post-war Labour government was William Jowitt, who had been a contemporary of Clement Attlee at preparatory school.

A self-effacing and well-liked former barrister and Asquithian Liberal, Jowitt had converted to the Labour Party in order to become Attorney General in the National Government of 1931. Attlee made him Lord Chancellor in 1945, but while his party pursued socialist policies in the House of Commons, Jowitt was stoutly conservative on the woolsack in the Upper Chamber. He thought only the legislature could define principles which society should uphold. The role of the judge, in Jowitt's opinion, was to apply precedent and to articulate what the law was by interpreting statutes only on their plain meaning. Judicial creativity was not the role of judges. He did not want the European Convention on Human Rights, which his government had ratified by treaty in 1949, to be any part of English law. He believed it would compromise the sovereignty of Parliament.[5]

The post-war senior judiciary of the 1950s had hardly changed from its pre-war obsession with deference and status where 'the majesty of the law, embodied in the circuit system, moving from assize town to assize town, accompanied by Lords-Lieutenant, trumpeters, pikemen, marshalls and the butler, became a symbol for the irrelevance of the judiciary's role in modern England.'[6] The judiciary was becoming irrelevant because their power was unused. It is a singular feature of post-war political and legal history that while the government of the day, a reforming government of Clement Attlee from 1945 to 1951, was laying down the law in Parliament, the judiciary was deliberately declining a role for itself in scrutinising or reviewing in the courts the decisions of the executive giving effect to Parliament's intentions.

There were two important cultural reasons for this. First, in the period following wartime stringencies there was a general acceptance of rules and regulations which often smacked of totalitarianism. Douglas Jay, who served as a senior minister in both Attlee's government and that of Harold Wilson in the mid-1960s, wrote in 1937 that the necessities of life should be subject to planned distribution by the state in nutrition and health; just as in the case of education, the gentleman in Whitehall really does know better what is good for people than the people know themselves.[7] The Supplies and Services (Extended Purposes) Act in 1947 was designed to ensure the whole resources of the community were available for use in a manner best calculated to serve the interests of the community. This was patently authoritarian and there was an outcry from the liberal press. The judges, on the other hand, were silent. There was not an appetite among the public for challenging central authority in the early 1950s, and certainly not an appetite among judges to make rulings on the impact of sweeping powers on individual citizens.

The second reason that the judiciary were becoming irrelevant is different, but of equal importance. Both the judiciary and the senior civil service consisted of men (they were exclusively men) who were of the same clerisy; educated men, sharing common assumptions, whose loyalties were to the institution they had aspired to join. Entrants to the bar, and thereafter candidates for the bench, were, like their counterparts in the civil service, some of the brightest graduates from Oxford or Cambridge. Judges regarded those in the executive branch of government as their social and intellectual equals. If judges did not attempt to question the actions of the executive they were not, in their opinion, leaving a void. The intentions of the government were implemented by men from the same schools and universities as the judges themselves. Such men could be trusted to run the country without a judge looking over their shoulder.[8]

The senior civil service at this time consisted of men who had been at university, invariably either Oxford or Cambridge, between 1919 and 1949. It was a coterie of clever – although not overtly intellectual – men who shared common assumptions about public duty, who believed in loyalty to colleagues and who, on the whole, did not want radical change. These men valued government by discussion and consensus, with policies created through a process of objective reasoning and rational inquiry. Their thought processes were not particularly original, but neither were they revolutionary. They had nearly all been educated at public schools, where the overriding ethos was to obey. They were, in short, the establishment in Whitehall, the 'network of people with power and influence who rule the country'.[9]

When Roy Jenkins went to the Home Office in 1965 to take up his appointment as Home Secretary, he found a rigid, hierarchical structure with a 'defensive pattern of consistency' in which he received advice only in a coordinated minute, signed by the permanent secretary. This was the redoubtable Sir George Cunningham, whom everybody, Jenkins included, was required to address as 'Sir George'. It appeared to the new Home Secretary that nothing had changed within the Home Office for a period of twenty-five years.[10]

During this time judges were content to work by according benign obedience to the fidelity of law, without any aspiration to attempt legal reform. As the legal historian Robert Stevens has explained, during this period there was no public or administrative law to speak of and 'the legal system was increasingly irrelevant to the functioning of modern England'.[11]

While the executive and the judiciary enjoyed a cosy relationship of mutual admiration, politicians liked to remind everybody that judges occupied a separate world from their own. Judges did not have the requisite social origins, training or experience to attempt to make law. Their task was simply to apply the laws that Parliament had made. Politicians wanted them to be just the servants of Parliament.[12]

An example of the increasing irrelevance of the courts in doing justice in administrative and local government law occurred when some functions of two rural district councils were subsumed into a larger administrative unit, the Newport Corporation in the early 1950s. An issue arose about the level of compensation payable to the district councils who had lost income as a result of the merger. The relevant legislation was obscure and badly drafted and Lord Justice Denning (then a newly appointed appellate judge who would later become one of the country's best-known judges) said that the courts should not put an 'ultra-legalistic interpretation' on words in a statute if the result would cause injustice. In Denning's opinion the courts should strive to find what the intentions of Parliament had been in drafting legislation in order to make proper sense of an enactment. He was given a stinging rebuke by the Lord Chancellor when the case was taken to the House of Lords (which at that time was the highest appeal court). Lord Simonds said it was not the law of England that it was the duty of the court to divine the intention of Parliament. To do so would usurp the legislative function under the thin disguise of interpretation. If the legislature had not made their intentions clear then only the legislature could fill the gap by passing a further act of Parliament.[13]

In the 1950s, judicial self-restraint appeared to have won a decisive victory over judicial activism, and judges voluntarily curbed their own power to review administrative decisions.[14] Professor Sir William Wade, Britain's foremost constitutional expert in the 1960s and 1970s, put it more bluntly:

> During and after the Second World War a deep gloom settled on administrative law ... the courts and the legal profession ... showed little stomach for ... imposing law upon government ... It was hard to understand why, in the flood of new powers and jurisdictions that came with the welfare state, administrative law should not have been vigorously revived, just when the need for it was greatest.[15]

The judiciary was something of a backwater within the Constitution in the 1950s and was in danger of losing respect. While the bench in the 1950s contained its share of 'scholarly, fair and decent men, it also had more than its share of cantankerous, prejudiced, intimidating and boorish judges constrained by no retirement age'.[16] The English judiciary in the 1950s remained shackled in the past, cocooned in its own customs and traditions, scared of political controversy and frightened to stand up to the executive. When a barrister called John Widgery QC was promoted to the bench in 1961 there was disgruntlement that he would retain his military moustache (which he did) as the remainder of the bench were all clean-shaven.[17] Conformity enhanced trustworthiness. In the event, the moustachioed Widgery went on to become Lord Chief Justice – to the chagrin, no doubt, of his clean-shaven colleagues.

The government and the civil service were trusted by the judiciary to carry on with their business on the strict understanding that the traditions and customs of the law were left alone by government. This arrangement suited the governing party and the civil service perfectly. Politicians and civil servants could sleep easy at night knowing there would be no threat to the way that they chose to govern from the judiciary. When the *Daily Mirror* commented that 'from the judges downward, the legal profession is antiquated in its thinking, its procedure, its language and its dress', everyone knew the editor was taking a friendly swipe at the slightly comical way the judiciary chose to present themselves.[18]

Small changes in judicial attitudes began to reveal themselves in the later 1960s. In a rather obscure case about compensation for British companies in Egypt whose property had been sequestered during the Suez crisis, the House of Lords abandoned the formalistic approach to statutory interpretation. They decided that the courts should, at last, give a purposeful interpretation to statutes. The decision pointed the way for the courts to regain the initiative in public law cases by looking at the intention of Parliament, not just to give a literal interpretation of the words on a page.[19]

It was not until 1972 that Britain's most senior judge, Lord Reid, finally made it clear, in a speech, that judges did more than simply declare what the law was, as enacted by Parliament: they also made law.

There was a time when it was thought almost indecent to suggest that judges made law – they only declare it. Those with a taste for fairy tales seem to have thought that in some Aladdin's cave there is hidden the common law in all its splendour and that on a judge's appointment there descends on him knowledge of the words 'open sesame'. Bad decisions are given when the judge muddles the password and the wrong door opens. But we do not believe in fairy tales any more.[20]

The common law was not something merely *ex post facto*, as Bentham had witheringly described it; a law made after the event, when litigants who had been through an experience went to court to try to discover what the judge would say about it. The common law was always there. It had grown up through usage and custom, owing nothing to Parliament, and was therefore independent, and such independence is a bulwark against tyranny. The common law is also flexible and is able to apply and adapt precedent to new facts presented in new cases.

In 1974, Sir Leslie Scarman, then a High Court judge who was to become a Law Lord and chairman of important inquiries, thought that the development of the common law might have run out of steam. In excoriating language, he identified weaknesses of the common law and cast blame on the failure of practitioners, academics and his fellow judges on the bench for having a lack of sensitivity to the changes that were taking place in society:

The law is very much the esoteric business of lawyers. It is neither easily accessible nor easy to understand when found. It is resistant to change: encapsulated in the forensic process, jealously guarded by those tireless workers in the legal hive, the teachers and the practitioners, it can have no greater sensitivity to the winds, let alone the gentle breezes, of change than have the judges and the profession who administer it … Social change is currently a most formidable threat to the English legal system, as we know it today … It appears to need new law, new principles, new remedies, new machinery and new men … It is no longer sufficient for the law to provide a framework of freedom in which men, women and children may work out their own destinies: social justice … requires the law to be loaded in favour of the weak and exposed.[21]

Sir Leslie Scarman was extraordinarily far-sighted. Almost all of his criticisms of the complacent attitudes which existed throughout the legal establishment have since been addressed and to a great extent remedied. Even his enthusiasm for a recognition of entrenched rights were taken up later by fellow judges and legal commentators. Scarman believed strongly that English law had much to learn from foreign jurisdictions. He highlighted a trend which could be traced back to the creation of the International Labour Organisation in 1919 and the European Convention for the Protection of Human Rights and Fundamental Freedoms in 1950. Each sent a clear message: if rights were declared to be fundamental then no body or group (including a sovereign Parliament) could diminish them. Applying this message to Britain, Scarman acknowledged there was a problem. This was what he called 'the helplessness of the law in the face of the legislative sovereignty of Parliament which makes it difficult for the legal system to accommodate the concept of fundamental and inviolable human rights'.[22]

Scarman had identified a problem that would, in the next forty years, bring politicians into conflict with the judges. Charters from continental Europe and broadly generalised declarations of rights from America just do not fit into English constitutional arrangements. If individual rights are to be laid down in a written document and applied and interpreted by judges, then what role is there for elected politicians to amend, alter or abolish a charter? In simple terms, Scarman had identified a power struggle but the field of battle had not, in 1974, been established. In fact, the battle lines were not drawn up until Margaret Thatcher came to power in 1979.

THE ARRIVAL OF MARGARET THATCHER

Scarman presented his argument at the Hamlyn Lectures, which coincided with Margaret Thatcher's arrival on the political scene in February 1975 as leader of the Conservative opposition in the House of Commons. Her arrival was as unexpected as it was enthralling. With a no-nonsense energy, Thatcher set about shattering the political consensus that existed between many middle-of-the-road Conservatives and their opposite numbers in the moderate wing of the Labour Party. Thatcher's instinctive suspicion of consensus had a profound effect both on politics and on the relationship between elected politicians and judges. Shortly after her election as Conservative leader, succeeding Edward Heath, Thatcher interrupted a rather tedious policy seminar by reaching into her handbag and holding aloft a book called *The Constitution of Liberty* by F. A. Hayek and announcing, to the astonishment of those present, 'This is what we believe.'[23]

The book in question had been written in 1960, but Hayek's philosophy was further developed over a period in the 1970s, culminating in a three-volume tome, published in 1982, called *Law, Legislation and Liberty*. Hayek, a Nobel Prize-winner who was born in Vienna but became a British subject in 1938, was one of the most profound thinkers of the twentieth century and, like Thatcher herself, an enemy of consensus. It is beyond doubt that Hayek had a significant influence on Margaret Thatcher's political beliefs and those of her acolytes and colleagues.

Hayek set out to provide a new and comprehensive statement about liberal principles, justice and political economy. His task was to debunk theories, originating in the Enlightenment, that societies arose from the conscious and deliberate decisions of individuals. This was a fallacy. In order for something to be designed or planned, the designer, usually a government, must know all the true facts which allow a decision to be made, but this is a delusion as human activity is made of millions of individual decisions, all of which cannot be known by everybody else. The evolution of order among peoples is therefore spontaneous. In Hayek's view there should be the absolute minimum of broadly general rules of organisation, to permit spontaneous order to flourish.[24] Hayek likened spontaneous order to the common law of England which provided basic freedoms in the eighteenth century. The common law was not authoritative in setting out rules for obedience but existed to oversee a set of rules enabling men and women to live together in orderly relations. The judge acted as a preserver of the peace which spontaneous order had produced. However, the consequences of spontaneous order can never be predicted and therefore the results of spontaneous order cannot always have been intended. In Hayek's mind there is not a purpose or a value in the rule of law. A state of affairs does not have any intrinsic value which is independent of the choices made by individuals. It is neither just nor unjust. Law evolves in the same way as societies evolve and permits the decisions of individuals to flourish. The law, for Hayek, did not have a single purpose but only countless different purposes for different individuals. The judiciary had no role in deciding how society ought to behave.

When Margaret Thatcher became a prominent politician in the mid-1970s, the views of Sir Leslie Scarman and those of F. A. Hayek could hardly be more different. Scarman had warned that the common law was failing to address problems of distributive justice and was mapping a future for the common law based on a charter of rights, whereas Hayek maintained that such universal rights were a fallacy and logically impossible. *The Mirage of Social Justice* was published in 1976, within two years of Scarman's Hamlyn Lecture, and Hayek's trenchant opinions were expressed in uncompromising terms. The word 'law', for Hayek, meant only a safeguard for the freedom of an individual and he argued that it should not be used as a term defining conduct of individuals towards each other in a social context.

It was fundamentally and morally wrong, according to Hayek, to impose social justice on spontaneous market order. For Hayek, there could be no such thing as inherent rights for an individual. There was only a right to live a life within his or her chosen domain, which was recognised by a corresponding obligation from another, which might involve government, to respect that right. There can be no right, in the sense of a claim, to be super-imposed on spontaneous order. This would imply somebody has a corresponding duty to transform spontaneous order into an organisation assuming power to control the results. This, for Hayek, is not only logically impossible but positively dangerous since the organisation assuming power would inevitably become socialist or totalitarian in nature. When Margaret Thatcher famously declared 'there is no such thing as society', she was quoting almost verbatim from Hayek: 'We are not members of an organisation called society, because the society which produces the means for the satisfaction of most of our needs is not an organisation directed by a conscious will, and could not produce what it does if it were.'[25] Hayek also believed that morality was an entirely private matter. If an individual did good works it was because of the goodness of his private heart, not because he was bound to the beneficiaries of the act by ties of mutual obligation.[26]

This conflict between politicians who were followers of Hayek and lawyers who became inspired by Scarman therefore began in the mid-1970s, but few noticed the tectonic movements in the political and legal plates beneath them at the time. Hayek was not a well-known figure outside of his own cloistered academic environment, and Scarman was a serving judge, and judges express their views on legal topics only when invited to do so, and then only in legal lectures on rare occasions. Neither man was exactly a public figure; still less was either recognised as a trailblazer for a struggle for supremacy in a war of ideas that did not break out until the 1990s.

In his memoirs, a close confidant and Cabinet colleague of Margaret Thatcher, Nigel Lawson, summarised her unique contribution to politics as 'free markets, financial discipline, firm control over public expenditure, tax cuts, nationalism, "Victorian values" … privatisation and a dash of populism'.[27] It was a shrewd summary. Thatcher was far from being a populist in the modern sense of the term. She had just enough of a dash of it for her successors to pepper it up to full flavour. This fully cooked populism broke out in the 1990s.

When Margaret Thatcher entered Downing Street on 4 May 1979, she was determined there would be no 'collectivist' theories of social justice, which she associated with socialism. Her government would enlarge the freedom of the individual and expose the fallacy that 'social justice' was more equitable than justice to the individual. She was a strong advocate of what she called the 'rule of law', but she did not believe the rule of law itself secured justice. For her, justice required that certain fashionable heresies were defeated, and it was the responsibility of those in public office to defeat them. The first heresy, according to Thatcher, was the notion that if there was sufficient intimidation by a determined minority, the law would not be used against them. This, she called the 'collective immunity' from a legal process. Here, she had in mind picketing by trade unions. The second heresy was what she called the 'superiority to the law' by those who felt strongly about individual issues like nuclear weapons or animal liberation.[28] Here, she had in mind the Greenham Common women, who were camped at an American airbase in Wiltshire to protest against nuclear weapons, and animal rights demonstrators who invaded scientific laboratories.

Margaret Thatcher was conscious that Parliament itself could not be relied upon to repudiate these heresies: 'Parliaments act by majorities and majorities are not always right.' The rule of law, she maintained, could not stop a parliamentary majority from acting unjustly, as the courts had no alternative but to administer any law passed by Parliament. Freedom, according to Thatcher, can be guaranteed neither by Parliament nor by the courts. Freedom depended on an unwritten moral code which had a quality to impel Parliament to use its majority as a trust, to pass laws in accordance with concepts of fairness and justice. 'It is this code that maintains the rule of law.'[29]

Underpinning this unwritten code was a notion of respect for the rule of law. In the Conservative Party manifesto for the 1979 general election there were bold promises to restore respect for the rule of law which was 'the basis of a free and civilised life'. The Conservatives promised to restore a lost respect by re-establishing the supremacy of Parliament and giving priority to the fight against crime: 'We will see that Parliament and no other body stands at the centre of the nation's life and decisions, and we will seek to make it effective in its job of controlling the executive.'[30]

Some features of Margaret Thatcher's political outlook were important in defining what was to become the relationship between politicians and judges under her successor, John Major. First, she envisaged no role for the courts in controlling the behaviour of the executive. This was exclusively the responsibility of Parliament, but Parliament could not be relied on to repudiate the heresies which imperilled the freedom of the individual. The judges had no role in this since their job was to carry out the will of Parliament. It was only the unwritten moral code which placed restraint on the supremacy of Parliament, not the rule of law. The moral code provided 'liberty in a strong social order'.[31] This social order comprised thrift, respect for authority, family values and individual freedom within a moral compass based on tradition. It was the individual, who was self-sufficient, loyal to friends and robust against enemies, who embodied this invisible and unwritten moral code. In addition, there was a faith in government to do the right thing: 'Her instincts were rooted in the legitimacy of a single all-powerful executive subject only to periodic election.'[32]

While Margaret Thatcher wanted a strong executive at the heart of government, people as a whole were becoming more 'aware of their rights as consumers; were more mobile and changing their jobs more frequently; and were becoming less deferential of authority'.[33] Ten years later an American academic reviewed these promises. He concluded that Thatcher's legacy was more 'law and order' than rule of law, placed individual rights over collective rights and promoted an unqualified support for the police.[34]

There was, however, a fundamental paradox about Thatcherism. On the one hand, Margaret Thatcher wanted to rein in collective action, reduce trade union power and break up state monopolies. On the other, she relied on a strong centralised state with a powerful executive to push through her reforms. In reality, what society needed as much as anything else was a strong and independent judiciary to uphold rights and oversee the ever-growing powerful executive.

This is exactly what happened. While the Thatcher style wanted strong, central control where the 'moral code' set the limits on individual autonomy, the public were beginning to understand that they also had power. The ideal nation state for Thatcher was one which was deregulated, with private enterprise replacing the dead hand of publicly owned institutions. This coincided with a new liberated citizen as well. Class barriers were breaking down, sexual taboos were being broken and the citizen as consumer began to realise that they had rights. A powerful cadre of government officials still existed in the free environment that Thatcher was designing. The corollary of this development was that the citizen was ready to confront bureaucrats with as much vigour as Thatcher was trying to dismantle state-run industry. State power could be challenged in the courts in a remedy called judicial review.

JUDICIAL REVIEW

Judicial review is a means whereby an aggrieved citizen can seek to have a decision taken by a public body overturned on the grounds that the public body had exceeded its lawful powers. A judge who hears a judicial review application is not concerned with the merits of the decision, only whether it was taken within the rule of law. The public body is then obliged to think again and to try to frame the use of power in a legal way.

The remedy of judicial review became a method of challenging decisions which produced conflict. In the 1970s and 1980s there were conflicts between central and local government, for example in the dispute about whether to retain or abolish grammar schools. The public resorted to the courts if they believed public bodies exceeded their powers. The huge growth in the number of tribunals inevitably led to challenges in the High Court where a person was aggrieved by the fairness or lawfulness of a tribunal decision. A growing scepticism about the right of the powerful to rule over the powerless became a discernible trend within society and consumers were becoming more confident in asserting their rights against producers.[35] Another senior lawyer went further and argued that recourse to judicial review by litigants was an understandable response to the powers of the corporate state in Britain, which, since 1945, had imposed more and more power on officials. This allowed the civil service to acquire huge levels of power over administrative tribunals. Judicial review realigns the polarities of state power by using the full sovereignty the courts possess to oversee the practices of tribunals.[36] For example, if a social security tribunal is created to mediate between the state and the citizen in the provision of benefits for those who are in hardship, the tribunal cannot simply be part of the executive arm. The tribunal must apply basic principles of fairness and justice in reaching a decision; the reasons for the decision must be clearly understood; and the ground rules for the decision must be known in advance. The Queen may make law in Parliament, but the Queen's courts interpret and apply the law. One central point has to be borne in mind: all judicial review decisions recognise the fundamental importance of parliamentary sovereignty in Britain's constitutional arrangements. The courts always try to honour this obligation by maintaining the 'appropriate balance' between judicial intervention and judicial restraint.[37]

During the period of Thatcher's administration, conflicts between the judiciary and the executive became a regular occurrence. The judiciary were becoming powerful, but their power had emerged through the social, cultural and political changes which were taking place within society. But it was a use of power that could challenge the lawfulness of executive decisions directly that would involve ministers of the Crown themselves. This is what rankled politicians and laid the foundations of the current suspicions that many politicians, egged on by populists, have of the judiciary.

IMMIGRATION AND THE CASE OF 'CITIZEN M'

There is no greater use of state power than in the immigration and asylum system. Any person without a United Kingdom passport may be admitted or refused admission to the country and even if admitted may later be deported and never allowed to return. Such a situation occurred in September 1990 when a young 24-year-old citizen of Zaire (now the Democratic Republic of the Congo) applied for political asylum after he had entered the United Kingdom on a flight from Nigeria. Known only as 'M', his application for asylum was based on the fact that he had organised a teacher's strike in Zaire and had been imprisoned for this activity. He feared for his future safety if he was ever to be sent back to Zaire. His application was considered by Home Office civil servants but was rejected on the grounds that there was no evidence to support the fact that he had been imprisoned for trade union activity in Zaire. As was his right, he challenged this decision, but the Court of Appeal refused to quash the deportation order, which was due to take place later the same day, on 1 May 1991.

What happened next was speedy and rather confusing. From his confinement in Pentonville Prison, Citizen M was able to instruct new solicitors, who made a dash to the High Court at 5.30 p.m. and found a judge who could hear a fresh application to quash the deportation order, based on new grounds. By this time, M was at Heathrow and was about to board a plane to Paris to connect with a flight to Kinshasa, the capital of Zaire. The judge could hardly embark on a full hearing so late in the court day, so, relying on what he believed to have been an undertaking by the barrister representing the Home Secretary that M would not be put on the plane pending his decision, he adjourned the case to the following day. In fact, counsel had not given the undertaking because he had no instructions to give it, nor could the solicitor for the Home Office request the airline to hold M's departure, as he was in contact with the wrong terminal at Heathrow. In the muddle, M flew to Paris and in no time at all was on a night flight to Kinshasa.

Once M's solicitors learned of this development, they contacted the judge at his home. Such an occurrence is perfectly normal, as there is always a duty judge who is able to deal with urgent and pressing matters available at all hours. The judge believed the Home Secretary had deliberately disobeyed an order of the court and issued a judicial direction over the telephone, relayed to the British Embassy in Kinshasa, that M be returned to the United Kingdom as soon as he arrived. At around midnight, while M was 35,000 feet above the continent of Africa, the judge made a written order. The judge's order stated that it was a disgrace that, contrary to an undertaking by counsel for the Home Office, lines of communication to prevent failed asylum seekers being removed pending a full hearing had not been used. As a consequence, the Home Secretary and his officials must procure the immediate return of M to the United Kingdom. If necessary, ordered the judge, he should be held at Kinshasa by British Embassy staff until a return flight could be arranged. This order was sent by fax (emails were hardly used at that time and not by government departments) to the Home Office. Hardly surprisingly, there was nobody at the other end to receive it.

The next day, 2 May 1991, the minister of state at the Home Office responsible for immigration and asylum cases was waking up to the fact that there had been an unusual flurry of activity overnight and a High Court judge appeared to be rather cross. Meanwhile, in Kinshasa, M was in the care of the British Embassy after his flight had arrived in the early morning and the staff there were studying timetables for flights back to the UK. In Whitehall, there was no time to lose and an urgent meeting between the Home Secretary, Kenneth Baker, and his minister of state was arranged for the afternoon at short notice. The Home Secretary took the view that as M's appeal against the deportation had been refused once by the Court of Appeal (which was true), the deportation was sound in law and therefore M should not be flown back to the United Kingdom. The British Embassy in Kinshasa were told to abandon the plans to send M back to Britain. Later the same day, the Home Secretary received advice from counsel that he should appeal, forthwith, the judge's order made in the small hours of the previous day.

At the end of twenty-four hours of hectic activity it is likely that neither the judge who made the order nor the Home Secretary who chose to ignore it realised that they had embroiled themselves in a case of considerable constitutional importance. What was at stake was a question of whether the Home Secretary himself could be impleaded for a contempt of court. On the face of it, Baker had known of the order and had chosen to ignore it, but was the order valid in the first place? Could a Secretary of State, in high office under the Crown, be a person, like any other, who could be in contempt of a court order? The Home Secretary's reason for not complying with the order was that, in his view, the judge had no jurisdiction to make it. M was far away on a flight over a foreign land. This was a misconception. An order of the court is valid unless patently beyond the power of the court to make it, unless and until it is complied with or overturned on appeal.

After mature reflection, the constitutional importance of the case turned on what the words 'the Crown' mean. True enough, the sovereign is immune from being sued or prosecuted and Parliament is immune from being sued or prosecuted for anything said or done in the course of its own proceedings. Equally, judges cannot be sued or prosecuted for anything done in connection with a case they are trying, but is the Home Secretary the 'Crown', or is he an individual acting in an official capacity, given to him by virtue of his office? The argument put forward by Kenneth Baker was that he was responsible only to Parliament if he failed in his capacity as a member of the executive. It was only Parliament who could censure him. The courts were the judicial arm of the executive and submission by a minister of the Crown to the order of the court was voluntary, not compulsory under the rule of law.

The judge who heard the case agreed and concluded that the relationship between the executive and the courts is one of trust only. On appeal, more senior judges disagreed. The Court of Appeal (and later the House of Lords) was clear that, on the facts, the Home Secretary had interfered with the administration of justice by removing from the jurisdiction of the court a person with whom the Home Secretary was in dispute. The key point for the

court to decide was what the consequences were for a Home Secretary who interferes with the administration of justice? For mere
mortals, who are not Secretaries of State in Her Majesty's government, the consequence is proceedings for contempt of court, and
these were exactly the proceedings that lawyers for M were taking
against Kenneth Baker MP. The House of Lords decided that it was
fundamental to the rule of law that orders of the High Court were
respected by the executive in the same way that the courts would
respect the acts of the executive providing that both work within
their respective legal frameworks. The highest court in the land decided that a Secretary of State was liable to be sued for contempt of
court just like everybody else.

This case was an important one in many respects. First, it was
not enough to rely on trust to define the relationship between the
executive and the judges. The rule of law required the relationship
to be firm, predictable and clear. The lessons are that if trust breaks
down, as it does when something goes wrong or the public lose
confidence in their elected representative, then the rule of law steps
in. But trust cannot be the foundation of good practice all of the
time. Rules of law are essential to ensure that trust is not a mere
backstop, a convenient tradition, a disguise shielding behaviour
which is unlawful.

BORIS JOHNSON JOINS THE CONTROVERSY

The reverberations of the case of the anonymous failed asylum
seeker M called for a response. Who better to take on this task than
Boris Johnson, who was then a journalist at the *Spectator* maga-
zine? In a long piece, published in June 1995 to coincide with the
release of the film *Judge Dredd* (the helmeted character who had
power to convict, sentence and sometimes execute wrongdoers in a

dystopian future of mega-cities), Johnson argued that judges were acting like 'frustrated politicians which some of them may very well be'. He speculated that there could be a reintegration of the judiciary and the executive unless judges were put firmly back in their box.[38]

Making use of his classical education, Johnson referred to the fact that the ancient Hebrew rulers Othniel, Deborah and Shamgar wielded power because they combined leadership with judgeship. With confident flamboyance, linguistic flourishes and reckless exaggeration, Johnson took aim at the High Court judges and described how they lived 'complete with butlers, cooks and parlour-maids' and then targeted the huge financial rewards of barristers in their 'pleasant, Oxbridge-college-style Inns'. Pitted against this privileged elite were the hard-working politicians in Parliament who embraced the admirable causes of 'frustrating scroungers' and keeping 'a couple of Kashmiri murderers in jail'. Johnson's language was pure populism: 'scroungers' and 'murderers' were being kept at bay by the politicians while the judges were busy trying to stop the politicians from doing their job. Judges, according to Johnson, should go back to being just 'snaggle-toothed Wykehamists' (students at the public school Winchester College), who kept out of politics. Unless they did, one of them would 'force the generals to welcome homosexuals into the ranks'. Thankfully, this prophecy, provided by a judge, proved to be correct.

Boris Johnson's broadside reflected another trend within Thatcherism: a dislike and suspicion of the professional elite in general. The legal profession was perceived as being elitist and unaccountable and the judges at the top of it were using their elite power to challenge an elected government. The cosy privilege of lawyers and judges who overstepped into political territory needed cutting down to size. Judges were especially elitist and unaccountable as they used their power to undermine the executive, but intellectuals in general were not exempt from the withering stare of disapproval from Thatcher.

In 1985, the University of Oxford had refused to award Thatcher an honorary degree, which was an almost unprecedented snub, since she was the first Oxford-educated Prime Minister since 1945 to be denied the honour. The late polymath Jonathan Miller called Thatcher a 'philistine of odious suburban gentility and saccharine patriotism, catering to the worst elements of commuter idiocy'.[39] The intellectual snobbery of this remark was, no doubt, hurtful, but it was not untypical of the contempt with which academics and many lawyers viewed the tendencies of the Prime Minister to impose change on institutions that were occupied by elites. The tendencies to try to reduce the power of elites gave birth to a strain of populism which was to emerge in the mid-1990s. This kind of populism distrusted experts who occupied elite positions in public life. Boris Johnson in his *Spectator* article had succeeded in planting a narrative in the public mind that the judiciary was becoming too strong, too unaccountable and too undemocratic.

LORD BINGHAM'S ANSWER AND THE CASE OF THE UNIFICATION CHURCH

The truth was a little different. As Lord Bingham has explained, no constitutional democracy can function without judicial review: 'Far from challenging the authority of Parliament, as is sometimes suggested, judicial review buttresses the authority of Parliament by ensuring that powers conferred by Parliament are used as Parliament intended.'[40]

It was not true that judges were undemocratic or unaccountable. That was constitutional nonsense. Judges are unelected as they owe fidelity only to the law and not to the electorate, whose opinions may change during a judge's tenure of office. A judge represents no body of opinion or majority view. A judge must do justice to every person in all communities regardless of the political complexion of that community. The truth was that politicians feared the power of judges. These simple points seem often to have eluded politicians, especially those who fancy themselves as tribunes of the public, who like to hit the headlines by trying to expose the foibles of unelected judges.

In October 1995, the founder of the Unification Church, Sun Myung Moon, a citizen of South Korea, applied to enter the United Kingdom for the purposes of a religious and private meeting with his followers, who were colloquially known as 'the Moonies'. He wished also to address a meeting of about 1,200 guests at the Queen Elizabeth II Conference Centre in central London. Before his visit, some newspapers, particularly the *Mail on Sunday*, had expressed horror that such a man was to visit London. There was a fear that 'the Moonies' were a threat to the British family life. The Home Secretary refused entry clearance to the Rev. Moon on the grounds that his presence in the United Kingdom was not conducive to the public good. This was a judgment that could be made, under our Constitution, exclusively by the Home Secretary, and his decision was final. There was no avenue for appeal unless there was an appeal to a judge to declare the exclusion order unlawful. This required judicial review proceedings to be pursued.

Rev. Moon argued that the Home Secretary's decision was irrational as four years earlier he had been granted entry clearance into the United Kingdom by an adjudicator. The question, therefore, was whether the Home Secretary had a continuing obligation to comply with the earlier decision to admit him, or whether there was a clear and obvious reason to depart from it. This could be a new event or a new discovery of a past event capable of giving grounds for a change of mind. However, as the judge found, there were no new events giving grounds for a change of mind. In addition, Rev. Moon had been given no opportunity to respond to the Home Secretary's reversal of an earlier judicial decision. The judge added, 'This is precisely the unpopular applicant for whom the safeguards of due process are most relevant in a society which acknowledges the rule of law.'[41]

This rider should have given comfort to those who value the primacy of law over politics, but the next day an MP denounced the decision as 'extraordinary' and an example of the contempt with which some members of the judiciary seem to treat the views of the House of Commons and of the general public.[42] This, of course, was wrong on all counts. The decision to refuse entry to Rev. Moon had been taken by the Home Secretary, not by the legislature, and as far as a tirade in the *Mail on Sunday* is concerned, it is a matter of opinion as to whether or not it represented the views of the public. In the event, the legal challenge was something of a damp squib. The Rev. Moon abandoned his plans to visit the United Kingdom.

MICHAEL HOWARD AND THE CASE OF JAMIE BULGER

The Home Secretary whose decision was quashed in 'the Moonies' case was Michael Howard, who was, arguably, Britain's first truly populist politician in power. Born in south Wales, he chose to become a Conservative at a young age, which was an unusual choice for a gifted child in the Principality who had ambitions to enter Parliament. A quick-witted and affable man with an easy smile and natural charm, Howard went to Peterhouse College, Cambridge, and studied economics before switching to law. Among his contemporaries at Cambridge were Kenneth Clarke, who preceded him as Home Secretary, and John Selwyn Gummer, who also went on to hold high office. Howard had made his reputation as a formidable advocate in planning cases with a capability to combine levity with serious argument, and he had the intellect and the eloquence to take him to the highest ranks of Queen's Counsel. But he really wanted to become a politician. He achieved quick promotion in Margaret Thatcher's second administration and became a member of her Cabinet within six and a half years of entering Parliament.

Michael Howard's time as Home Secretary was beset with controversy. He had a reputation as a committed reformer who wanted to reverse 'progressive theories of the 1960s and 1970s' that 'made excuses for crime and seemed to blame everyone apart from the criminal'.[43] Crime had been rising inexorably between 1980 and 1993 – the period presided over by Margaret Thatcher and then John Major from 1990 – and Howard was determined to reverse the trend. *The Sun* greeted his appointment as Home Secretary with the words: 'At last we've got a Home Secretary who is on the public's side.'[44] At the Conservative Party conference in October 1993, Howard introduced a shopping list of reforms to help the police, make it easier to convict those on trial for criminal offences and a plan to build more prisons. 'Let us be clear. Prison works,' he declared to the rousing cheers of the audience. *The Sun* could hardly contain itself: 'What a great day for people power,' it gushed.[45] Howard had succeeded in making the Conservative Party unequivocally the 'law and order' party. A senior retired judge reflected on Howard's career and commented that he made 'illiberal and populist decisions' which as a QC he must have known were vulnerable to attack, but as a politician he would not mind too much if his views chimed with his party supporters.[46]

Tony Blair, Howard's opposite number as shadow Home Secretary, had to tread water in an attempt to keep his party's policy
afloat by declaring that he was 'tough on crime and tough on the
causes of crime' at the Labour Party conference in Brighton in 1995.
But this was no match for the genuine article. The Conservatives
were now out in front as being tough on crime, unlike the man-
darins in the Home Office, who were the last relics of a defeatist
post-war consensus in the eyes of Howard and his allies.

Michael Howard had identified a rather more progressive civil
service than the one that Roy Jenkins had encountered during
his time at the Home Office. In fact, a near revolution in outlook
had taken place in the twenty-seven years which separated Jenkins's and Howard's tenures in that particular corridor of power.
The historian Peter Hennessy has suggested that the sea-change
in outlook within Whitehall happened when the 'establishment'
became a 'meritocracy'.[47] The meritocratic generation were those
born around the time of the Education Act 1944. The expansion
of free education allowed the supple, concealed soft power of the
public school 'establishment' to be shared with a generation that
valued, above all, their own ability to succeed on merit. Ironically,
Michael Howard had himself benefited from being a member of
the meritocratic generation, but the civil service was full of similar
individuals. Like Howard himself, the meritocratic generation were
in positions of power and authority during Margaret Thatcher's
premiership between 1979 and 1990.

The best-known of the new breed of civil servants was Clive Ponting. He was a senior civil servant in the Ministry of Defence who
leaked a document from his department to a Labour MP which
revealed that Parliament had been misled about the circumstances in which an Argentinian cruise ship, the *General Belgrano*, had

been sunk by British naval forces during the Falklands War in 1982. Ponting was prosecuted under the Official Secrets Act. His defence at his trial at the Old Bailey in 1985 was that it was in the public interest for such a document to be in the public domain. Despite the judge's legal directions that this was not a valid defence as 'public interest' was only a matter for the government to decide, the jury acquitted Ponting. The case provided another demonstration of the good sense of the jury system which could put deference aside.

Other meritocrats included women such as Caroline Slocock, who became Margaret Thatcher's private secretary, and Kate Jenkins, who went on to become director of the Prime Minister's efficiency unit in 1986. At the Home Office, a cerebral and liberal-minded man named John Halliday held a senior position. He wrote a key report called 'Making Punishments Work' in 2001, which reviewed the criminal sentencing framework in England and Wales and went on to form the basis of the Labour Party's criminal justice policy.[48] Halliday's thinking was the polar opposite to that of Michael Howard, which held that prison worked.

The civil service had become much more progressive and open-minded, in contrast to the politicians in power, who were embracing populism. In 1995, the Conservative Party chairman, Brian Mawhinney, told the party conference that people should let judges know when they were dissatisfied with them. 'Magistrates and judges are good people,' he declared, 'but they do not act in a vacuum. They are your representatives, so praise them when you agree with them and let them know if you are dissatisfied.'[49] This was disingenuous populism. Judges and magistrates should be representative of the people, but they cannot represent the people, in the sense of being accountable to the people at an election. Judges and magistrates are accountable only to the law by doing right to those who appear before them without fear or favour, affection or ill-will according to law. This is the oath taken by every judge and magistrate in the land.

The rule of law and populism make for uneasy bedfellows. The rule of law is different from law and order. Law and order is the province of political decision-making. The rule of law is above politics. As Lord Denning was fond of reminding us, 'Be ye never so high, the law is above you.'[50] Michael Howard did not bear these words in mind when he had to make an important decision in a case which became known to all as the Jamie Bulger murder.

This was a horrific case which is etched in the minds of everybody who knows what happened on 12 February 1993. Jamie Bulger was nearly three years old when he was taken shopping by his mother. The pair went to New Strand Shopping Centre in Bootle on Merseyside and when shopping Denise Bulger took her eye off her son for a second or two. Jamie had seemingly disappeared completely among the crowds of shoppers. After twenty-four hours of parental agony, the police released a grainy, somewhat blurred CCTV image of a young child, Jamie, being led away by two other children, who looked to be about ten or eleven years old. The images were played over and over on television and the still pictures appeared in every newspaper. Two days later, Jamie's dead body was found on a little-used freight railway line in Walton, Liverpool. He had been killed in a prolonged and violent attack. Bricks and stones had been thrown at him and he had been kicked in the face and body. He had been beaten on his buttocks and the foreskin of his penis showed signs of having been pulled back. But perhaps the most horrific aspect of the murder was that his killers had left Jamie's tiny body across one of the tracks on the railway line so that his dead body would be severed if a train were to come by. Mercifully, the pathologists later concluded that the baby was dead before his body was cut in half.

The killers were two schoolfriends, Robert Thompson and Jon Venables, who were at the time known only as 'Child A' and 'Child B'. There was incontrovertible scientific evidence which placed them at the scene of the killing. As children, each aged almost eleven at the time of the murder, they were just over the age of criminal responsibility. Their identities became known only after the trial had concluded. The prevailing view was that the crime was a metaphor for society as a whole: a symbol of declining standards, loss of values, lack of respect, family breakdown, the failure of the welfare state and moral vacuum.[51] It certainly attracted enormous public attention. The trial of the boys at Preston was watched closely by the media. Both had pleaded not guilty and each unconvincingly attempted to blame the other for Jamie's death, although neither boy gave evidence in their own defence. In passing sentence, the judge described the murder as an act of 'unparalleled evil and barbarity' and stated that their conduct was 'cunning and very wicked'. The popular press were near unanimous in their condemnation and the two boys were described as being 'thoroughly evil'.

The sentence the judge imposed was a foregone conclusion. The trial judge, Mr Justice Morland, had no choice. The boys were guilty of murder and abduction and the only sentence that could be passed was one of detention at Her Majesty's pleasure until the Home Secretary was satisfied that they had matured sufficiently to be rehabilitated into society and no longer posed a danger to others. This kind of sentence had two elements: a penal element or 'tariff', which is the length of detention deemed necessary to meet the requirements of retribution and general deterrence; and the rehabilitative element, the time it takes for the children to be safely rehabilitated back into society. Mr Justice Morland was of the opinion that the penal element should be eight years, to reflect the ages of the boys. Had the boys been adults, he would have suggested they remain behind bars for eighteen years before being considered for parole. The judge had therefore recommended they remain behind bars for at least eight years. It would be for others to decide, as the boys developed and matured, when they would actually be released.

As with every sound judgment, justice had been tempered with mercy, but this judicious approach angered the popular press to a pitch of unprecedented fury. No sooner had the judge's opinion been made known than a petition was organised by the *Sun* newspaper. A coupon was placed in an edition of the paper which read: 'Dear Home Secretary, I agree with Ralph and Denise Bulger that the boys who killed their son James should stay in prison for LIFE.' In total, 21,281 readers cut the coupon out and sent it to Michael Howard. *The Sun* also publicised other attempts to put pressure on Michael Howard, for example, reporting that 80,000 people had contacted a TV station demanding that the killers 'must rot in jail' for the rest of their lives. The local MP submitted a petition signed by 5,900 members of the public demanding that the 'tariff' should be twenty-five years. A further petition signed by 278,000 members of the public urged the Home Secretary to keep the boys behind bars for the rest of their lives.

Mr Justice Morland's recommended tariff was subject to the agreement and approval of the Lord Chief Justice, Lord Taylor. In the solitude of his chambers in the Royal Courts of Justice, the Lord Chief Justice wrote to the Home Secretary stating that, in his opinion, the minimum period for punishment and deterrence should be ten years, therefore increasing, slightly, the sentence handed down by the judge at the boys' trial.

Michael Howard had received legal advice and had received petitions, letters and pleas from the public. In a letter to the boys' solicitors in July 1994, Howard said that the tariff element would be increased to fifteen years. His reasons were that in order to maintain confidence in the criminal justice system he had to have regard to public concerns, which were evidenced by *The Sun*'s coupons and the petitions and letters supporting detention for life without the possibility of parole. As a result, he increased – by 50 per cent – the tariff the Lord Chief Justice had suggested. This decision was challenged on the boys' behalf in judicial review proceedings.

The question that the lawyers for Thompson and Venables wanted an answer to was: 'What does "detention at Her Majesty's pleasure" actually mean?' Is this the same as a life sentence, which is the compulsory sentence for murder in the case of an adult? It was the complications of the law on this point that drew Michael Howard into conflict with the courts. If 'detention at Her Majesty's pleasure' was exactly the same as life imprisonment, then the Home Secretary could fix the tariff period. On the other hand, if a sentence for a child was different, then the Home Secretary should keep the length of detention under review during the period of a child's development and growing maturity. Setting the length of incarceration in stone at such a tender age would fetter the discretion of future Home Secretaries who would be in office during the detention period.

Parliament had not considered the ramifications of this distinction and Howard was confident that he had the power to fix a tariff for the Bulger murderers. His difficulty was that there was no previous example of a Home Secretary using the power in the case of a child murderer. His predecessors had never done what he had done.

The decision for the courts, ultimately the appellate committee of the House of Lords, was whether Howard had acted lawfully in heeding to public clamour for vengeance. By a majority, the country's top judges decided that he had not. The House of Lords described Michael Howard's role in fixing the tariff as a quasi-judicial one. He was perfectly entitled to take into account general public confidence in the justice system, but when he considered the tariff in an individual case the Home Secretary's responsibility was to beware of ill-informed public opinion. As a judge when sentencing in an individual case should ignore a public campaign encouraging him or her to increase a particular sentence, so the Home Secretary had a duty to balance considerations of public interest against the dictates of justice. The Home Secretary was required to adopt a detached approach. He had not done so as his reasoning placed undue credence and weight on the public clamour for a tough approach.[52]

The Jamie Bulger case put into sharp relief the tension between a populist use of executive power and the rule of law. The judges exhaustively examined the rationale behind the sentencing of children and young persons for crimes which, if committed by an adult, carried a life sentence. Their conclusions provided restraint to the use of power which was unduly influenced by public opinion, which was not necessarily informed about the facts and circumstances of the case under consideration. In other words, public clamour for vengeance in the Jamie Bulger case was populist. This desire for a more stringent sentence was a generalised view, which was proclaimed to be the view of 'the people' when, in reality, it was the view of those who had chosen to sign the petition or had chosen to send *The Sun*'s coupon to the Home Secretary. As Tom Bingham has said, 'While public opinion is capable of being generous and tolerant it is also capable of being vengeful and intolerant. Public opinion is an unreliable source of protection to those most in need of it.'[53] Popular opinions should not be cast aside as being

unworthy – many others who did not sign the Jamie Bulger petition might agree with the signatories – but by the same token they
do not become an instruction to elected politicians in the name of
the people. The temptation for populists is to take hold of opinions
they would like to hold themselves, and to rely on the public as
providing the legitimate endorsement of those opinions.

An essential feature of the rule of law is to ensure that when members of the executive are exercising powers conferred on them, they
use those powers in good faith, fairly and for the purpose for which
the powers were conferred.[54] Executive decisions about punishment
for children need detachment and objectivity, weighing the interests
of the public against the interests of the children affected by the decision. In the Jamie Bulger case, the rule of law provided a brake and a
restraint on the populist instincts of the Home Secretary.

CONCLUSION

In the 1990s, the rule of law played an important part in the events
surrounding an asylum seeker from Africa, an unconventional church
leader from South Korea and two child murderers from Merseyside.
Each one of the individuals at the centre of these cases may, rightly, be
worthy of condemnation for their activities and behaviour. But that
is not the point. It is easy to be intolerant about migrants, child murderers and unusual religious sects. On the whole, the British 'people'
want immigration strictly controlled, child murderers incarcerated for
a very long time, and religious fanatics stopped from trying to convert
them to their faith. The rule of law does not exist to make a judgement on whether any of these objectives are laudable or whether it is
right or wrong for politicians to pursue them. The rule of law exists to
ensure that the pursuit of political objectives which impinge immediately and directly on the lives of individuals are pursued lawfully.

The 'rule of law' and 'law and order' are different things. Margaret Thatcher's political philosophy did not include any particular role for the courts in overseeing the use of power by the executive. For her, it was only an invisible 'moral code' that protected and enhanced individual freedom and provided a guide to the executive in its use of power. Thatcher and her political heirs attached importance to law and order when it came to crime and disorder and endorsed the rule of law when it reflected the moral code. But her moral code – consisting of respect for authority, thrift, family values and loyalty to friends – was too value-laden to be the 'normative umbrella' of the rule of law. It was, in a sense, too political a philosophy, which for many was its strength. Law does not have a political philosophy. It has an anchor in values which have an enduring quality, transcending changing political attitudes of the time.

Margaret Thatcher's distinctive moral code was on the wane by the time John Major succeeded her in 1990, but his version of it, called 'back to basics', was only a temporary phenomenon. Major had tried to promote values of 'neighbourliness, decency and courtesy' as an antidote to features of Thatcherism which appeared to champion selfish acquisitiveness. This was Major's attempt to stamp his personal moral outlook on the Conservative Party and the nation.[55] Unfortunately, his laudable suggestions coincided with some embarrassing personal revelations about the private lives of some of his colleagues in the House of Commons. These were splashed in prurient detail in the tabloid press as evidence of a scandal. He was mocked for promoting morality in the face of immorality by the people he worked with. His 'moral code' was as short-lived as his premiership, which ended when Tony Blair won a landslide victory in 1997.

When the Labour government enacted the Human Rights Act in 1998, the power of judges was enlarged, and the full implications of this will be discussed in Chapter 5. But as politicians began to absorb the change that a prominence for human rights was presenting, they realised that political power had to be protected if judicial power was about to be enlarged. It was the arrival of human rights which prompted many to complain about judicial power. Fear of the power of judges had begun long before the Labour government decided to bring in a Human Rights Act. Judges had begun to be feared as soon as they emerged as fully fledged creatures from their chrysalis of quiescence in the 1970s and 1980s.

This was the period when power of the executive had been increasing while the confidence of individuals to try to challenge it was growing as well. This clash was the cause of the growth in judicial review applications, which we discussed earlier. Another area of controversy was the use of prerogative or executive power within the lawful boundaries of the British Constitution. For politicians, the Constitution is strong but flexible and the use of prerogative powers by the executive allows for firm government, subject only to accountability to Parliament. For judges, on the other hand, the Constitution is a fundamental part of the rule of law and it is within the province of judges, not just Parliament, to ensure that the executive complies with the law of the Constitution. A clash between judges and the executive was incubating within our constitutional and legal frameworks. It burst into life when citizens began to rely on human rights law to challenge executive decisions and when the executive attempted to curb human rights in terrorist cases. At the epicentre of these clashes was the Constitution itself, which came to be tested in the fallout from the referendum in 2016. The scene was set for a battle royale between judges and politicians. The skirmishes which developed into open warfare are discussed in the succeeding chapters and begin with the rule of law and the Constitution.

CHAPTER 4

POPULISM, THE LAW AND
THE CONSTITUTION

The run-up to the general election in December 2019 was as fre-
netic as it was fractious. Opinions were strongly held, dialogue
and consensus were impossible and the fabric of the Constitution
was fraying along its seams. Central to the argument advanced by
Boris Johnson was to ask the electorate to decide whether the EU
referendum result in 2016 had sent a direct message to him to implement the result in any way he chose, or whether the message was
that Parliament should be able to implement the result as it thought
best. Boris Johnson wanted the general election to be about a resolution to this question and his argument carried the day. But in
doing so Johnson's winning side had deliberately or inadvertently
embroiled the country in a controversy that went to the heart of the
rule of law in the United Kingdom.

From the moment the referendum result was interpreted as a
'mandate' in 2016 to the occasion when the Supreme Court ruled
that the Prime Minister's attempt to prorogue Parliament was null
and void in 2019, politicians and judges were engaged in a dispute
about the place of the rule of law in the governance of the country.

The leaders of the Leave campaign in 2016, Boris Johnson, Michael Gove and Dominic Cummings, now occupy positions at the heart of government, but despite the combined intellect of these powerful men they have completely overlooked the fact that 'taking back control' cannot possibly restore the British Constitution to what it was before Britain joined the EU in 1973. The social, political and legal developments which have occurred in the forty-seven years since Britain gave up elements of its national sovereignty in order to become a full member of the European Economic Community (as it then was) have been so profound that the clock simply cannot be turned back.

Understanding the meaning of the words 'sovereignty of Parliament' and 'rule of law' has occupied the minds of academics ever since Albert Venn Dicey made the study of the Constitution his field of research in the nineteenth and early twentieth centuries. Thanks to a group of pro-hunting campaigners who wanted fox hunting to be preserved by challenging the legal validity of the Act of Parliament that banned it, judges were compelled to consider the essential meaning of these words.[1] Lord Steyn, one of the Law Lords who unanimously dismissed the fox hunters' argument, stated that while the sovereignty of Parliament was a 'general principle of the Constitution', the principle was a construct of law which had been created by judges.

This case was only one of many where the tensions between the law made by judges in the courts and the law made by politicians in Parliament have been exposed. Such tensions only grew once Britain became a member of the EU after the Maastricht Treaty of 1992 created the European Union. The EU became a higher legal order as member states had to apply their obligations under the treaty uniformly throughout the Community and English judges had to recognise that Community law had supremacy over national laws. However, this principle existed long before the EU was created at Maastricht. Under the old common market, the Treaty of Accession, signed by the United Kingdom in 1972, Community law prevailed over national law if there was a conflict between two legal systems. Conflict might arise in the operation of a uniform market which functioned in all member states. The supremacy of EU law in these situations did not prevent the United Kingdom from retaining its own levels of tax and insurance, and its own health, education and legal systems and its unique Constitution, franchise and first-past-the-post voting system.

The United Kingdom used its own sovereignty to allow Community law to be part of its domestic law in the European Communities Act 1972. Despite the political rhetoric it will now be virtually impossible for Britain to 'take back control'. In the years between 1973 when Britain joined the EEC and 2020 there has been so much fundamental change in Britain that returning to a pre-1973 state of affairs will be a daunting task. In their hearts politicians know this, which partly explains why there is so much fear within the present government about the power of the judiciary. In order to grasp fully the flaws in the argument that leaving the EU will enable the British Parliament to go back to where it was before 1973, we need to understand a little history.

THE BRITISH CONSTITUTION

The Constitution of the United Kingdom is unwritten, but the general notion of parliamentary sovereignty became established in 1689 when there was a significant constitutional settlement after the Bill of Rights was enacted. This endorsed into law a general political consensus embodying the Tory view that sovereignty was the 'king in Parliament' with the Whig view that the people were represented by those who took their place in Parliament.[2] So developed the eighteenth- and nineteenth-century conception of representative democracy in Parliament. There was a contract or compact that people were governed by laws they had consented to because they had conferred upon their elected representatives the authority to make them. By the middle of the nineteenth century the great scholar of parliamentary practice Erskine May was able to state that the legislative authority of Parliament was subject to no limits other than those that were incidental to its sovereign authority, the willingness of people to obey or their power to resist.[3] Sovereignty in the British Constitution is held within Parliament, not by the executive in Downing Street or by civil servants in Whitehall. The British Constitution, with parliamentary sovereignty at its heart, has grown organically and gradually and the people have become united in a shared experience, an immemorial usage and a common practice of consenting to laws made by Parliament. The British way was not to devise a constitution by the application of reason and then to write it down. The British way was to allow a constitution to evolve and to sustain it by recognising it.[4]

This self-sustaining nature of the British way of doing constitutional law has many merits, notably flexibility, but it has one severe disadvantage. An uncritical acceptance of flexibility and adaptation as the supreme virtue of the Constitution does not properly recognise the conditions in which the justification for our Constitution actually becomes a part of the definition of that very Constitution.[5] In other words, when we learn and understand that the supremacy of Parliament means that Parliament can enact any law it chooses except one to limit its powers, what does that mean? Does that mean a law to limit its powers is a genuine exception or is it just an exemplification of the doctrine? Another problem is that in the British unwritten Constitution there is nothing to distinguish a legislative measure which might be described as constitutional, such as a law permitting a referendum to be held, and a political convention, such as the occasion for a prorogation of Parliament. The grey area between true constitutional law and mere custom and practice makes the British Constitution exceptional and is a void which is open to occupation. Unscrupulous politicians may take up the space between the law of the Constitution and the political reality of it because the 'law' of the Constitution also embraces traditions of behaviour which sustain it. If these traditions are not observed, the terrain may be taken over by politicians who pay scant regard to convention and good behaviour.

This point is of critical importance in understanding how and why the clash between politicians and the judges arose in the fallout from the 2016 referendum. There is now something of a constitutional crisis in Britain. Judges have become the target of abuse and the Conservative government has plans to update the Human Rights Act and administrative law to restore a 'proper balance between the rights of individuals, our vital national security and effective government' and also to ensure the law is not 'abused to conduct politics by another means or to create needless delays'.[6] Johnson's government is proposing the forming of a 'Democracy and Rights Commission' to examine these issues. In the government's view, one of the strengths of the UK Constitution is its ability to evolve, but as times have changed, so have Parliament, government and the judiciary.

The politics of the Conservative Party of Boris Johnson is an unusual sort of conservatism. Unlike his predecessor John Major, who followed in the tradition of pragmatism and a respect for British institutions, Johnson is a radical populist who is no longer prepared to allow the effluxions of evolution to point the way forward. He believes that there is now an urgent need for radical constitutional reform, as we live in a period when we need rapid change. This should include cutting the judiciary down to size. But Johnson is behind the times. The rapid changes have already taken place, long before his new 'global Britain' will show its true identity. Devolution has taken place in Scotland, Wales and Northern Ireland; the use of proportional representation has been introduced for elections to the devolved assemblies and, until 2019, the European Parliament; the Human Rights Act 1998 has been passed; and the Constitutional Reform Act 2005 has transformed the relationship between the judiciary and the executive. The judiciary is now transparently independent with the Lord Chief Justice as its head, and the highest appellate court now occupies its own building and is called the Supreme Court. Alongside these developments, the power of the judiciary has grown organically, in step with social changes that are making citizens bold enough to challenge the use of power if it is used by the executive in a manner in which Parliament did not authorise or contemplate. In order to question the legitimacy of power, the citizen was obliged to turn to the judges. Hence the rise of judicial power which was described in the last chapter. We are now entering what can only be described as a power struggle between the executive and the judiciary where trust between the two is at breaking point.

UTILITARIANISM

The origins of the crisis can be traced back to the utilitarian movement of the late eighteenth and early nineteenth centuries. Until the utilitarians applied their considerable intellectual skills to

dissecting the meaning of the word 'law', British lawyers and politicians were content that the common law, made by judges in the
courts, should hold sway while Parliament did its job constrain-
ing monarchical absolutism. In an age when there was a paucity
of legislation impinging on the liberties of the individual citizen,
this seemed to work reasonably well, until Jeremy Bentham, born
in 1748, arrived on the scene.

A precociously intelligent child from a wealthy family, Bentham
entered Queen's College, Oxford, at the age of twelve and following
his father's advice was called to the Bar in 1769. However, to prac-
tise law was far too limiting for the formidable imagination and
indomitable energy of Bentham. He wanted to tear up the world
as he saw it and to start again with a clean sheet. Not noted for
his modesty (he contacted both President James Madison of the
United States and Alexander I of Russia offering to rewrite their
respective constitutions), he was, in many ways, a man ahead of his
time. He was obsessed with codes, definitions and categories and
he was bitterly dismissive of anything he designated a 'fallacy'.

For Bentham, only logic, reason and the clear use of language
could be applied to the problems of the world, which, for him, were
legal in character. 'If one branch of knowledge be in its nature more
interesting than another it should be this of Law, on the breath of
which ... everything that can bear the name of interest depends.'[7]
But law had to be *defined*. Law was something laid down by government that issued commands and prohibitions; the law had to
be defined and categorised and satisfy the test of utility. It was the
job of the government to point out 'what we ought to do as well
as to determine what we shall do. On the one hand the standard
of right and wrong, on the other the chain of causes and effects.'[8]
Nature had endowed the government with two sovereign masters:

pain and pleasure. Bentham embarked on divisions and subdivisions of what 'pain' and 'pleasure' actually meant and he did not believe in any abstract concepts such as 'rights'. Rights did not exist because they could not be satisfactorily defined and therefore they could not be real. His denunciation of rights in *The Handbook of Political Fallacies* is famous; he described them as being rhetorical nonsense, elevated nonsense and 'nonsense upon stilts'.[9] Here, Bentham set the distinctly English rule of law on a separate path from the road taken in continental Europe at the end of the eighteenth century.

Bentham deplored the French Declaration of the Rights of Man of 1789 as a 'perpetual vein of nonsense', both emotional and overtly rhetorical. He thought that passions were an enemy of reason. Bentham helped establish a peculiarly English meaning to the words 'rule of law'. First, law could only be understood in terms of commands and prohibitions, and this, necessarily, meant that law had to originate in Parliament, not from tradition in the common law. Second, law must not consist of fictions; concepts that did not have a definable meaning. For Benthamites, it was the source of law which was important, not its content or value.

An academic lawyer named John Austin, who became professor of jurisprudence at London University, was Bentham's neighbour in Queen Square Place, Bloomsbury. Austin was greatly influenced by Bentham as he developed his theory of 'positive law'. Austin argued that law was essentially a command, emanating from a determinate sovereign body whose powers were legally unlimited. He also believed in the importance of clarity of expression and the need for speech to have meaning. He later wrote a panegyric on the British Constitution where he praised 'our present incomparable Constitution for the existence of order and liberty in the British Isles'.[10]

DICEY AND THE LAW OF THE CONSTITUTION

While Austin was a little-noticed university lecturer and occasional pamphleteer, Albert Venn Dicey was winning prizes at Balliol College, Oxford, achieving a fellowship at Trinity College, Oxford, and then, in 1882, election as Vinerian professor of law at the university. His great work, the *Introduction to the Study of the Law of the Constitution*, was first published in 1885 and went into eight editions, the last in 1915. Dicey was a figure of such importance it is almost impudent to question the wisdom of his analysis and opinions. He is credited with coining the expression 'rule of law' and he is cited by every modern commentator on matters constitutional.[11]

In essence, Dicey sought to analyse and describe the source of power in British constitutional arrangements and he argued that the only way to understand a constitution that was unwritten was to reveal the true meaning of the words 'legislative sovereignty', the 'rule of law' and 'conventions' by careful study. Power derived from the sovereign power of Parliament, which was supreme as all laws made by Parliament had to be enforced in the courts. Parliament was all-powerful as no other person or body could make a law which overrode it. The sovereignty of Parliament, therefore, was the 'very keystone of the law of the Constitution' in the strictly legal sense. Dicey was alive to political realities and he went on to argue that Parliament was restrained, politically, from passing absurd or tyrannical laws. This restraint was political, not legal. Dicey had faith that the electorate would not elect a tyrannical legislature.

The rule of law, according to Dicey, had three elements in the British Constitution. First, no person in Britain could be punished or suffer a penalty except for a distinct breach of the law established in the courts. Secondly, every person, whatever his rank or position, is subject to the ordinary law of the land. Thirdly, the general principles of the Constitution are determined by judicial decisions brought by private persons in individual cases. It is these decisions, Dicey maintained, which provided the liberties enjoyed by British citizens.

These rights are part of the unwritten Constitution, but they are not rights given by the Constitution. According to Dicey, if rights were acquired and preserved by judicial decisions over time and became binding under the doctrine of legal precedent, it would be difficult for an authoritarian regime to undo them by the stroke of a pen.

This third principle was one of Dicey's most important observations. He sought to distinguish the superiority of the British Constitution from both the administrative law of France (*droit administratif*) and the federalism of the United States, each of whose systems Dicey also studied closely. Dicey, therefore, articulated a particularly British 'rule of law' which, according to him, was superior to anything attempted elsewhere. The liberties of English citizens existed because they were not trespassed upon by Parliament passing laws restricting them, and the courts, by treating everybody who appeared before them equally, upholding them. Like Bentham before him, Dicey believed in the British way of doing things. The final piece of Dicey's framework were constitutional conventions. These were those customs, practices and maxims not recognised as laws but enforced by the courts as a survival of the discretionary monarchical authority. They were the general agreements of public men about the 'rules of the game' to be borne in mind in the conduct of public affairs.[12]

Dicey's views now seem too firmly based on a Victorian perception of political realities to have a modern resonance. He believed that the untrammelled power of Parliament was the key to England's power and glory within a global empire, while at the same time asserting that there was a residual right of the people to resist the will of Parliament if a law passed by it was sufficiently odious. Dicey was a die-hard unionist and he favoured resistance on the streets if home rule legislation passed by Parliament was not endorsed in a referendum. In Dicey's Victorian mind, 'the unhappiness of the Irishman was less important than the Constitutional satisfaction of the Englishman.'[13] To the modern eye, these views jar as much as Dicey's fulmination against women's suffrage, which he made plain in the eighth edition of the *Introduction to the Study of the Law of the Constitution*.

According to Dicey, the words 'rule of law' do not have any inherent meaning beyond the formality of law. The fundamental weakness in this conception to the modern reader lies in his failure to appreciate that the rights of minorities could not be protected without a strongly based legal system that could stand up to the tyranny of the majority. Taken to its logical conclusion, parliamentary sovereignty only means a partisan majority in Parliament, enabling the majority party to warp the law to interfere with fundamental liberties and the rule of law.[14] A former Labour politician, Richard Crossman, once boasted to an American audience that British politicians did not believe in natural law: 'If we don't like a law, we just change it.'[15]

A Constitution worth its name should be able to provide checks and balances against an all-powerful executive backed by its party supporters in Parliament. But in Dicey's conception there could be no rights against Parliament, as it was for Parliament alone to change or abrogate a citizen's existing rights. Dicey relied on conventions to provide the scenery for political actors to behave properly. The second fundamental weakness of Dicey's analysis was his failure to appreciate that the actions of the executive are accountable to the courts for their lawfulness and not just to Parliament for their permission to exercise power and authority over the lives of ordinary citizens. For Dicey, there was no distinction between the notion of public law – the law applied by the courts to ensure the executive acted only within the law made by Parliament – and private law, which consisted of disputes between citizens or companies which were resolved in the courts.

Jeremy Bentham, John Austin and A. C Dicey each set down a clear roadmap for navigating a way through the terrain of the British Constitution. The supreme authority was Parliament, whose laws the judges should apply and interpret. Constitutional law did not involve any consideration of the content of law. There was no distinction between a law which was 'constitutional' and any other law that was passed by Parliament, and the focus of academic commentary was on the procedures for law-making by Parliament, not the values passed down in the laws themselves. Values or rights were a foreign concept, dismissed by both Bentham and Dicey with equal contempt. Finally, for a period of over 100 years it did not dawn on politicians or judges that the executive had an accountability to law, not just an accountability to Parliament.

THE MODERN MEANING OF THE RULE OF LAW

Nowadays, a different meaning to the words 'rule of law' is generally accepted among lawyers. In a public lecture in 2006, Lord Bingham, who was then the country's most senior judge, set out some core principles which encapsulate the words 'rule of law'. First, law must be intelligible, clear and predictable. Second, all persons and authorities within the state, whether public or private, should be bound by and entitled to the benefit of laws publicly and prospectively promulgated and publicly administered in the courts. Third, law should apply equally to all, except when objective differences justify differentiation, for example where particular laws should apply to children or the mentally ill. But for law to have meaning, differentiation must be rational and objectively justified and not based on spurious reasoning. Fourth, law must afford adequate protection of fundamental human rights. Lord Bingham acknowledged that these principles are not universally accepted as representing the words 'rule of law' but he gave an example of why protecting fundamental rights is essential to law:

> A state which savagely repressed or persecuted sections of its people could not in my view be regarded as observing the rule of law, even if the transport of the persecuted minority to the concentration camp or the compulsory exposure of female children on the mountainside were the subject of detailed laws duly enacted and scrupulously observed.[16]

Here, Bingham parts company with Dicey. Bingham accepted that there was an element of vagueness about this aspect of his definition as 'the outer edges of fundamental human rights are not clear-cut'. But he justified its inclusion as

> within a given state there will ordinarily be a measure of agreement on where the lines are to be drawn, and in the last resort (subject in this country to statute) the courts are there to draw them. The rule of law must, surely, require legal protection of such human rights as, within that society, they are seen as fundamental.

This modern departure from Dicey contained two important new ingredients to the rule of law in Britain. First, there is such a thing as fundamental rights, and second, it is the job of the courts to enforce them. Bingham then developed this new departure by dealing with power:

> Ministers and public officers at all levels must exercise the powers conferred on them reasonably, in good faith, for the purpose for which the powers were conferred and without exceeding the limits of such powers ... The historic role of the courts has of course been to check excesses of executive power, a role greatly expanded in recent years due to the increased complexity of government and the greater willingness of the public to challenge governmental (in the broadest sense) decisions. Even under our Constitution the separation of powers is crucial in guaranteeing the integrity of the courts' performance of this role.

Sir Stephen Sedley has made this point rather more philosophically. He has argued that the rule of law 'signals a shared ideal that individuals and society should not be subject to the whim of the powerful, and that their rights and obligations should be determined by laws made by an elected legislature which respects fundamental rights'.[17]

These former senior judges emphasise a departure from Dicey. Bingham places the principles of judicial review as having their foundation in the rule of law, and Sedley reminds us that rights are for society as a whole, not just the individual. Both underline the central point that law, as administered by judges, has a central role in protecting fundamental rights as well as curbing the excesses of executive power. For Dicey, tyranny was prevented by politics not law, and politicians could be trusted not to exceed their own authority. Long-standing conventions, according to Dicey, would ensure politicians did not exceed their legal authority. These observations are, however, inherently vague. This is not the fault of

Dicey. His inability to go beyond vagueness and his reliance on convention to explain the British Constitution is a direct result of the nature of our Constitution.

DICEY AND A CONSTITUTIONAL CONUNDRUM

In a penetrating modern analysis, Professor Vernon Bogdanor has explained why Dicey had to resort to vagueness in his constitutional interpretation.[18] Dicey had not recognised the difference between national sovereignty and parliamentary sovereignty. Politicians in 1973 believed that Britain was sharing only national sovereignty with other nations when the country joined the EEC, but in a series of legal cases in Europe and in Britain since then it is plain beyond doubt that the European Union made laws for the operation of a 'common market' independently of Parliament. Was our Parliament, therefore, still sovereign when we departed from the EU on 31 January 2020? If Community law meant uniform rules in all member states, surely this limited the sovereignty of Parliament, which Dicey had said was supreme? Or does parliamentary sovereignty just go on and on, irrespective of the laws it chooses to make? However, one chooses to debate and answer these questions, Bogdanor is very clear about one thing: when the United Kingdom entered the EEC in 1973, the parliamentary legislation that permitted it, which was passed in 1972, transformed the character of the British Constitution. Now judges are recognising that the freedom to legislate under the principle of absolute sovereignty of Parliament is being qualified in other ways, notably in applying the Human Rights Act 1998 to decisions made by public bodies.

It is ironic that one of the catchphrases that helped the Leave campaign win the 2016 referendum – 'take back control' – is now so illusory. As Bogdanor has observed:

The Britain of today is a land of much greater liberty than the Britain of 1972. So, although many Brexiteers feel with some confidence that Brexit will restore the sovereignty of Parliament, such a restoration will go against the trends of the last forty-five years. It is unlikely that Britain will revert to the constitutional position of 1972. The past is indeed another country.[19]

Another constitutional misunderstanding by those who are now in government and who campaigned for Leave in the EU referendum relates to the legal status of the referendum within our Constitution. The referendum itself was something of a novelty. A referendum serves not to replace the machinery of government but only to supplement it. In a referendum the people take on a third chamber of the legislature, in addition to the lower and upper houses. For a referendum choice to be implemented there are three hurdles to surmount, not two.[20] A third chamber must be added to the House of Commons and the House of Lords: the people. A constitutional democracy, like Britain today, is founded on the key principles of participation, representation, accountability and recall. Any person who is not legally ineligible may participate in a general election and seek election as a representative for a defined locality, known as a constituency. That person, if elected, is accountable to the electorate and may be recalled in a subsequent election and replaced by another representative. These features do not exist when a referendum is held. The only participation for ordinary citizens in a referendum is the right to vote in it. No person represents the result and no person is subject to recall. A referendum vote represents an anonymous mass of opinion expressed directly to the executive. That is why, for basic constitutional principles, a referendum must be a supplement to parliamentary democracy, not a substitute for it.

POPULIST MISUNDERSTANDINGS

Parliamentary democracy legitimises dissent; there is a formal constitutional role for Her Majesty's loyal opposition. Parliaments are periodic and no Parliament can bind its successors. These essential points clash with the concept of referendums and so if a referendum is held it must be accommodated within established constitutional procedures and customs.

This basic point eluded many politicians after the 2016 referendum on Britain's continued membership of the EU. For example, Jacob Rees-Mogg relegated the role of Parliament to that of considering only the details surrounding the actual leaving of the EU; the decision was in a 'mandate' provided in the referendum and such a mandate bound Parliament.[21] He made the point even more clearly five months later by declaring in Parliament, 'Let us not say "respect" the electorate: let us say "obey" for we will obey the British electorate.'[22] The Prime Minister was no less populist in her address to the Conservative Party conference in October 2016. Theresa May claimed that the result was clear and that it was the outcome that 'the people' had voted for. In fact, in Scotland 62 per cent of the electorate had voted for Remain and in Northern Ireland 55.8 per cent had voted for Remain. The result in the United Kingdom as a whole was narrow: 51.9 per cent had voted Leave, 48.1 per cent Remain. May was adamant that only the executive would take the decision to invoke Article 50 and after doing so her government would not give a running commentary or a blow-by-blow account of the negotiations; she interpreted the referendum result as a 'mandate'; she predicted that neither Parliament nor the courts, nor the devolved assemblies in Scotland, Wales and Northern Ireland, would play any part in the implementation of the result. As if this message were not populist enough, she included in her speech the following swipe at the political and media elite: 'Just listen to the way a lot of politicians and commentators talk about the public. They find their patriotism distasteful, their concerns about immigration parochial, their views about crime illiberal, their attachment to job security inconvenient.'[23]

Following the shock of the referendum result, politicians lost their heads: they forgot their constitutional heritage and embarked on populist rhetoric and sloganising. It was a shameful period in political and constitutional history and it provoked a clash with the judges who, by virtue of their political neutrality, were able to keep their eye on the constitutional ball. This, in turn, produced a political reaction which posed a real and pressing threat to trust in the rule of law. It centred on the ancient constitutional doctrine of the 'prerogative'.

THE CONSTITUTIONAL PREROGATIVE

Constitutional prerogative powers are powers, in the unwritten Constitution, retained by the monarch but exercised on her behalf by the executive. The most important use of the prerogative is the power of the government to make international treaties with other countries, but the deployment of the armed forces is also ordered by a minister of the Crown exercising the prerogative. Judges and ministers are appointed by the Crown under the prerogative.

After the EU referendum result, there arose a clash between the ancient established doctrine of parliamentary sovereignty and the equally ancient practice of the use of the prerogative. Few politicians in the government had expected that the electorate would vote to leave the EU. The government and the civil service were quite unprepared for the constitutional and legal shock that the result had inflicted on the corridors of power in Westminster and Whitehall. In order to embark on the process of leaving the EU, the government had to invoke Article 50 of the Treaty on European Union, but this could only be done 'in accordance with its own [the UK's] constitutional arrangements'.[24] Could the start of the process to leave the EU be done by the use of a foreign affairs prerogative or was an act of Parliament necessary to authorise a notification to the EU of Britain's intention to withdraw?

ENEMIES OF THE PEOPLE

This question could only be answered by judges. At some risk to her own personal safety, an investment manager named Gina Miller took on the government to seek clarification on what was meant by the words 'constitutional requirements' in Article 50. No sooner had she embarked on this inquiry than she and others supporting her became the victims of vitriolic abuse. The abuse was so extreme and so threatening that the High Court had to issue a warning that if the case – which was due to start at the beginning of the legal term in October 2016 – was disrupted by abuse, those responsible would be in contempt of court. Such a pre-trial order is unusual but was an illustration of the feverish mob-based populism that was infecting the country in the weeks following the EU referendum in the summer of 2016.

The key point in the case was whether a change to British constitutional arrangements, which leaving the EU would involve, could be brought about solely by ministerial or executive action (the government's case), or whether such a change required the explicit authority of Parliament (Ms Miller's case). Lord Thomas, the Lord Chief Justice, and two senior Lord Justices of appeal heard the arguments and the important conclusion was made that the executive was deemed to be subordinate to the rule of law. The subordination of the Crown to law was the foundation of the rule of law. If the prerogative was to be used lawfully (as the government lawyers had argued) then the government was obliged to demonstrate that this relic of absolute power had been contemplated when Parliament decided to join the EU. Leaving the EU, the court ruled, was just as important a constitutional change as joining it had been. As nobody except Parliament itself can nullify or change any previous primary legislation, it followed that only Parliament could start the process of undoing what it had done when the UK joined the EU in 1973. The referendum was advisory only in law and, in one sense, irrelevant; if the prerogative could be used to invoke Article 50, then the prerogative did not need the authority of a referendum to do so.[25]

For lawyers, this ruling had been predictable and, to a degree, comforting. The court was applying the meaning to the words 'rule of law' in the way it had been explained to them by Lord Bingham in his 2006 lecture.[26] The judges were holding the executive to account. The laws and liberties of the country we live in have been handed down to us by the common law and by Parliament. The two, in conjunction, provide the rule of law. Most people, one might think, would find it comforting to have those principles confirmed in a judgment about the EU referendum. However, populists do not think like lawyers. The court's judgment was reported widely in the media, mostly responsibly, but the *Daily Mail* splashed the story under the banner headline: 'Enemies of the People: Fury over "out of touch" judges who have "declared war on democracy" by defying 17.4m Brexit voters and who could trigger constitutional crisis'.[27] Branding senior judges as 'enemies of the people' was, for many, the most chilling newspaper headline in living memory and evoked memories of the jackboot and the outstretched-arm salute. Historically, the 'enemies of the people' were those whom the revolutionaries in France condemned to death during the Reign of

Terror in 1794 for not being sufficiently revolutionary. Later, the term was revived by Stalin, who declared that the 'enemies of the people' included not only capitalists but communists on his own side who had fallen below his own strict standards of revolutionary zeal. Like their French forebears, they were also executed.

It must be presumed that the editor of the *Daily Mail* knew what he was doing when this article was written, but it chimed with opinion in the Conservative Party. Many Members of Parliament, 'led by an ex-justice minister', believed it was 'an "unholy alliance" of judges and embittered Remain backers that could thwart the wishes of 17.4 million Leave voters'. The ex-justice minister in question was Dominic Raab MP, now Foreign Secretary in Boris Johnson's government. The journalist who wrote the story, James Slack, is now Boris Johnson's official spokesman in 10 Downing Street. According to the *Daily Mail*, the 'outpouring of rage against the High Court's shocking "judicial activism" was so strong at Westminster that there were calls for a review of the way senior judges are appointed'. Douglas Carswell MP described the ruling as 'shocking judicial activism – these judges are politicians without accountability'.

The Prime Minister, apparently, was enraged that the ruling might force her to reveal more than she had done, hitherto, about her broad negotiating aims. She expected the Supreme Court to reverse the ruling. In fact, the ruling was confirmed by the Supreme Court, as many others had expected.

This vitriol that was directed at anybody who dared to stand up to a powerful executive was an expression of populism. It was the fury of a section of the adult population of England (Scotland and Northern Ireland voted to remain in the EU) that the most important demonstration of democratic opinion was the referendum result.

This was an expression of direct democracy, not representative democracy, and direct democracy is the form favoured by populists.

The depressing aspect of this is that many clever and responsible Members of Parliament associated themselves with this sentiment. In doing so they were undermining features of our liberal democracy and, with it, trust in the rule of law.

Within a few weeks of the referendum result the language of many prominent Leave supporters had become entirely populist. For example, Jacob Rees-Mogg described the result of the referendum as a mandate, a victory, an instruction. He likened the referendum result to the Battle of Agincourt, waged in 1415.[28] It was a singular ill-chosen comparison. The victory at Agincourt was short-lived. Within forty years, France, under the spell of Joan of Arc, had recovered its self-respect, the English army was in retreat and Jack Cade and his followers were marching on London to mock their rulers for their supine behaviour in not resisting the French properly.

Not only was Rees-Mogg's historical comparison far-fetched but his argument was at odds with the organic growth of our Constitution, which placed the sovereignty of Parliament as its centrepiece. The European Union Referendum Act 2015 had faithfully adhered to this central principle by saying nothing about what should happen if the majority voted to leave the EU. In law, the 2016 vote was purely advisory, as has been authoritatively stated by the Court of Appeal on several occasions.[29]

Just as Agincourt did not have the consequences that King Henry V intended, so the referendum of 2016 has had unforeseen results. If the mandate of the people was a victory then parliamentary sovereignty had been vanquished. A victory for one side inevitably involves defeat for the other. Few responsible politicians have been as rash as Rees-Mogg and most have favoured a compromise.

Few would want to take the path towards a complete defeat for an institution so cherished and important as the authority of the British Parliament. According to Liam Fox MP, 'Parliament subcontracted its sovereignty on the issue of whether we stayed in the European Union or not to the people of this country. Parliament said ... we will not make a decision on this; you, the British people, will make the decision.'[30] This was an extraordinary statement as it was constitutional nonsense. Parliamentary sovereignty is a constitutional absolute, not a tradeable asset, and Parliament had not, by the Act of Parliament which permitted the referendum, diluted its own sovereignty. Parliament could no more subcontract its own sovereignty than the Queen could subcontract her monarchical authority to her staff at Buckingham Palace.

A populist interpretation of events was taking over from a reflective, liberal one. The seeds of this development had been sown some years previously. The coverage of the Gina Miller case by the *Daily Mail* was chilling and shocking, lacking all appreciation for the actual legal and constitutional issues that the case had involved, but it was not altogether surprising. Complaints about so-called judicial activism had first surfaced under the Labour government when David Blunkett was Home Secretary and continued under Michael Howard's stewardship at the Home Office. The referendum result in 2016 was given an almost sacred status by populists who had an instinctive attraction to direct, rather than parliamentary, democracy. The Miller case thrust into sharp relief the discontent that was simmering among sections of the political class about the essential principles underpinning the rule of law.

A populist view of the political and legal landscape in Britain had taken root within the senior ranks of the government. Almost as shocking as the 'Enemies of the People' piece in the *Daily Mail* was the muted, almost inaudible, reaction to it by the government. The minister of the Crown who has a specific responsibility to uphold the rule of law is the Lord Chancellor. Traditionally, the holder of the office was a senior lawyer who took a place in the House of Lords in order to be a member of the government. Since the Constitutional Reform Act 2005 there is no longer a requirement for the Lord Chancellor to have a legal background and they may be a member of the House of Commons, rather than the House of Lords.

At the time of the Miller case, the Lord Chancellor was Liz Truss MP. On appointment, she took an oath which stated that:

In the office of Lord High Chancellor of Great Britain I will respect the rule of law, defend the independence of the judiciary and discharge my duty to ensure the provision of resources for the efficient and effective support of the courts for which I am responsible. So help me God.[31]

The judiciary, as a body, were constitutionally restrained from entering the fray to call for a robust defence by the Lord Chancellor, but the Bar Council requested a clear statement from Liz Truss in view of the *Mail*'s article, which it described as being an 'unprecedented attack which undermines the rule of law'. Despite this clear invitation, Truss's response was barely adequate. It took three days for her department to issue the briefest of statements, which said:

The independence of the judiciary is the foundation upon which our rule of law is built and our judiciary is rightly respected the world over for its independence and impartiality. In relation to the case heard in the High Court, the government has made it clear it will appeal to the Supreme Court. Legal process must be followed.

This response was shameful. The judges in the Miller case were doing no more than their constitutional duty by listening impartially to the arguments and giving a judgment according to law. Lord Igor Judge, the recently retired Lord Chief Justice, is reported to have stated that Liz Truss's response, in her capacity as Lord Chancellor, was so lame that it was likely that she had acted unlawfully as she had, apparently, consulted the Prime Minister about her response when she should have acted independently.[32]

The *Daily Mail's* assault on the judiciary was vicious, and yet it had the support of many MPs and no doubt also many members of the public. It called for a prompt and unambiguous statement from the Lord Chancellor condemning the unwarranted attack on her judges and spelling out for those who did not know already the role and function of an independent judiciary in a democracy underpinned by the rule of law.

It was probably fear that prompted the Lord Chancellor to issue such an inadequate statement, strongly hinting that the decision would soon be overturned by the Supreme Court. As the BBC's political correspondent Ben Wright put it, 'It would be a very brave (or foolish?) minister to criticise the press for writing what they like about Brexit. And many voters will share the anger of some newspapers about the decision of the court.'[33] Fear of the power of the press and fear of the reaction from voters probably held sway in the Lord Chancellor's mind over her constitutional duty to 'defend the independence of the judiciary'. If this was indeed the case then a new populist era of politics has arrived. Trust in the ability of the Lord Chancellor to uphold the responsibilities of that high office was disappearing within the ranks of judges and lawyers in practice as barristers or solicitors.

The arrival of populist politics marks a clear break from the past. The pre-populist consensus was firmly based on norms of parliamentary democracy, a pluralistic and lively free press, an active civil society, the rule of law through an independent judiciary, professionalism in the public sector, stable majority governments counterbalanced by the protection of minority rights.[34] Populism has scant regard for firmly based political norms. The protection of minority rights and the need for tolerance and mutual respect have passed from politics into the purview of the rule of law and from MPs to the judiciary. At the same time, populist simplicity, which reduces complex global problems to platform rhetoric, have entered the political mainstream. These are tectonic shifts and have consequences for the rule of law and the Constitution.

The first casualty in the fracturing of the old consensus was Parliament itself, the jewel in the constitutional crown, according to Dicey. The general election of 2017 deprived the Conservatives, led by Theresa May, of their parliamentary majority and May was forced to govern under a 'confidence and supply' agreement with the Democratic Unionist Party of Northern Ireland. Having negotiated a Withdrawal Agreement with the EU, May had to obtain parliamentary approval for it. As her Cabinet, her party and MPs in the House of Commons were bitterly divided, there was little chance that this would happen. She failed on three attempts to get approval for her deal. By March 2019, 'Britain was facing its greatest challenge since the constitutional crisis of 1909–11'.[35]

The crisis was a political one caused by the challenge of leaving the EU in a way that would not inflict damage to the economy, security and international standing of the United Kingdom in the process. The fears and doubts among the public about the consequences of leaving the EU had, to a large extent, been reflected in the result of the 2017 general election. It was the electorate which produced the hung parliament after the election. However, like the shoddy workman who blames his tools, Theresa May chose to blame the institution of Parliament for her own misfortunes. In March 2019, May made a speech to the nation in which she put herself on the side of the frustrated public when she stated, 'You are tired of the infighting, tired of the political games and the arcane procedural rules ... I am on your side.'[36] Here, May was reverting to the populist instincts she had displayed at the Conservative conference in 2016. The message was clear. Being on the side of the people meant being against the institution of Parliament. In truth, the MPs, whom the electorate had chosen as their representatives, were doing their job. Far from playing games with arcane procedures, members had seized the initiative in cross-party cooperation and had voted by 321 votes to 275 to press the government not to leave the EU without a deal.

In September 2019, the institution of Parliament was further traduced, this time by the Attorney General, no less. By now, the mood in the nation was one of bitter disagreement as to whether the Brexit impasse could be broken by threatening the EU that Britain would walk away without a deal or whether exit day should be postponed in order for an agreement to be reached. These were matters of political judgement, but Geoffrey Cox QC blamed the institution of Parliament for the state of affairs in which his government found itself. 'This Parliament is a dead Parliament,' he told the House of Commons. 'It should no longer sit. It has no moral right to sit ... This Parliament is a disgrace.'[37]

These remarks, coming from a law officer of the Crown, whose responsibility it is to tender impartial legal advice to the government, are almost as chilling as the 'Enemies of the People' article by the *Daily Mail*. They demonstrated contempt for an institution which is the bulwark of the Constitution and exhibit an anger that elected representatives should be able to thwart the power of the executive. Geoffrey Cox is no fascist, but it was Oswald Mosley, the leader of the fascists in the 1930s, who described Parliament as 'the false liberty of a few old men to talk forever' and he thought, as fascists do, that power should not depend on the 'intrigues and manoeuvres of conflicting parties, but on the will of the nation, directly expressed'.[38] If the executive were ever to thwart the will of the legislature then the rule of law is gravely threatened and fascism would have arrived. Fascism thrives when a single leader follows the views of 'the people' directly expressed.[39]

THE PROROGATION DECISION

The second casualty caused by the fracturing of the old consensus was the collapse of the customs, maxims and conventions which Dicey held so dear as essential elements of the Constitution. The prerogative power of the monarch to prorogue Parliament has traditionally been entirely non-controversial as it would be exercised only on an occasion when there was a consensus, born of custom, that the time had come for the Queen to open a new session of Parliament. On 28 August 2019, Jacob Rees-Mogg, Lord President of the Council, and other Privy Councillors visited the Queen at Balmoral. They came away with an Order in Council, made on the advice of the Prime Minister, that Parliament should be shut down from a day no earlier than 9 September (but no later than 12 September) until 14 October 2019.

This was no routine prorogation. A fundamental change to the Constitution was due to take place on 31 October, as this was the date Britain was due to leave the EU. However, Parliament had also enacted a measure that if the government could not obtain assent from Parliament as to the terms of withdrawal (or Parliament assented to leaving without a deal) by 19 October, the government was obliged to seek an extension beyond 31 October. Therefore, it was obvious that members of both Houses of Parliament would be anxious to be heard on the crucial and important question of when, and on what terms, the United Kingdom would leave the EU.

On the day Rees-Mogg obtained the Queen's permission to prorogue Parliament, he wrote an article in the *Daily Telegraph* under the headline: 'Our constitution is robust. No harm will come from respecting the will of the voters'.[40] He informed his readers that prorogation in the current circumstances was not in the slightest bit abnormal, there was no constitutional crisis and nothing was happening that did not have 'historic precedent and a happy outcome'. In reality, the decision to prorogue, and thereby close down Parliament for five weeks at a critical and important time, was intensely controversial. A former law officer, Dominic Grieve MP, described the decision as 'deeply questionable and frankly pretty outrageous', while the former Justice Secretary David Gauke MP said the decision was setting a dangerous precedent. Although many Conservative members and supporters were worried about the political repercussions, and sections of the press, especially *The Guardian* and the *Financial Times*, complained that prorogation was an affront to democracy, few believed that Boris Johnson had acted unlawfully. For example, Will Hutton, a respected commentator and author, despaired that while the nation wallowed in a constitutional crisis, it was unlikely that any challenge in the courts to the decision would be successful.[41]

Constitutional lawyers, on the other hand, were thinking differently. In his blog on 31 August 2019, Paul Craig QC, professor of English law at the University of Oxford, exposed the gaping hole in the government's arguments for seeking a prorogation.[42] If it was necessary for a new programme of parliamentary business to be prepared then civil servants could be instructed to begin preparations. No prorogation was necessary. If, on the other hand, prorogation was required because the existing session had been a long one, why was it necessary to put a constitutional convention to the test for the sake of a few weeks? Craig also pointed out some constitutional truths. The courts have always protected parliamentary sovereignty from being undermined by the use of the prerogative. For example, during the First World War a posh hotel next to the Thames in London was requisitioned for defence and war purposes by regulations made by an Act passed in 1914, but the regulation, used by the executive under prerogative powers, did not allow for compensation. The hotel took the government to court and the Court of Appeal and the House of Lords decided that a Victorian Act of Parliament which had not been repealed and which did allow for compensation in such cases could not be cast aside by the use of the prerogative at a later date. Craig argued that the government's reasoning to prorogue Parliament diminished the foundation principle of parliamentary sovereignty in exactly the same way.

Three days later, Paul Craig and five other constitutional experts, supported by fifteen others, wrote to *The Times* and invited the government to recognise its mistake in shutting down Parliament. The letter pointed out that the British Constitution depended on conventions and if accepted norms were not observed, the integrity of the system was undermined.[43]

The decision of the Supreme Court on 24 September confirmed the fundamental constitutional principles that the academic lawyers had been highlighting. The first fundamental is that by advising the Queen to prorogue, the Prime Minister had a constitutional responsibility; he was not just acting in a political capacity. His use of the prerogative was a use which the law allowed; the question was whether there was a lawful limit to the use of the power and if so, whether the use of it was properly a matter for the court to determine. The Supreme Court decided that an unlimited power of prorogation was incompatible with the fundamental principle of parliamentary sovereignty as, theoretically, if there was no legal limit the Prime Minister could prorogue Parliament for as many months as they wanted or prorogue Parliament to stop an unpopular Bill in its tracks before it received royal assent.

So, what is the relevant limit? The Supreme Court ruled that prorogation is unlawful if it has the effect of frustrating or preventing Parliament carrying out its constitutional functions as a legislature responsible for the supervision of the executive *without reasonable justification*. The court might have found in the Prime Minister's favour had he put before the court a reasonable justification for choosing a period of thirty-four days for prorogation instead of the usual ten days or less. Johnson himself did not place any reasons of his own before the court. An official in Downing Street had put a rather limp and unconvincing memorandum to the Prime Minister in August, which he had signed off, but this totally ignored any consideration of what MPs might have wanted to do in the period that they were being denied, nor what parliamentary time would be needed to approve any new withdrawal agreement, nor the impact of prorogation on the special procedures for scrutinising delegated legislation. As Lady Hale caustically observed:

Nowhere is there a hint that the Prime Minister, in giving advice to Her Majesty, is more than simply the leader of the Government seeking to promote his own policies ... It is impossible for us to conclude ... that there was any reason – let alone a good reason – to advise Her Majesty to prorogue Parliament for five weeks.[44]

Boris Johnson's reaction to the judgment, which was a humiliation for him, was to counterattack. In political terms the judgment was a devastating blow to the populist narrative which maintained that there was, within the British Constitution, some higher authority than Parliament, namely 'the will of the people'. By the winter of 2019, Boris Johnson was firmly in the populist tent following a barn-storming tour of the country in his campaign to become Conservative Party leader. He could not meekly accept the judgment lying down. He commented, 'I think if judges are to pronounce on political questions in this way, there is at least an argument that there should be some form of accountability. The lessons of America are relevant.' He was wrong on two counts. First, the Supreme Court was not pronouncing on political questions. All important decisions made by the executive have a political hue to them, but this has not inhibited the courts from exercising a supervisory jurisdiction over those decisions. Many if not most of the constitutional cases in British legal history have been concerned with politics in that sense.[45]

Second, the lessons from America are relevant only to the extent that politicisation of the judiciary should, at all costs, be avoided. Judges are trusted to act fairly and impartially because they are different from politicians. Their philosophies and values are expressed in their judgments and are there for all to see, and are assessed by an independent and non-political appointments commission if a judge is to be promoted. If a political and legal culture allows for political considerations to be taken into account in judicial appointments then this may be exploited by the unscrupulous. Recently, President Trump and his conservative allies in the Senate celebrated their success in achieving the appointment of forty-five conservative judges to the nation's appeals courts. This meant that one-quarter of all appellate court judges in the United States will have been installed by President Trump.[46]

Johnson's response to the judgment was echoed by others. In the House of Commons, the Attorney General Geoffrey Cox accused the Supreme Court of converting a political convention into a legal principle: 'This House will, in the coming years and months, have to reflect on the implications and on whether it is content to leave that position untouched.'[47] Geoffrey Cox was a member of Boris Johnson's government, which at that time had no majority. Now that Johnson's party commands a large majority the word 'House' should now be transposed to 'executive'. Another senior Conservative MP, David Davis, has written: 'The lesson we should learn is how to ensure judgments reflect the majority national interest of the day, without making judges themselves political.'[48] Quite how Davis believes this constitutional somersault could be achieved remains to be seen. Judges have never, and should never, give judgments in the 'national interest of the day'. They do, and always will, give judgments according to law, and law and the national interest do not always walk hand in hand. The national interest will always be a subjective view of those who say something is a national interest, but law is founded on precedent or on statutory interpretation.

Plainly, there has been a breakdown in trust between members of the executive in Boris Johnson's government and the Supreme Court on this occasion. They are uncomfortable about legal rulings which they feel trespass upon their territory. The Queen's speech for the new session of Parliament in December 2019 promised a 'Constitution, Democracy and Rights Commission'. The purpose of this commission had been explained more fully in the Conservative Party's manifesto. It proposed to update administrative law to ensure there is a proper balance between the rights of the individual, national security and effective government. It also promised to ensure 'judicial review is not abused to conduct politics by another means to create needless delays.'

To date this commission has not been set up, so neither its membership nor its terms of reference are known, but the promise to set up the commission is worrying in itself. What, exactly, is the mischief Boris Johnson wants to excise from our system of law and justice? Governments often suffer when judicial reviews are taken, so, in a sense, every government must dread being taken to court by an aggrieved citizen, but if you are usually on the losing side in a match of football you should not advocate changing the rules so you can do better next time. You should up your game instead.

IS THERE SOMETHING ROTTEN ABOUT OUR CONSTITUTION?

The first question therefore must be: 'Is there something rotten in the state of justice and law in the United Kingdom which offends against the traditional tenets of our unwritten Constitution?' In other words: 'Are the courts too powerful, have judges overreached themselves?' In his Reith Lectures, Lord Sumption answered the question in the affirmative. He claimed that 'in the last half-century the courts have developed a concept of the rule of law, which penetrates well beyond their traditional role of deciding legal disputes and into the realm of legislative and ministerial policy'.[49]

Here, Lord Sumption is relying on a narrow concept of law which Lord Bingham challenged in his 2006 lecture, as discussed earlier. In Lord Sumption's view, providing that law is clear and not retrospective and providing that the law is interpreted by an independent judiciary to citizens who have access to the courts then no further elaboration about the meaning of the words 'rule of law' is needed. The rule of law is thus independent of any discussion or debate about whether a law is good or bad, just or unjust. That is the province of politics, not law. Debate about rights and entitlements is really a debate about a conception of rights or a conception of democracy. It is not a debate about the purpose and content of the rule of law.[50]

In Sumption's mind there is a clear dividing line between law and politics, and judges have, for fifty years or more, been straying over the line. This begs the question of where, actually, the line between law and politics should be drawn, if indeed there is a compelling case for a dividing line in the first place.

In 1992, Lord Goff, a senior Law Lord, said, 'Although I am well aware of the existence of the boundary, I am never quite sure where to find it.'[51] In 2005, Lord Bingham, as senior Law Lord, had to grapple with the whereabouts of the boundary in a case involving terrorism which is discussed in more detail in Chapter 6. He said that the court should consider demarcations between political and legal functions by looking at the relative constitutional competence of each in deciding the point at issue in the individual case. The more purely political (in a broad or narrow sense) the question is, the more appropriate it will be for a political resolution, leaving the court with a small or negligible function. Conversely, the greater the legal content of any issue, the greater the potential role of the court, as under the Constitution the courts, not politicians, must resolve legal questions.[52]

Politics is a different activity from law. Politics allows different groups to co-exist together in the same nation without living under tyranny or anarchy. Politics provides a way that free societies are governed through public debate and periodic elections.[53] The accountability of politicians to the electorate gives them authority to make important decisions on our behalf. Politics is not the implementation by the executive, local authorities or other public bodies of political choices made by a legislature. In order to carry forward legislative choices, officials are invariably given a measure of discretion as to how the political decision should best be implemented. The courts are acting properly when they rule on the legality of the implementation of those decisions.

Lord Sumption had observed, in an earlier lecture, that judges should be aware of the boundary otherwise the public may expect the law to be an engine of social improvement, which is beyond their constitutional role.[54] He summarised the merits of liberal democracy in a modern state in providing basic standards of public amenity, guaranteeing minimum levels of security, regulating economic activity and protecting the individual against misfortune of every kind, from the expansion of regulatory offences to the creation of new civil torts. He then argued that protection at this level 'calls for a more intrusive role for law' as traditional restraints, like religion and social convention, have lost much of their former force. However, this observation simply restates the fact that law develops incrementally alongside social and cultural developments within society itself. If society's demands mean law has become more intrusive, this is hardly an argument for judges to try to push back the very developments society has thrown at them.

Sir Stephen Sedley, a retired Lord Justice of Appeal, has pointed out that it is important not to conflate the implementation of parliamentary instructions with the practice of politics in the chambers of the House of Commons and the House of Lords. Law, or public law as it is better called, can only exercise legal control over the executive, not on proceedings within the Commons or Lords where politics is carried out[55] The boundary between law and politics is the place where the executive, local government or quangos overstep their mark by acting outside or beyond legal powers given to them by Parliament.

Not all judges have supported Lord Sumption's general thesis that judges are in danger of overreaching themselves. Lord Dyson, who sat in the Supreme Court as well as becoming later Master of the Rolls, has said, 'I am not aware of a widespread sense of unease that judges are routinely overstepping the mark and impermissibly quashing executive decisions ... I am unaware of any major policy issue whose merits have been resolved judicially.'[56]

This was an opinion that Lord Sumption seemed to hold himself in a lecture he gave in 2014.[57] Here, he acknowledged that long before the Human Rights Act, English courts would routinely give 'anxious scrutiny' to administrative decisions when a litigant complained the decision conflicted with a fundamental right. Traditionally, the courts have kept a narrow focus on making this judgment as it is often beyond the job of a judge to assess the executive justification for interfering with a fundamental right. 'The breadth of the decision-maker's discretionary margin of judgment will vary with the significance of the right being interfered with and the nature of the decision.'[58] The complaint Lord Sumption made about this approach is that judges have been too reticent to admit that this balancing exercise provides an inhibition from going too far into making political judgments. However, in this opinion, made in 2014, Sumption does not criticise the notion of anxious judicial scrutiny, nor the application of it by the House of Lords or the Supreme Court.

Sedley was concerned that Sumption's general thesis in the Reith Lectures harmed the standing of the judiciary and confidence in the rule of law.[59] As Lord Bingham has explained, a judge is not overstepping the boundaries of judicial responsibility by declaring that a particular executive decision was one which no sensible authority acting with due appreciation of its responsibilities would have decided to adopt, providing judges approach their task with caution as two reasonable people can reach different conclusions and no judge must substitute their decision in place of an executive one. By contrast, if judges were to exercise powers properly belonging elsewhere, they would usurp their authority.

The boundaries may not be easily articulated, as Lord Goff said, but High Court judges and those above them are lawyers of the highest integrity who take their constitutional duties seriously. Few are bold enough to stray beyond the limits of the fine boundary line and if they do the Court of Appeal or Supreme Court can correct them. If judicial power is exercised properly to hold ministers, officials and public bodies to account then judges exercise the constitutional power the rule of law requires.[60] The holding of the executive to account is not crossing a forbidden boundary. It is an essential function for the judiciary in a liberal democracy.

What is forgotten by those who fear encroachment by judges onto the turf occupied by politicians is that the politicians themselves have become thoroughly muddled about their own source of power. The entry by the United Kingdom into the EEC in 1972 inevitably changed traditional perceptions about what the supremacy of Parliament meant. In addition, social and cultural changes in the period since then have undoubtedly enlarged the sovereignty of Her Majesty's courts of justice. The tensions that the passage of time has created between politicians and judges are unlikely to be resolved quickly. The decision of the Conservative government of 1970–74 to pass the European Communities Act 1972 let the genie out of the bottle. Frantic attempts in 2020 to put the genie back in are unlikely to be successful in 'taking back control', nor are judges likely to abandon their role that natural developments in law and the expectations of society have placed upon them.

CHAPTER 5

HUMAN RIGHTS: WHY WE NEED THEM AND WHY POPULISTS HATE THEM

In December 2013, Chris Grayling made an appearance before the Joint Committee on Human Rights of the UK Parliament, a committee consisting of MPs and peers. As Grayling was, at the time, the Secretary of State for Justice and Lord Chancellor, the members of the joint committee were no doubt interested in what he had to say. He told the committee that Great Britain had benefited from a common law system dating back hundreds of years. For this reason, he did not think that the Strasbourg Court of human rights had made our country a better place than it would have been otherwise.

The court he was referring to, the European Court of Human Rights (ECHR), was established in January 1959 under Article 19 of the European Convention on Human Rights to ensure that all contracting states to the convention observed their obligations. The court sits in Strasbourg and is often called the Strasbourg Court. There is one judge for each contracting party, which means that there are now forty-seven judges at the court. Nominations for membership of the court are made by each contracting state but the appointment decision is taken by the Assembly of the Council of Europe. The court, consisting of a small group of judges, sits in chambers, the most authoritative of which is the Grand Chamber.

Chris Grayling was expressing a traditionally held view that it was alien to British traditions for there to be a written document setting out rights. However, this was a view that had been going out of fashion for at least twenty years among judges, practising lawyers and Labour and Liberal politicians. Grayling, in his capacity as Lord Chancellor, was making a party-political point. He was articulating a political objection to the European Court of Human Rights which had been a constant theme of Conservative Party policy in the months and years before his appearance at the joint committee. In fact, Grayling wanted to go further than official party policy and he expressed the view to a senior judge that he wanted the United Kingdom to withdraw from the European Convention on Human Rights entirely.[1] Opposition to human rights was being orchestrated by the popular press for many years before Chris Grayling's appearance before the joint committee.

In 2006, David Cameron, then leader of the Conservative Party, had become sceptical of the value of the Human Rights Act 1998 as it had failed, in his view, to properly protect the rights of citizens.[2] This scepticism was articulated in the Conservative Party manifesto for the 2010 general election when his party promised to replace the Human Rights Act with a new Bill defining British rights. In 2015, his party promised to break the link with Strasbourg and make the Supreme Court 'the ultimate arbiter of human rights matters'.[3] Ironically, by 2019 this faith in the wisdom of the Supreme Court by a Conservative Prime Minister had changed dramatically. Boris Johnson had to suffer the indignity of having his decision to prorogue Parliament declared unlawful by the Supreme Court, as was explored in Chapter 4.

By 2012, the Conservatives had a new and important ally in their dislike of the European Court of Human Rights. In an interview with the *Daily Telegraph*, a former ambassador to the United Nations from the United States stated that the United Kingdom should not submit to the jurisdiction of the Strasbourg Court. In the former ambassador's view, the court represented an infringement of British sovereignty and, in his opinion, British politicians needed to ask themselves whether they wanted Britain to be a truly sovereign nation or not.[4] The casual reader would be entitled to assume that this view came from a senior diplomat, giving an objective assessment from his vantage point of being a member of an organisation trying to promote an international rules-based order. This was not the case.

The former ambassador in question was John Bolton, a figure barely known in Britain at that time and hardly a household name in the United States. He became ambassador to the United Nations under President George W. Bush for a brief period in 2005–06, but he was, and still is, a vocal 'nativist' and neo-conservative who supported regime change in Venezuela and Cuba and is, in general terms, a foreign policy 'hawk'. He was National Security Advisor to President Trump from April 2018 until September 2019. In his comments about the Strasbourg Court, Bolton was articulating the populist view which is sceptical of the value of international institutions and a rules-based order in the world. The consensus of successive administrations in the United States since 1945 had been to champion international institutions like the World Bank and the International Monetary Fund as a means of ensuring a semblance of world financial stability while other international bodies like NATO and the Southeast Asia Treaty Organization would endeavour to preserve peace. The role of the United States was to be a leader within these bodies. Bolton, on the other hand, is a believer in the 'Monroe Doctrine', which places the United States as the sole player in world affairs, exercising economic and military strength in situations only where US interests are directly engaged. The single interests of the United States as an independent sovereign state are more important than the collective interests of international institutions.

This 'populist' world view has, since 2012, become a familiar narrative in the tabloid press concerning the status and legitimacy of the European Court of Human Rights. In October 2014, James Slack, home affairs editor of the *Daily Mail*, wrote that it was time for our judges to ignore the 'crazy decisions' of the European Court that allows 'foreign killers and rapists' to 'avoid deportation'. In the same article, Chris Grayling, still Secretary of State for Justice, stated that people 'are fed up with human rights being used as an excuse for unacceptable behaviour' and Dominic Raab MP, then a prominent Conservative backbencher, said that the Strasbourg Court represented 'mission creep' and has wrought damage to the 'wider democratic process'.[5]

The *Daily Mail* became almost apoplectic with fury over a 'human rights farce' involving a Lithuanian citizen, Kestutis Matuzevsius, who had been arrested on a European arrest warrant in the United Kingdom and was deported back to Lithuania to stand trial for murder. The case was completely unremarkable, except for the fact that Matuzevsius had unwisely sought to challenge his deportation before the ECHR on the grounds that his state of mental health should have prevented the United Kingdom court from deporting him. The Strasbourg Court found no difficulty in deciding that this argument was 'manifestly ill-founded' and dismissed his human rights application. However, the *Daily Mail* took the view that the claimant had wasted taxpayers' money in making his human rights application, thus rendering the proceedings in Strasbourg a 'farce'.[6]

This is a perplexing and deeply concerning comment on the case. It was Sir William Blackstone, the famous eighteenth-century legal scholar, who coined the adage 'it is better that ten guilty persons should escape than one innocent person should suffer'.[7] This phrase illustrates the important principle that the process of law should always strive to protect the innocent rather than serve the interests of the general will by convicting all who might, in the view of some, be guilty. The same principle applies in applications by aggrieved citizens to the European Court of Human Rights. It is better that 98 per cent of cases brought by individuals against decisions of the United Kingdom are dismissed (as they are) than one meritorious case slips through the net and a deserving citizen is denied his or her fundamental rights.

The populist narrative does not see a basic legal framework in this way. Instead, for them applications to the court are made by rapists, criminals and murderers who are somehow using the ECHR as a vehicle to frustrate the British judicial system. For example, the *Daily Express* often uses inflammatory language when reporting cases heard in Strasbourg.[8] This narrative is not confined to the print media. At the Conservative Party conference in 2011, Theresa May, who was Home Secretary at the time, told the audience that in addition to drug dealers and robbers whom the Human Rights Act protected from deportation there was an example of an illegal immigrant who could not be deported from the UK because he had a pet cat.

She was referring to an otherwise unremarkable case heard in December 2008 where an immigration judge had decided that the Home Office had failed to properly apply its own guidance in treating the applicant as having a relationship akin to marriage with his partner. It was purely coincidental that the family unit included a pet cat. May's remarks echoed a tabloid press narrative that human rights had become a term of abuse and decisions of the European Court of Human Rights were either mocked as being farcical or treated seriously as a source of menace to ordinary people. In the populist scheme of things, human rights are for those with a shared identity of being 'outsiders' in society – criminals, immigrants, foreigners – whereas for the ordinary person human rights are an expensive irrelevance, soaking up taxpayers' money.[9]

When human rights became a subject of political debate fifty years ago it was not a party-political issue, still less an opportunity for populist rhetoric. One of the first Members of Parliament to raise the need to entrench basic liberties in a written law was the Conservative Lord Lambton in 1969. Quintin Hogg MP (later Lord Hailsham and Lord Chancellor under Margaret Thatcher) was also fearful of an erosion of liberty when he warned, in a paper for the Conservative Party in 1969, that Parliament had become virtually an 'elective dictatorship'. By the mid-1970s, many parliamentarians in all three parties agreed that there was a need to entrench human rights, though others disagreed.[10]

CODIFYING HUMAN RIGHTS

During the mid-1980s, a consensus had grown in favour of incorporating the European Convention on Human Rights into English law. In 1985, the House of Lords gave the Human Rights Bill a second reading, enabling the House of Commons to debate it. By now, the Conservatives were in government, and the Bill was opposed by the Solicitor General, Sir Patrick Mayhew. The Bill had been moved in the Commons by a Conservative, Sir Edward Gardner QC, who said the language of the European convention 'echoes down the corridors of history. It goes deep into our history as far back as the Magna Carta.'[11] On that occasion ninety-four MPs, fifty-eight of whom were Conservative, voted to give his Bill a second reading.[12] It failed only for technical reasons, as fewer than 100 MPs had voted for the 'closure' of a private members' bill.

When the Scottish barrister John Smith became leader of the Labour Party, he persuaded his party to back a new human rights law in 1993, the same year that Lord Bingham, Master of the Rolls, wrote a persuasive article in a legal journal which advocated incorporating the European Convention on Human Rights into English and Scottish law.[13] A formidable array of the senior judiciary in the House of Lords agreed with Lord Bingham. *The Times*, *The Guardian* and *The Economist* all favoured incorporation. In 1994, Anthony Lester, the barrister who had first argued for a Bill of Rights in 1969, was now Lord Lester of Herne Hill QC, a Liberal Democrat peer. His unsuccessful attempt to introduce human rights legislation in the House of Lords was supported by, among others, the Lord Chief Justice, two former Lord Chancellors and two former Home Secretaries.[14] By the time of the general election of 1997, the Labour Party was fully committed to constitutional reform and after his victory Tony Blair published a white paper entitled 'Rights Brought Home: the Human Rights Bill'.[15] However, for the first time the argument for incorporating the European Convention on Human Rights into United Kingdom law was becoming party-political. The Conservative Party manifesto for the 1997 election had made clear the party's opposition to incorporation:

We do not believe there is a case for more radical reform that would undermine the House of Commons. A new Bill of Rights, for example, would risk transferring power away from

Parliament to legal courts – undermining the democratic supremacy of Parliament as representatives of the people. Whilst this may be a necessary check in other countries which depend upon more formalised written constitutions, we do not believe it is appropriate to the UK.[16]

It was hardly surprising, therefore, that in the House of Commons the Conservatives voted against incorporation in 1998. Sir Brian Mawhinney, speaking from the opposition front bench, said:

> The Bill is not even about giving human rights to our citizens – they have them already. Whether intentional or not, the Bill is about diminishing the sovereignty of Parliament; it is about weakening our democracy and changing fundamentally the balance of the separation of powers between the Executive, the legislature and the judiciary. The result will be a further increase in the power of the Executive, the diminution of Parliament and the politicisation of the judiciary.[17]

These were respectable, if somewhat misguided, constitutional arguments, but they were not couched in chauvinistic, nationalistic, anti-European language. This language began to surface approximately eight years ago, in 2012. The current debate about human rights has degenerated (with some honourable exceptions) into a shrill and distasteful dispute. On one side are ordinary people, who do not need cumbersome laws to protect their interests. On the other are a litigious minority who exploit the taxpayer and the availability of human rights remedies to further their own unpopular causes. But, in one sense, the very sound of the high-pitched shrieks of this disagreeable discourse has forced liberals to examine, again, from first principles the arguments that underpin the need for human rights.

THE CORE ARGUMENTS FOR HUMAN RIGHTS

Almost everybody would agree that personal autonomy, the aspect of humanity that allows for reflectiveness, self-awareness and a natural instinct to explore one's own relationship with the outside world, is valuable in its own right. Yet we cannot acknowledge the inherent value of personal autonomy without asking why it is absolutely necessary as a precondition for becoming a full human being. Is it valuable because it contributes generally to the good of society? Or is it valuable only in a way which enhances the life of the individual? May an individual pursue the choices inherent in possessing personal autonomy without a society providing the framework within which the choices may be made?[18] The pathways to answering these questions often provide a starting point for a possible future parting of the ways between conservatives and liberals.

One of the greatest intellectuals of the twentieth century, Isaiah Berlin, argued that it is not enough to say individual liberty is preserved unless someone else, a lawmaker or a parliament, authorises its violation. Interdependence within a society entails some loss of liberty, as free action will necessarily be limited by law. But, at the same time, there must be a certain minimum liberty which cannot in any circumstances be violated. A frontier must be drawn between the area of private life and that of public authority. These 'frontiers' have been given different names by different people. The essential point, Berlin maintained, is that society erects these frontiers in a way that enables them to be widely accepted. By being widely accepted they become an essential part of what is meant by being a human being.[19]

Joseph Raz developed Berlin's point a little further. Man's capacity for personal autonomy and self-directed action can only occur within a social infrastructure. This is an environment which provides the conditions in which an individual can make choices.[20] In a further refinement, David Feldman has argued that liberties provided by a minimalist state may mean more to some than to others. If those with economic advantages can use their advantage to purchase opportunities which are denied to others, liberties are not enjoyed equally.[21] This, inevitably, leads to the state becoming involved in issues surrounding personal autonomy. Without the state, vulnerable people will need help to enjoy their autonomy and society has a broad responsibility to provide the infrastructure for everybody to exercise their own personal autonomy.

If the starting point is a recognition by the state that there is such a thing as personal autonomy then the state must inevitably recognise that there are certain things which are beyond the power of the state to arbitrate on. They are within the sphere of personal autonomy, which is private, and the use of power by the state is a public function. This is not to exclude the power of the state to make rules for our behaviour; it simply means that within the private sphere, individual private choice outranks social preferences.

This might appear to be a scenario which creates an obvious tension between democracy and an individual's exercise of autonomy, but this will not arise if the delimitation between the public and the private is itself a democratic decision. It is here that the importance of democracy to the rule of law and individual rights enters the debate. It is difficult to imagine a properly functioning democracy without freedom of expression, a free press, a right to vote, a right to protest and petition Parliament, and freedom from arbitrary arrest and detention without trial. These rights are fundamental to democracy. They could not be taken away without undermining the very democracy which legitimises public decision-making.[22]

Once the boundaries have been set within the democratic process, the courts have a role both in keeping the public sphere within its delineated boundary and in ensuring individuals are able to make use of their autonomy. The rule of law sets down the zone in which individual autonomy, or the exercise of personal rights, is immune from government interference. The flip side is the corresponding duty on the government and state institutions to enable autonomy to be enjoyed and to protect the exercise of autonomous rights by the individual citizen. This principle is, in general terms, the philosophical foundation of a mature and civilised democracy. This is the context in which the European Convention for the Protection of Human Rights and Fundamental Freedoms has been ratified by the United Kingdom. As Anthony Lester has written, 'It is a public acknowledgement of our shared humanity.'[23]

EUROPEAN CONVENTION ON HUMAN RIGHTS

The European Convention on Human Rights, which was written in 1950, grew from a new invigorated idealism following the end of the Second World War, from the defeat of fascism and a determination by the international community that the carnage brought about by genocide and political tyranny should never occur again. In 1941 in the United States, President Franklin D. Roosevelt trumpeted his 'four freedoms': freedom of speech, freedom of worship, freedom from want and freedom from fear. After the war, politicians and diplomats applied their own skills to the drafting of the Universal Declaration of Human Rights in 1948 as well as the European Convention on Human Rights, but also the Convention on the Prevention and Punishment of the Crime of Genocide 1948 and the

Geneva Convention 1949 within a political consensus which believed that such documents were valuable and necessary. They all attempted to provide the 'frontiers' that Isaiah Berlin was writing about.

The reaction to the catastrophes of the Second World War cannot be overstated. As the writer and philosopher Hannah Arendt has written, 'anti-Semitism and totalitarianism, one more brutal than the other, have demonstrated that human dignity needs a new guarantee which can only be found in a new political principle'.[24] She meant the new guarantee should be one of rights.

The above conventions set down rights which form the bedrock of democracy and attempted to outlaw the obvious and deliberate flouting of them, whether in peacetime or in war. This way of looking at the role of rights involved an aspiration towards high standards which should be universal and should exist across borders. The new mood revived old Roman notions about 'natural' law but adapted for contemporary needs. It said an individual's agency within society could be used against the state in which he or she lived. This was quite new, certainly for the United Kingdom, as written statements setting out rights, even bare minimum rights, were alien to British political traditions.

There are only two documents in British legal history which have attempted to define a citizen's rights: Magna Carta 1215 and the Bill of Rights 1689. The British way has been to rely on an unwritten Constitution which details how laws are made, not the values contained in the laws themselves. Parliament is supreme and can, in broad terms, do what it likes. Parliament alone decides what interference there should be in the liberties of the subject. Without a written constitution there are no principles of English law which possess any fundamental moral claims over and above any other law enacted by Parliament. An unwritten constitution provides no protection from the misuse of power by the state, nor from the decisions of the executive and public bodies if they act in a way which is incompatible with convention rights. Human Rights protect human agency against a future use of oppressive power by the state, but this was not recognised in British constitutional arrangements until the enactment of the Human Rights Act 1998.[25]

THE HUMAN RIGHTS ACT 1998

The Human Rights Act 1998 broke new ground in attempting to create 'a more explicitly moral approach to decisions and decision-making' and 'a culture where positive rights and liberties become the focus of concern of legislators, administrators and judges alike … where there would be a greater concentration on substance rather than form'.[26] The 1998 Act is a skilfully drafted statute, reflecting a pragmatic compromise between the full 'incorporation' of the European Convention on Human Rights into English law and the age-old British attachment to its parliamentary supremacy. The supremacy of Parliament is not undermined as this 'constitutional orthodoxy' is accommodated.[27] The executive is required to issue a statement that, on the balance of probabilities, any new legislation is not incompatible with basic convention rights.[28] In reality, this is not difficult.

There are three categories of rights in the convention. The right to life (except death as a result of lawful war), the prohibition of torture, slavery and servitude and the right not to be punished by a retroactive law are absolute rights. But the right to marry and the right to liberty and security are limited rights, as they may be restricted in explicit circumstances, for example to put obstacles in the way of 'sham' marriages. Lastly, there are rights which are qualified, for example the right to freedom of assembly and association. The right may be qualified in a balancing exercise by the courts where there is a clash between a group exercising a right of peaceful assembly, for example climate change protestors, and the protection of the rights and freedoms of others, for example passengers on public transport. The duty of the courts when interpreting legislation is to interpret it 'so far as is possible to do so', in a way which is compatible with convention rights.[29]

Far from it being a shock to the system, English judges were quick to embrace the new culture that was introduced in the Human Rights Act 1998. Lord Bingham gave no fewer than eight reasons why the Human Rights Act was both important and necessary. First, the Act did not invent new rights and freedoms we had not previously been entitled to: it made those rights enforceable in a British court. Prior to the Act, an aggrieved citizen had to take his case to the Strasbourg Court. Second, the Act did not transfer power from politicians and administrators to judges; a judicial decision after the Act came into force could have been made before. Third, the Act is drafted to preserve supreme legislative authority to Parliament. Fourth, the Act does not elevate individual rights above community rights; legitimate communal interests have to be taken into account in deciding where individual rights begin and end. Fifth, the Act does nothing to diminish a citizen's duties and responsibilities as members of society, as these are already fully prescribed in statute or common law. Sixth, the European convention provides a floor, not a ceiling, to citizens' protection. The convention does not prevent a sovereign Parliament from providing additional rights if it chooses to do so. Seventh, in Bingham's opinion the decisions of the Strasbourg Court are no more foolish than some decisions in our domestic courts, and the many wise decisions of the court are as wise as those made in domestic courts. He left his last and best point to the end:

Convention rights deserve to be protected because they are the basic and fundamental rights which everyone ought to enjoy simply by virtue of their existence as a human being ... Are any of them trivial, superfluous or unnecessary? There may be those who would like to live in a country where those rights are not protected, but I am not one of their number.[30]

Another eminent and recently retired judge, Lord Dyson, has commented that the convention did not present difficulties to English judges in interpreting decisions of the Strasbourg Court as the European court's approach to interpreting the convention was analogous to the English method. Further, the text of the European convention was itself admirable.[31] Lord Mance, a former Supreme Court Justice, has emphasised the global nature of modern world realities where supranational principles and international law have an impact on law, commerce and communities generally and it is simply unrealistic to believe English law could isolate itself from Europe and the wider world. Forty-seven nations are now members of the Council of Europe, including many that were previously communist states.

The British common law system stands almost alone in being unconstrained by a written constitution. Strasbourg case law has had a beneficial effect on purely domestic English law: homosexuals are not banned from the armed services and aliens suspected of terrorist activities cannot be detained without trial. Alleged terrorists wanted by foreign countries cannot be deported if they face a real risk of torture or inhuman treatment in their home nation.[32] These last two benefits of the European convention to maintaining a civilised liberal democracy in Britain are discussed fully in Chapter 6.

JONATHAN SUMPTION'S OBJECTIONS

These are well-argued justifications for the values enshrined in the European convention being applied to new legislation. Judges have an obligation to take account of (but not slavishly follow) decisions of the Strasbourg Court and therefore domestic law has not been taken over by a foreign court. But the European convention is not universally popular with senior judges. By common consent, Jonathan Sumption, a recently retired Supreme Court Justice and a former barrister of eminence, is one of the most persuasive and intelligent lawyers of his generation. At the Bar, he hardly ever lost a case. His Reith Lectures in 2019 were a tour de force of intellectual brilliance and the book which followed, *Trials of the State: Law and the Decline of Politics*, is packed with original and thought-provoking material.[33] Sumption goes to the heart of the matter when it comes to the influence of the European Convention on Human Rights on English law: is it legitimate, he asks, for democracies to create a body of law that is independent of democratic choice and protected against abrogation or amendment by a democratic legislature? As with all skilled advocates, he frames the central question in the way which is most likely to receive the answer he wants to hear.

Sumption's chosen central question is built upon a structure which he has devised as his premise. He is interested in finding a solid foundation for why law is legitimate in itself. In simple terms, what is it that makes law valid? Law is legitimate, according to Sumption, only if it derives from consent, and this comes 'from the general body of citizens'. This general body is within the body politic or simply 'politics' as Sumption calls it. Therefore, in Sumption's carefully layered argument law and politics occupy separate spaces in society and they must never be mixed up or confused. Law may be one thing, but politics is definitely something else. Law's legitimacy comes from politics and 'it is the business of citizens and their representatives to decide what the law ought to be'.

Few could disagree with this general statement of representative democracy which, for Sumption, is the 'constitutional mechanism' for making law. The next piece of Sumption's structure is his argument about values and fundamental rights. It is here that Sumption becomes controversial in his explanation of values and rights within a representative democracy.

According to Sumption, fundamental rights can only exist in a valid legal system. If they have legitimacy, what is the 'transcendent authority', independent of democratic legitimacy, that gives a validity to fundamental or inalienable rights? There is no such transcendent authority, but equally rights cannot exist in a vacuum. They have to be created. In the absence of any transcendent authority, notions about the inherent values underpinning law are self-validating. Any political regime can call itself democratic, even if it is not, and here he gives the example of the former German Democratic Republic (GDR). The European Court of Human Rights in Strasbourg, like the old GDR, employs a concept of democracy as a general term of approval for a set of political values and therefore the Strasbourg Court has self-validated its own set of values. The values that Strasbourg has developed in its own judgments should be ones made democratically by the 'general body of citizens'.

Strasbourg's self-validation means that democratic choices within individual states are constrained by the values set by the court. According to Sumption, this is fundamentally objectionable because if liberal values are given a privileged constitutional status then this claim to privilege is conceptually no different from similar claims of communism, fascism or Catholicism. The Strasbourg

Court exists independently of democratic choice and its judgments cannot be changed or amended by member states. The qualified rights within the convention produce acute problems for Strasbourg judges, as they force them to make political judgments, not legal ones.

ARE THESE OBJECTIONS SOUND?

The first objection to this analysis is that most people would not naturally associate the repressions of the highly centralised and controlling regime of the GDR with the European Court of Human Rights. They are different institutions in every conceivable way, except in Sumption's categorisation of self-validation. The German Democratic Republic had no generalised body of citizens who could provide any legitimacy, through free elections and freedom of expression, for its existence. It existed only by the exercise of brute force and the curtailment of liberties. The regime had absolute power.

Curiously, in an argument which seeks to find common ground between the defunct German Democratic Republic and the European Human Rights Court in Strasbourg, Sumption does not disagree with the broad concept of fundamental rights. His acknowledgement that fundamental rights do exist is qualified. He supports fundamental rights providing they are so generalised that no reasonable person could disagree with them. His first fundamental right is the right to social existence itself, such as freedom from arbitrary detention, physical injury and death and access to an independent court. His second is the right associated with democratic existence, freedom of thought and expression, assembly and association and the participation in elections.

The problem for Sumption is that these are the 'frontiers' which Sir Isaiah Berlin had in mind as being so widely accepted that they become an essential part of being human. But Berlin did not contemplate them as being legitimate in the sense that Sumption insists legitimacy is necessary for something to become a law. Berlin thought that his frontiers could be natural rights, the word of God, a natural law or even the demands of utility, yet Sumption maintains such things have no inherent legitimacy as there is not, in modern times, any 'transcendent authority' other than laws made by the 'general body of citizens'. Why should a concept like fundamental democratic rights not have a legitimacy of its own through culture, history and the general experience of inhabiting a community?

Strasbourg case law may not come from any elected general body within a nation state, but the decisions of the European Court of Human Rights apply some very broad principles that were accepted by the United Kingdom when they signed the convention as being essential, in the way described by Isaiah Berlin.

The second objection to his attack on the legitimacy of the Strasbourg Court is his assumption that democracy and the art of politics will provide, by their nature, the liberties and freedom necessary to sustain it. If democracy must be sustained then where are the boundaries between law and politics? Giving teeth to generalised political tenets of democracy needs lawyers and judges to keep ambitious politicians on the straight and narrow, not veering away towards autocracy. In the English unwritten Constitution both Parliament and the judges are sovereign in their own spheres. Judges are obliged to apply law made by Parliament, but Parliament is not above the law.[34] Sumption is far too optimistic in concluding that the 'only effective constraints on the abuse of democratic power are political ... active citizenship, a culture of political sensitivity and the capacity of representative institutions to perform their traditional role of accommodating division and mediating dissent'.[35]

Sumption displays the same touching faith in politics to uphold and sustain the values of democracy as Bernard Crick did in 1962 in his book *In Defence of Politics*.[36] Crick was able to praise the art of politics in 1962 Britain as being 'an adaptable, flexible and conciliatory activity, providing a market-place and price mechanism for social demands, existing within settled order, tolerance and diversity'. This is a description of politics from a bygone age where 'Western' concepts needed a robust defence against communist ideology promulgated from behind the iron curtain and from single-party nationalism emerging from newly independent countries in Africa. The world is now a completely different place where human agency and autonomy clash with remote multinational conglomerates. Trust in politics is vanishing while populism is doing its best to rid politics of conciliation, flexibility and adaptability.

In today's Britain politics is not only a collectivist activity where classes and powerful interest groups find their voice in political parties and loyalties are handed down through generations. Politicians must appeal to individuals, whose own ideological loyalties are fluid and whose opinions are often formed via social media, which is quintessentially an individually targeted method of communication. Social media enables the individual to express themself in ways unthought of even in the recent past while at the same time retaining enormous, largely unregulated, power to itself. The rights and responsibilities of the individual within a political environment are now as important, if not more important, than the economic clout, or lack of it, of groups identified by wealth, social class, geographical location or occupation. Yet, it is precisely in the area of the individual's relationship to the wider political community that the British Parliament has proved to be so weak.

THE MORAL VACUUM IN PARLIAMENT

Sumption insists that the problem about applying the European convention in British courts lies in 'transforming controversial political issues into questions of law'.[37] However, it is equally valid to argue that the problem exists within politics. Parliament too often avoids making important decisions and leaves the job of finding a solution to the courts. There is no better illustration of Parliament's failure to confront a controversial moral issue than the topic of assisted suicide. In the bad old days of the early 1960s when the application of the criminal law was cruel and unfeeling – as was discussed in Chapter 2 – Parliament enacted the Suicide Act 1961. This Act made it a crime, punishable with up to fourteen years' imprisonment, for any individual to help somebody else to commit suicide. The Act did not discriminate between what is sometimes called 'mercy killing' and heartless acts which more closely resembled murder. Plainly, the blunt instrument of this law has not kept pace with society's development and the fact that, medically, many people can remain alive while earnestly wishing that they could die.

Moral issues are there for all to see. Does human autonomy permit a relative to kill a loved one who has expressed an unequivocal and voluntary wish to die because to continue living is intolerable and unbearable? If so, should the law always permit this, or only in certain circumstances? If so, in what circumstances? Is the resolution of these questions exclusively a matter for Parliament? If so, what are the consequences if Parliament fails to admit that there are questions that need answering?

In 2008, Debbie Purdy was suffering from primary progressive multiple sclerosis which had deteriorated to such an extent that she had lost all ability to carry out tasks for herself and experienced choking fits when she drank liquid. She wanted to know whether

her husband Omar Puente would be prosecuted under the Suicide Act 1961 if he helped her to die at a time of her choosing. She knew a time would come when life for her would be intolerable. She was able to ask the courts to answer this question as Article 8 of the European Convention on Human Rights was engaged. The justices in the House of Lords did not have any function in changing the law on assisted suicide, as it had been made in Parliament, but they could consider the guidance which the Director of Public Prosecutions had published for complying with Parliament's law in Debbie Purdy's application. The judges concluded that the guidance was unclear and they gave judgments requiring the Director to issue offence-specific guidance to provide consistency and clarity for those who wished to know whether they risked prosecution for the crime of assisting suicide.[38] Lord Hope explained that judges do have a role to play if the application of a law made by Parliament by the Director of Public Prosecutions lacks clarity and consistency. The court held back from declaring that the Suicide Act 1961 was incompatible with the European Convention on Human Rights, but new guidance clarifying the circumstances when a prosecution would or would not take place was issued.

The limits of judicial law-making are illustrated in another case. Tony Nicklinson was fit and healthy until he became paralysed from the neck down after he suffered a severe stroke which resulted in 'locked-in syndrome'. He could move only his head and his eyes. He earnestly and sincerely wished to end his life with dignity but could not do so without assistance and assisting a suicide was a crime under the Suicide Act 1961. He sought a declaration from the courts that this crime was incompatible with Article 8 of the European Convention on Human Rights, the right to respect for private and family life. When a High Court judge refused this application, Nicklinson was devastated and declined food. He died of natural causes in August 2012. The Supreme Court did not consider the ethical, legal and moral aspects of the case until 2015 and the justices did not reach unanimous conclusions. The majority, of which Lord Sumption was part, concluded that it was not part of the British Constitution for any court, including the Supreme Court, to usurp Parliament's prerogative to deal with moral issues. Lord Sumption made the point that the decision-maker is bound to be influenced by their personal opinion about the merits of assisted suicide and therefore it is appropriate that the decision-makers should be those who represent the community as a whole. It was not the province of the courts to make decisions about moral dilemmas. As the political scientist Anthony King put it, 'So much for the notion that Britain's judges, aided and abetted by the Strasbourg court, have become rapacious seekers after power.'[39] Neither the Purdy nor the Nicklinson cases support Lord Sumption's argument that the higher courts in Britain have converted political questions into questions of law.

In September 2015, the House of Commons debated the Assisted Dying (No. 2) Bill, which had been passed in the House of Lords on a second reading but could not proceed further because of the general election. The Bill had been drafted by Lord Falconer, a former Lord Chancellor and Secretary of State for Justice, who had consulted widely, and contained safeguards to allay fears that terminally ill patients might feel under pressure to make a decision to end their lives. The Bill stipulated that doctors could be allowed to help a terminally ill person to end their life if, first, the patient was terminally ill with less than six months to live; second, two doctors had been satisfied that the patient had the capacity to make an informed decision; and third, a judge had made a declaration that two doctors had solemnly gone through the necessary steps and that the patient's decision was voluntary and informed. The case of Tony Nicklinson would have satisfied these provisions. Despite these safeguards, the Bill was rejected by MPs by 330 votes to 118.

This decision left the law made by Parliament in 1961 still in place. The Suicide Act 1961 exposed any friend or relative (or indeed sympathetic doctor) to prosecution for assisting the commission of an offence if they fulfilled the wishes of their loved one or patient to end their life. At the end of his first Reith Lecture, 'Law and the Decline of Politics', Lord Sumption was asked by a member of the audience what the point of the Suicide Act 1961 was as it prolonged suffering, produced moral anguish and had the potential to send a deceased's loving relatives or faithful family doctor to jail. He replied, 'I will tell you exactly what I think about this. I think that the law should continue to criminalise assistance in suicide and I think the law should be broken from time to time.'[40] This was a brave answer to a huge moral dilemma, but an extraordinary one for a former senior judge to have given. Judges who make and apply the law are liable to be labelled hypocrites if, at the same time, they condone breaches of law. His answer exposed a weakness in a central plank of his general thesis.

In reality, the opposite conclusion to Sumption's arguments can be drawn from the 'right to die' cases in the Supreme Court. The simple truth is that politics cannot always arbitrate satisfactorily when the rights and duties of citizens clash with the intentions of a democratically elected legislature when the legislature shies away from contemporary moral concerns. Parliament cannot always be relied on to make or unmake laws that impinge directly on morally difficult questions. These may involve autonomy or even hard questions about behaviour which should or should not be made criminal. This cropped up when the Supreme Court had to consider what Parliament, or politics, had meant when the Sexual Offences Act 2003 made it a requirement – which could not be challenged or reviewed – that any offender convicted of a sexual offence and sentenced to thirty months' imprisonment or more had a lifelong duty to inform the police about their personal address or any plan to travel abroad. The offender in question in this case was a boy who at the age of eleven sexually violated a younger child. The Supreme Court had no difficulty in deciding that Parliament had gone 'over the top' in legislating for a burdensome obligation to be lifelong in every case, without exception, as the offender had no opportunity to demonstrate that he was no longer a public risk. The notification requirement was disproportionate to Parliament's general objectives of preventing the commission of further offences.[41]

If politics has been unable to grapple with these acute moral difficulties then how is the void to be filled? If, as Sumption argues, the Strasbourg Court lacks legitimacy, what harm has this apparent legitimacy gap caused to the United Kingdom? Lord Dyson, who was a judge for twenty-three years and held office as a Supreme Court Justice and Master of the Rolls and has presided over scores of cases involving human rights, has said, 'On the whole the case law of the European Court of Human Rights has strengthened and enriched our human rights law.'[42]

There is a big difference between the use of the Human Rights Act by judges and political decisions made by people whose livelihoods depend on success in the polling booths. Judges can only deal with the facts and data placed before them and reach decisions based on legal precedent and reasoning for people whose lives are affected by generalised political intentions. When judges apply the Human Rights Act to actual cases they can put 'flesh on the bare bones of what we say we believe in – fairness; justice; and inclusivity – testing our claims against very specific, and often heart-rending facts. Critics of rights legislation are much more comfortable keeping their views at arm's length from the facts.'[43]

IS THERE TOO MUCH JUDICIAL ACTIVISM?

The second strand of Lord Sumption's attack on the European Court of Human Rights, the first being its legitimacy, is a criticism of the judicial activism displayed by the reasoning of Strasbourg judges. This, Sumption contends, has converted the convention into a 'dynamic' treaty, which is something Britain did not sign up to when the United Kingdom ratified the convention in 1951. Sumption's point is that the large body of case law generated by over 20,000 applications to the court in six decades has gradually and stealthily resulted in new rights being invented which were not on the printed page of the original convention. The result is 'non-consensual' legislation being imported from the court at Strasbourg to the law of the land in Great Britain. He relies on the court's interpretation of Article 8 of the European Convention on Human Rights. Article 8 provides the right to respect for private and family life. According to Sumption, this was not drafted as a 'right' to encompass almost everything that could possibly intrude into a person's personal autonomy. New rights, which the UK Parliament did not enact, have been bolted on to the convention by the judges at Strasbourg.

Before dealing with the substance of this argument, it is necessary to get some terminology clear. It is not the treaty which is dynamic; it is the interpretation of the treaty as 'a living instrument' by the Strasbourg judges. As a signatory of the treaty the United Kingdom has an obligation under international law to give effect to Strasbourg decisions taken against the government which were successful. This obligation existed quite independently from either dynamic interpretations or the Human Rights Act 1998. It is this interpretation of the convention made by the treaty that Sumption finds difficult to justify. But there is a simple answer to this objection.

The European Convention on Human Rights came into being when a body called the Council of Europe was created by the Treaty of London 1949. Under the Vienna Convention on the Law of Treaties 1969, the treaty must be interpreted in good faith in accordance with the ordinary meaning to be given to the terms of the treaty in their context and in the light of the object and purpose of the convention. There is nothing 'dynamic' or controversial about this, as the international method of interpretation accords with the canons of interpretation used by English judges. For example, a word such as 'family' cannot be defined satisfactorily in a way which will last for all time and encompass shifting social and cultural attitudes. In 1975, the Court of Appeal in London heard a case where an elderly woman, Olive Fox, had received an eviction notice from her landlord because her long-standing partner, Jack Wright, to whom she was not married, had died. Had she and Jack been married she would have been protected from eviction under the Rents Act 1920 then in force. A judge in the county court upheld the landlord's claim to push her out of her home as an earlier, older case, decided by judges who had been born in Victorian times, held that an unmarried couple 'masquerading as man and wife ... to avoid neighbours' gossip', could not, in law, be classed as a family.[44] With eminent good sense, and applying traditional methods of interpretation, the Court of Appeal held that the county court judge was wrong as there had, by 1975, been a revolution in society's attitudes towards unmarried partnerships. What mattered was the substance and reality of the relationship. If it was stable and, in truth, a family unit then the precise legal status of the relationship did not matter.[45] The court quashed the eviction notice.

If this decision can be used as an example of a 'dynamic' interpretation of the word 'family' in the Rent Act 1920, then it is not significantly different from the 'dynamic approach' of the Strasbourg Court. As Lord Nicholls has put it, 'The common law is a living instrument of law, reacting to new events and new ideas, and so capable of providing the citizens of this country with a system of practical justice relevant to the times in which they live.'[46] Curiously, it is the 'living instrument' meaning given by Strasbourg to the interpretation of the convention that so concerns Lord Sumption.

The difference between domestic law as it existed before the Human Rights Act and the law made in Strasbourg is that under the European Convention on Human Rights applications originate from widely differing individual European nation states and cover a wide area of public policy. The Strasbourg Court inevitably has to take a somewhat intrusive view of the legislative regimes in different countries and in that way becomes drawn in to making generalised statements about the ground rules for acceptable practice. But this does not convert the court into an unaccountable overlord making extravagant demands on our own judges to slavishly follow every pronouncement made by the court. The answer to Sumption's broadside can be simply illustrated.

UK COURTS ARE NOT SLAVES TO STRASBOURG

Article 6 of the European Convention on Human Rights states that in a criminal trial the accused person is entitled to examine witnesses against him and obtain the attendance of witnesses against him. The Fourth Chamber (but not the Grand Chamber) of the

Strasbourg Court had decided in a case called *Al Khawaja* that if the 'sole, or at least, decisive' evidence against an accused consisted of written statements then the trial did not comply with Article 6. In the United Kingdom, Parliament had passed legislation to allow the written statements of witnesses who had died or who were in fear of testifying in open court to be read into the court record. However, the UK Parliament only permitted this if certain safeguards against depriving the accused of a fair trial were in place. A number of criminal trials had been conducted under this legislation, but there appeared to be a stand-off with Strasbourg looming.

In 2009, the *Horncastle* case was taken to the Supreme Court in order to ascertain whether the differences, if any, between Strasbourg and United Kingdom law could be resolved. Horncastle had been found guilty by a jury of inflicting grievous bodily harm on a man who had died, for reasons unrelated to this incident, before Horncastle's trial and his statement was read to the jury as United Kingdom law permitted in the circumstances of the facts. Lord Phillips, the President of the Supreme Court, gave the lead judgment and stated that the requirement under the Human Rights Act for UK judges to 'take account' of Strasbourg decisions applied normally, but if a domestic court has concluded that Strasbourg had not sufficiently appreciated or accommodated particular aspects of British practice it is open to our courts to decline to follow the Strasbourg Court. Lord Phillips rebuked the Fourth Chamber for introducing a jurisprudence that lacked clarity without considering whether there was a justification for imposing a rule of overriding principle on all European and common law jurisdictions.[47] The Grand Chamber did not uphold the Fourth Chamber in *Al Khawaja* and Horncastle's appeal to Strasbourg got nowhere. The court sensibly observed that there had been a good judicial dialogue between national courts and the European court on the application of the convention.

Horncastle was a criminal case, which Jonathan Sumption did not touch on in his attempt to categorise the European Court of Human Rights as in some way illegitimate. He did, however, put Article 8 of the European Convention on Human Rights under his microscope. He accused the court, in relation to this article, of 'mission creep' in its expansive interpretations of the convention.

Article 8 states:

> Everyone has the right to respect for his private and family life, his home and his correspondence ... There shall be no interference by a public authority with the exercise of this right except such as is in accordance with the law and is necessary in a democratic society in the interests of national security, public safety or the economic well-being of the country, for the prevention of crime, for the protection of health or morals, or for the protection of the rights and freedoms of others.

The article, therefore, is capable of embracing a whole range of subjects which might be included under the general heading 'family life', but it is a qualified, not an absolute, right. Article 8 was controversial when the United Kingdom was preparing to incorporate the convention into British law as it appeared to conflict with Article 10, which covers the right to freedom of expression. The press and media were concerned that they would be inhibited from reporting on events of public importance if it involved the private lives of prominent individuals. As it turned out, this clash faded away as the Leveson Inquiry recommended new ways of ensuring that journalists would no longer use outrageous methods, like phone tapping, to abuse their right to freedom of expression.[48] The Strasbourg Court has used Article 8 to protect an individual's identity, integrity and the right to form relationships with others, while Article 10 has been used by United Kingdom courts to justify the advancement of truth in the dissemination of ideas in a marketplace of self-expression. Each application of the principles enshrined in individual articles thrown up by the facts in different cases will lead to the core principles being enunciated in slightly different ways by the Strasbourg Court. This does not mean that the convention has been transformed from 'an expression of noble values into something meaner, a template against which to assess most aspects of the ordinary domestic order'.[49]

Lord Sumption's next criticism of Strasbourg is that the court has imposed 'standards of behaviour that people would not necessarily accept voluntarily'.[50] But what is the evidence for this and what, exactly, does he mean? Might they include, for example, unrestrained secondary picketing by striking trade unionists, unrestricted immigration, a right of political activists to cause as much disruption to the general public as they wish and, perhaps, same-sex marriage? At various times in our recent history these have been activities or practices that people have disapproved of. Yet, the Strasbourg Court has dismissed applications which have sought a convention right for each of these activities. All these topics of controversy are amply covered by domestic legislation and the 'margin of appreciation' principles have kept Strasbourg judges well away from these topics. During the Thatcher years, Parliament was not prevented from enacting legislation that banned secondary picketing or making new laws on public order by the language of the convention or its dynamic interpretation by the Strasbourg Court. As for same-sex marriage, this was legalised by Prime Minister Cameron and had nothing to do with Strasbourg. The convention, and its dynamic interpretation, does not require the United Kingdom to ease immigration controls or to make freedom of movement a convention right. On the other side of the coin, the convention, in the first protocol, provides that no person shall be denied the right to education. This essentially means that there is a convention right to education in existing educational establishments, such as fee-paying schools. Withdrawal from the convention would actually make the abolition of fee-paying schools easier.

Sumption's final point of criticism is to ask us to imagine a scenario when the United Kingdom would be forced, against its own settled will, to accept with gritted teeth a decision of Strasbourg with which our own legislature and our own procedures of domestic law were in conflict. Here he goes too far towards accommodating populism by asserting that defiance of Strasbourg is 'not an option *if* Strasbourg persists with an interpretation of a convention right with which the British Parliament and our courts disagree' (emphasis added). This paints a picture of a potentially all-powerful overbearing foreign tribunal wielding an authority more powerful than our own supreme Parliament. But Sumption does not give an example of Strasbourg persisting in an interpretation which would place the United Kingdom in breach of international law in this way. There is no Strasbourg decision which challenges the supremacy of Parliament in a power grab, but this is the spectre populists want us to believe. The case of *Horncastle*, mentioned earlier, illustrates this point very well.

THE POPULIST ATTACK ON HUMAN RIGHTS

Jonathan Sumption has a broadly liberal outlook, as is the case for most practising lawyers. His arguments are not the same as those adopted by populists. His argument, however, gives intellectual support to a crude populist attack. The first line of attack by populists has been to try to politicise human rights as a topic for party-political dispute. For example, Chris Grayling often calls the Human Rights Act 1998 'Labour's Human Rights Act', and commentary in the *Daily Telegraph* does the same.[51] This is, at best, only partially true. The right of petition by an aggrieved British citizen for an adjudication of their human rights claim to be heard in Strasbourg was introduced in 1966. This right was not abolished by the succeeding Conservative governments. The change the Labour Party made on coming to office in 1997 was to 'bring rights home' by enabling the aggrieved citizen to obtain a remedy in domestic courts, rather than having to go to Strasbourg for a ruling. However, by constantly calling human rights a 'Labour' policy, the territory is opened up for populists to occupy the terrain. This politicisation of human rights as a legitimate topic for political disagreement was vividly demonstrated in an argument about a relatively obscure subject: the ban on prisoners voting in elections.

It was Winston Churchill who said:

A calm and dispassionate recognition of the rights of the accused against the state, and even of convicted criminals against the state ... are the symbols which, in the treatment of crime and criminals, mark and measure the stored-up strength of a nation, and are the sign and proof of the living virtue in it.[52]

This humane statement of general principle was restated by the House of Lords in a 1982 judgment which confirmed that a convicted prisoner, in spite of his imprisonment, retains all civil rights which are not taken away expressly or by necessary implication.

This would appear to be a statement of the obvious: citizens who are in prisons remain citizens who (with rare exceptions) will return to the community, and they should be encouraged to maintain links with society, for their sake and ours.

Participation in society by exercising a right to vote is one way of maintaining links with society beyond the prison walls but in the United Kingdom the Representation of the People Act 1983 states that a person serving a term of imprisonment 'is legally incapable of voting at any parliamentary or local election'. This blanket legal incapability was tested when John Hirst, a prisoner serving a life sentence for manslaughter, complained to the European Court of Human Rights in Strasbourg. In October 2005, the court decided that the absolute ban on voting by all prisoners in elections in Britain is a breach of the European Convention on Human Rights. The court stated that the right to vote is a fundamental principle of a democratic society, not a privilege to be granted or taken away at the whim of Parliament in a 'blanket ban' imposed on all, irrespective of the nature of the offence and the length of the sentence. The Strasbourg Court declared that an 'automatic and indiscriminate restriction breached a vitally important Convention right', the right to vote.[53]

The Strasbourg judgment required the government to construct a policy which would approach the question logically, and to set down the boundaries justifying a complete ban. For example, the ban could have been imposed on prisoners serving a sentence of twelve months or more. Although Michael Gove, in December 2015, indicated that the government would shortly produce a substantive response to the judgment, no change to the Representation of the People Act 1983 has yet been introduced.

Votes for prisoners now appears to be the litmus test of whether you are a supporter or an opponent of the European Convention on Human Rights, even though, in the scheme of things, it is a relatively minor issue. Even if every prisoner exercised his or her right to vote the result of an election would not be affected, as, compared with the franchise as a whole, the number of prisoners is tiny. There can be no moral objection to a prisoner exercising a right to vote. A convicted criminal who has served their time can vote, as can one whose sentence of imprisonment is suspended. A remand prisoner (a person in custody awaiting trial or sentence) has been entitled to vote since 2000. Yet the Hirst judgment has been elevated to an issue of high importance. When he was Prime Minister, David Cameron was reported as saying that the Hirst judgment made him feel physically sick.

Withdrawing from the convention and repealing the Human Rights Act has been a rallying cry for populists for many years. According to Richard Littlejohn, a journalist for the *Daily Mail*, the European convention is a 'charter for crooks, terrorists, murderers, rapists and illegal immigrants – as well as being a goldmine for lawyers'.[54] The implication is clear: the convention is not for ordinary people. Populists want to make human rights unpopular as they supposedly benefit only troublemakers who take on the executive or criminals who should be behind bars. This populist rhetoric sows the seeds for a mindset which consigns convention rights to those on the fringes, the undesirables and undeserving within our society. In fact, the Human Rights Act has placed at the forefront of our culture a set of 'irreducibles in a culture that values tolerance and diversity ... human rights are owned by us all and set the basic rules for an open-minded politico-legal culture'.[55]

Littlejohn has castigated the United Kingdom judiciary, arguing that it 'regularly displays undisguised contempt for public opinion … the people who pay their wages'. He has implied that barristers who specialise in human rights law do so to cash in on the 'bonanza of cases' generated by the incorporation of the convention into domestic law.[56] He fails to mention that human rights barristers are usually far less well paid than those lawyers who undertake commercial, planning, tax or construction law. The sweeping generalisations of populism undermine trust in the rule of law and are rarely backed up by facts. For example, in July 2014 the *Daily Mail* reported a case heard in the High Court in London under the headline: 'Drug-dealing killer jailed for nine years for manslaughter can't be deported because he's illegitimate'.[57] In truth, the offender in question would have been a British citizen by birth (and therefore protected from deportation) had his parents been legally married. The judge sensibly concluded that this omission ought not to be the single deciding factor in a decision which would have wide-ranging consequences for the offender.[58] The headline was completely misleading and untrue.

CONCLUSION

Human rights as a feature of modern democracies grew from a realisation at the end of the Second World War that the conquerors of oppression must hold to a set of values which would help to ensure their defeated opponents could never gain ground again. The values contained within the European Convention on Human Rights have more than proved their worth. Communism went into retreat, new democracies have emerged and signatories to the convention have grown from six to forty-seven. The convention respects human dignity, equality and democracy. The values set out in the convention helped the transition from autocracy to democracy in Portugal, Greece and Spain in the mid-1970s. It asserts that rights exist for everybody, regardless of a person's life choices, and therefore is a strong antidote to the tide of populism, which is not an inclusive ideology. The adoption of convention rights by the United Kingdom sent a clear message to countries whose record on observing human rights is poor. By observing the convention, the status of the United Kingdom within the comity of nations is enhanced. The Human Rights Act 1998 permits the relationship between the individual and the state to acquire a new constitutional dimension. It accommodates the constitutional orthodoxy of the supremacy of Parliament with contemporary and internationally recognised rights.

The ferocity and determination of the populist attack on the values underpinning the convention requires an answer of equal firmness. It is not enough to disagree with populist arguments or sneer at their crudeness. Important constitutional debates loom in Britain. The government has proposed replacing the Human Rights Act with a British Bill of Rights and the possible dangers to our notions of liberal democracy in this proposal were discussed in the previous chapter.

The inviolability of minimum standards of liberty requires a stand to be taken by all who value them. Unless a stand is taken there is a danger that much of what we have taken for granted in terms of individual freedom and autonomy will be eroded under the shrill force of populism. The benefits that the European Convention on Human Rights has given us vastly outweigh some of the criticisms levelled at the Strasbourg Court. As Conor Gearty has put it, 'Human rights offer a route to a society where all are equal before the law ... where the basics of a decent life are regarded as the minimum to which each of us is entitled, whatever our birth circumstances.'[59] Another telling and convincing reason for

embracing human rights was given by Lord Bingham. When recit-
ing the rights contained in the convention, he asked, rhetorically:

> Which of these rights, I ask, would we wish to discard? Are any of
> them trivial, superfluous, unnecessary? Are any them un-British?
> There may be those who would like to live in a country where
> these rights are not protected, but I am not of their number.
> Human rights are not, however, protected for the likes of people
> like me – or most of you. They are protected for the benefit above
> all of society's outcasts, those who need legal protection because
> they have no other voice – the prisoners, the mentally ill, the gip-
> sies, the immigrants, the asylum seekers, those who are at any
> time the subject of public obloquy.[60]

Unless we are prepared to afford protections to all within our midst,
then the question arises: would this country be one worth living in?
Was the United Kingdom a better place when there was detention
without trial for alleged terrorists who were not British citizens; or
when homosexuals were banned from the armed services; or when
aliens could be deported and then suffer torture? What are the
values in the European convention that politicians such as Chris
Grayling believe have failed to make our country a better place?
Those are the questions that populists must ask themselves.

CHAPTER 6

ARMS OR ARGUMENTS? TERRORISM AND THE RULE OF LAW

Terrorism is an activity so repugnant that it occupies a unique territory in society's response to behaviour which is criminal and merits punishment. The notion that the terrorist can be punished is usually futile if the terrorist himself wants to die in his endeavours, as is often the case with Islamic terrorism, which is the focus of this chapter. Terrorism is a perverted creed, a mission to spread terror to convert social peace into a situation of fear to achieve a specific political goal. While the victims of terrorism are ordinary citizens, the ulterior aim is to influence the government under whom the citizen enjoys a peaceful existence. The motive is to advance the terrorist's own political, religious or ideological cause.[1]

Terrorism violates the usual norms of protest and dissent by seeking to weaken the enemy by attrition, by inflicting vengeance in order to provoke an overreaction and to undermine the legitimacy of democratic governments by coercive intimidation.[2] Terrorism threatens social peace domestically, while straining world order internationally. Terrorism falls neither into the category of criminal offences nor the definition of political protest.

Few doubt the need for special measures to tackle this threat for which neither traditional diplomacy on the international front nor ordinary processes for the investigation of crime on the domestic front are appropriate. Everyone has their own opinions on what the appropriate response should be. At one extreme, Marine Le Pen, leader of the National Front in France, has said the proper response is to halt immigration completely, give the police new powers and impose a complete ban on Islamist organisations. This solution was offered following the Bataclan concert hall attack in Paris in November 2015. She called for a national 'fight against terrorism'. This response caught the imagination of the French public and led to a surge of support for the National Front.[3] At the other extreme, the British academic and human rights specialist Conor Gearty has condemned special measures in the United Kingdom to tackle terrorism as 'depriv[ing] the criminal justice model of the space with which to breathe' and allowing a drift towards the use of administrative and executive powers without safeguards so that human rights laws are swallowed up to produce a kind of 'ersatz due process'.[4]

In Britain we have, with customary inclinations towards compromise, tried to navigate a middle course between these two approaches. A tough response was suggested by John Reid, who was Home Secretary in Tony Blair's third administration. He said in August 2006 that in order to tackle terrorism we could no longer have faith in 'traditional civil liberty arguments' and that legal 'orthodoxy' needed adaptation to deal with the new challenge posed by terrorism.[5] The following month, in a speech to the Labour Party conference, Reid said, 'It cannot be right that the rights of an individual suspected terrorist be placed above the rights, life and limb of the British people.'[6] Here, Reid appears to accept that terrorists can enjoy some rights but they are subservient to the rights of others. Tony Blair had made the same point in February 2005 when he and his government were trying to push legislation through Parliament to permit detention before charge for those suspected of terrorist-related crime to be a period of ninety days. He claimed that when there is a choice to be made between liberty or security, the duty of politicians is to put safety first.[7] The Prime Minister was suggesting that there is always a conflict between the rights of the individual suspect and those of society generally. He claimed that the responsibility of government was to put the safety of the public before the rights of the suspect. Parliament was not prepared to accept such a broad-brush distinction and Blair's proposal for a ninety-day detention period was rejected.

John Reid's predecessor as Home Secretary, Charles Clarke, was more nuanced and thoughtful in expressing the duty of government to put measures in place to protect the public. He said that a framework was needed to address the 'delicate balance' between the right of the public to be protected and the right of the terrorist to be protected from ill-treatment. But he went on to say that 'we cannot properly fight terrorism with one hand tied behind our back'.[8] Here, he recognised the choice was not a simple binary one between liberty and security but the rights of the terrorist had to be balanced with the rights of the community at large. However, to calibrate the scales properly, the executive could not be handicapped by having too many legal and human rights restraints limiting their ability to weigh the choices appropriately.

These varied responses to the threat posed by terrorism involve ethical issues of great importance to any democracy which claims to be liberal. Where is the boundary between the necessity of protecting the public from harm being plotted by the terrorist and the need to preserve the normal liberties that citizens have come to enjoy? Are traditional civil liberties so sacred they can never be abrogated, even in situations of national emergency? Are people who are in fear really free in the first place? Although ethics must inform any intelligent response to the terrorist threat, it is law which, in the end, must provide the answer. As Lord Atkin's celebrated aphorism puts it, 'amidst the clash of arms, the laws are not silent'.[9]

The most persuasive discussion about the ethical questions raised by counter-terrorism responses has been written by the Canadian philosopher and former politician Michael Ignatieff. His premise is that there can be no greater evil than the destruction of democracy itself and democracy involves security within which individual liberty is enjoyed. Democracy without rights is a contradiction in terms, but at the same time rights are not secure unless there is a democracy. What is unique and special about the terrorist threat is that it strikes at a basic right of an individual to live without fear.[10] Unlike ordinary crimes, most modern Islamist terrorism proceeds from a command or a 'fatwa' to kill infidels, which includes the populations of many countries who are not exclusively Islamic. Most Muslims condemn and deplore this perversion of Islam, but their denunciation does not undo the fatwas that are proclaimed in the religion's name. The fatwa is an interpretation of Islamic law which has been taken by some as legitimising the imposition of an extreme Islamist agenda by intimidation and coercion. If successful, democratic liberties, self-determination by women and choices for cultural and leisure pursuits by many would be destroyed. Defeat for the Islamist fatwa-based terrorist agenda is essential if democracy is to survive.

Ignatieff argues that, faced with this existential threat, society must decide what *lesser* evils, in terms of curtailments of liberty on grounds of necessity, may be justified in order to protect democracy from a *greater* evil, which is the destruction of democracy itself. Upon this foundation, Ignatieff maintains that there are certain fundamental liberties that cannot be curtailed, even on grounds of emergency or necessity. These are cruel and unusual punishment, torture, extra-judicial execution and the rendition of a suspected terrorist to another country for questioning. There are also fundamental procedural rights, the rights for a hearing before a judge, that should not, in a democracy, ever be suspended on grounds of necessity. Second, there is a fundamental principle of 'adversarial justification', which means that there must be some means of holding the executive to account in curtailing liberties if the 'necessity' for curtailing them is false. Third, any democratic state must obtain legislative consent for the use of emergency powers to protect democracy from its destruction. Providing a nation state holds fast to these fundamentals, Ignatieff argues that if the threat to democracy is factually true then a lesser evil of curtailing certain rights is morally justified to save the destruction of a greater right, the right to live in a democracy without fear.

The United Kingdom has adopted a distinctive British middle way in attempting to keep the population free of terrorist attacks. Unlike the United States, which largely abandoned the due process of criminal justice after the 9/11 atrocity, the United Kingdom has held on to most of the nation's legal structures. The country has chosen to treat alleged terrorists as criminals, not combatants, and has concentrated on trying to stop an attack by prevention in advance and to hold fast to common law traditions of denying the executive too many sweeping powers.[11] We have been less clear about observing ethical boundaries in the legal processes involved in our middle-way approach. This was vividly illustrated in the case of Paramjit Singh Chahal, a Sikh from the Punjab in India.

THE CASE OF PARAMJIT SINGH CHAHAL

Paramjit Chahal came to the United Kingdom in 1971 illegally but was given indefinite permission to remain under an amnesty arrangement that was reached a few years later. He was a strong supporter, like many Sikhs, of an independent Sikh homeland in Punjab, northern India. In 1983, there were incidents of violence at the Golden Temple in Amritsar in which a non-Sikh Indian policeman was killed. The following year, Indian Prime Minister Indira Gandhi was assassinated by her Sikh bodyguards, which led to revenge attacks in Delhi, where many Sikhs were killed in rioting incidents. Chahal had returned to Punjab during this period of instability and he visited the Golden Temple. He claimed that he was arrested and tortured by the Indian police but was then released without charge.

On returning to Great Britain, Chahal became an activist for Sikh separatism. He was suspected of being involved in a conspiracy among Sikhs in London to murder Rajiv Gandhi, Indira's son, who became Prime Minister of India after her assassination and who was due to visit London on a state visit in 1985. Chahal was arrested by police in London and questioned but was released without charge. At around the same time there was a violent disturbance at a Sikh temple in east London and Chahal was involved in the violence. He was convicted of the offence of affray and sent to prison for nine months, although this conviction was later quashed because there was a procedural irregularity during the case.

In 1990, the Home Secretary issued a deportation notice against Chahal on the grounds that his presence in the United Kingdom was no longer conducive to the public good for reasons of national security. He was then detained pending removal from the United Kingdom. The Home Secretary concluded that Chahal was a central figure of a terrorist network in the Punjab and that the violence at the London Sikh temple was motivated by a desire to take over the temple's funds in order to siphon them off to support Sikh separatists involved in terrorism in the Punjab. In those days there was a Home Office advisory panel, known colloquially as 'The Three Wise Men', which could advise the Home Secretary on the risk factors relevant to national security, but Chahal himself could not be legally represented before the panel, nor could he have access to any of the material relied on to support the contention that he was a security risk. Chahal could, however, seek judicial review of the deportation decision. He lost in the United Kingdom, where the courts upheld the Home Secretary's decision, but his case was eventually heard by the European Court of Human Rights at Strasbourg.

The Strasbourg decision was ground-breaking in two respects. First, the court ruled that the 'Three Wise Men' panel hearing breached Chahal's rights under Article 5(4) of the European Convention on Human Rights as his detention had not been decided by a 'court' that had the power to order his release if his detention was unlawful. The panel's task was only to advise the Home Secretary, which did not bind the minister, and Chahal had been denied legal representation and was not told of the case against him, as the reasons were founded on security considerations. Of greater long-term consequence, however, was the court's ruling in respect of torture. Article 3 of the convention places an absolute prohibition on the use of torture without qualification. The court ruled that Article 3 'enshrines one of the most fundamental values of a democratic society' and the principle extends to expulsion cases as any signatory to the convention has a duty to safeguard all persons against treatment which is prohibited. The court rejected the government's contention that terrorism in the Punjab had ebbed away to such an extent that it was unlikely that Chahal would be arrested if he were returned to India. Instead, the court placed weight on other pieces of credible evidence that abductions and executions of Sikh separatists were still going on, outside formal arrest and trial processes. There was a real risk of Chahal being subjected to torture if he were sent back to India and therefore the United Kingdom had failed to observe Article 3 of the convention.[12]

The Chahal case put into sharp relief two ethical principles which should lie at the heart of any measures to prevent terrorism. First, there are certain fundamental rights, such as the right not to be tortured, which cannot be abridged whatever the exigencies of the moment. Second, there is a fundamental right to a hearing before a court that has powers to make binding decisions. This is a principle so important to a liberal democracy that it cannot ever be taken away, whatever the private opinions of the security service are in relation to a person's risk. The Strasbourg ruling in this case underlined the need for an ethical framework for political and legal processes for those whose deportation was ordered if they were a security risk. The United Kingdom responded to the decision by creating a new entity called the Special Immigration Appeals Commission (SIAC) in 1997. It was a 'court' in the sense that it was a bench of three individuals presided over by a High Court judge and SIAC had a responsibility to uphold deportation decisions on grounds of national security or to overrule the Home Secretary if the commission disagreed with the exercise of his discretion. Essentially, SIAC was a further tier of appeal in immigration and deportation matters. A role for terrorism cases was not contemplated.

9/11 – THE WATERSHED MOMENT IN COMBATTING TERRORISM

Then came 11 September 2001 and counter-terrorism strategies entered a new phase for every nation on the globe. The atrocities in

New York, Washington and Pittsburgh when hijacked aircraft piloted by terrorists deliberately caused thousands of civilian deaths shocked and angered the world. In the United Kingdom it was imperative that the government was seen to act decisively. The government's chief legal adviser at the time was Lord Goldsmith, who reflected later that 'September 11th changed the legal landscape forever'.[13] He was right. The United Nations had recognised, in the aftermath of 9/11, that the attacks were an attack on the whole international community and the UN Security Council required all nations to take measures to prevent terrorism and to deny a safe haven for those who were planning, supporting or financing terrorism. Britain could hardly have refused to take the measures that the international community stated were needed.

The government's response was the Anti-Terrorism, Crime and Security Act 2001. The centrepiece of the legislation granted a completely new power to the Home Secretary to allow him to order the indefinite detention of foreign nationals suspected of being terrorists. The place of detention would be a high-security prison, usually HMP Belmarsh in south-east London. The legal landscape had certainly changed. Detention, let alone indefinite detention, was prohibited under the European Convention on Human Rights unless ordered judicially, with only one exception. The convention permitted the executive to order detention prior to deportation but only for so long as was necessary for the deportation process to take place. The conundrum posed by the government's new law was this: supposing a suspected foreign terrorist could not be deported, because he would face torture if sent home, how could the nation be protected? The answer would surely be to put him on trial for terrorist crimes in this country. But, here again, there was an obstacle. In many cases the material suggesting that someone was a terrorist or linked to terrorism came from sensitive intelligence sources and the security services have traditionally been unwilling or unable to make their methods public.

The government could derogate from applying the part of the European Convention on Human Rights which guaranteed a judicial hearing for indefinite detention if there was a 'public emergency' threatening the life of the nation providing the measures taken to avoid complying with a convention right were 'strictly required by the exigencies of the situation'. The government notified the European Commission that it was 'strictly necessary' to opt out of Article 5 of the convention covering the right to liberty and security due to the presence of 'foreign nationals' who posed a threat to the security of the United Kingdom.

The government made one nod towards protecting human rights by enlarging SIAC's powers. The Anti-Terrorism, Crime and Security Act allowed a detainee to appeal to the Special Immigration Appeals Commission but there were still some human rights obstacles. A detainee would not be allowed to know the nature of the material that led to their detention. Instead they would be allowed a 'special advocate' who could see the security-sensitive material but who could not inform the detainee of what the material was and could not take instructions on it. The detainee was allowed a personal barrister, but this legal representative was not allowed to see the material and so the detainee, although represented, would have a lawyer acting for him who did not really know what the case was about. As Lord Hope put it, some years later after nine detainees had taken their case to the House of Lords:

Indefinite imprisonment in consequence of a denunciation on grounds that are not disclosed and made by a person whose identity cannot be disclosed is the stuff of nightmares, associated whether accurately or inaccurately with France before and during the Revolution, with Soviet Russia in the Stalinist era and now associated ... with the United Kingdom.[14]

This was strong language and it made uncomfortable reading for David Blunkett, the Home Secretary who had introduced the 'stuff of nightmares' in Parliament. Although some judges expressed themselves robustly, the decision of the House of Lords that indefinite detention was incompatible with the European Convention on Human Rights was both logical and restrained. This important ruling was made in a case which became known as the *Belmarsh* case, so-called after the prison where the detainees were held. The House agreed, in a judgment delivered in December 2004, that it was the exclusive province of the executive to decide whether an 'emergency' existed in order to derogate from a convention right, but that did not mean the consequences of derogation did not raise questions of law for the courts to decide. If judges paid excessive deference to a ministerial decision to order extra-judicial detention then they would be abrogating their responsibility to apply the law. This meant that the judges could decide whether the decision to detain indefinitely was proportionate when weighed against the perceived risk. If, as the government argued, the detainees were free to leave the United Kingdom and live in any country which would accommodate them, how much of a danger did they really pose? Is it ethical simply to pass a difficult problem onto another country whose population may be put in danger? If the aim of the legislation was to detain only foreign terrorists, how was the nation protected if British-born terrorists were still at large? What was the logical comparator in singling out foreign-born suspects and neglecting the British-born ones who might pose an identical risk? Both posed a risk, yet neither could be removed, the foreigner because they were at risk of torture and the British one because they had a right of abode anyway. To the House of Lords, the government's distinction was illogical, unless the underlying reason was to make a religious comparison between 'Muslim' and 'non-Muslim', but such a distinction defied logic as well as being discriminatory. The House decided that the Home Secretary's plan for indefinite detention without trial was incompatible with the Human Rights Act 1998.[15]

The Home Secretary's reaction was defiant: 'The real threat to the life of the nation comes not from terrorism but from laws such as these.'[16] This off-hand and offensive dismissal of a carefully considered and reasoned judgment from the highest court in the land was a taste of what was to come. In the succeeding years, a gaping chasm began to appear between the intentions and beliefs of politicians in relation to tackling the terrorist threat and the determination of judges that counter-terrorism decisions must be made according to law. In fact, the chasm had begun to open some years earlier.

THE AFGHANI HIJACKING CASE

On a bleak cold night in February 2000, an aeroplane of Ariana Afghan Airlines was preparing to land at Stansted Airport. It was way off-course. It should have flown direct to Mazar-i-Sharif on an internal flight from Kabul, the capital of Afghanistan. A group of nine Afghan men had boarded the flight at Kabul and then forced the pilot to fly out of the country and after stop-overs in Tashkent and Moscow headed for Stansted, an airport more commonly associated with short European trips to holiday destinations. It emerged much later, during protracted legal appearances, that the hijackers were all members of a pro-democracy group called Young Intellectuals of Afghanistan which operated clandestinely in Afghanistan. The Taliban had occupied some cities in the country where there were many members. The hijackers had heard that four fellow members of the group had been captured by the Taliban and then tortured to extract the identities of other members. A few days before the hijacking seventeen members of their organisation were arrested by Taliban fighters.

In the days before 9/11, hijacking an aeroplane was seen as discomforting and potential dangerous and merited punishment, but it did not necessarily instil the fear that was generated after the 9/11 attacks. In the Afghan hijack nobody was hurt or killed, although the hijackers had guns and grenades with them. The nation watched in fascination as a stand-off between the hijackers and the British police which lasted for four days was beamed on to television from the perimeter of Stansted Airport.

Once the siege was over, the hijackers and a large number of passengers indicated that they would apply for political asylum, but Home Secretary Jack Straw was determined that everything should be done to prevent any asylum applications being granted. He told Parliament that he would take personal charge of the case and decide on the applications himself. He added, 'Subject to compliance with all legal requirements, I would wish to see removed from this country all those on the plane as soon as reasonably practicable.'[17] Those words 'as soon as reasonably practicable' would come back and bite the Home Office and Straw's successors as Home Secretary.

The criminal case against the nine hijackers seemed completely straightforward. They had been caught in the act. They were duly put on trial at the Old Bailey, but the men raised the defence of duress. That is to say, they did not deny the fact that they had hijacked the plane but they asserted that they only did so because they feared death or serious bodily injury unless they acted as they did to escape Afghanistan. It was during the Old Bailey trial that the background to the hijack plot was revealed and these circumstances, they claimed, amounted to duress. In law, the existence of duress is something the prosecution had to prove was untrue. A jury at the Old Bailey could not agree on the guilt of the defendants, except for one who was acquitted. A retrial took place and all were found guilty and received prison sentences. However, the trial judge had not given the jury legally incorrect directions on the law of duress and the Court of Appeal quashed their convictions. The men were now in legal limbo. They had not been found guilty of a crime and they were awaiting a decision to be granted or refused asylum on humanitarian grounds. Within weeks of their convictions being quashed the Home Secretary decided that they had not established a well-founded fear of persecution in Afghanistan and they remained liable for deportation.

The men appealed to an immigration adjudication panel in 2004 and their application to be granted asylum status was refused. The panel concluded that by hijacking a plane instead of escaping from Afghanistan across porous land borders they were excluded from protection under the 1951 Refugee Convention. However, the Afghans succeeded on the principles established in the *Chahal* case many years earlier, namely that to deport them back to Afghanistan would expose them to extra-judicial assassination by the Taliban, who had declared them enemies of Islam.

At first sight, it might seem strange that an adjudication panel considering an asylum claim concluded that the defendants did have an alternative means of escaping the Taliban (by crossing porous borders on foot) and yet the Court of Appeal had quashed their convictions for the crime of hijacking. The answer to this puzzle lies in the fundamental principles of criminal law. The first relevant principle is that no person should be found guilty unless the prosecution has proved their case beyond reasonable doubt, and the accused does not have a burden of proving their innocence. The second fundamental principle is that in a criminal trial the judge is responsible for directing the jury as to the law they should apply to their consideration of the facts. If the judge gives the jury wrong or inadequate legal directions then the jury's verdict is unsafe as it would have been founded on a legal misconception. The Court of Appeal exists to review a judge's legal directions if there is an appeal. If the appeal court concludes that there has been a misdirection, the conviction is quashed. This is basic law within a civilised legal system. An adjudication panel, on the other hand, decides factual issues on the balance of probabilities, which is a different standard from that applied in criminal courts.

The reaction of David Blunkett (who succeeded Jack Straw as Home Secretary in 2001) to the clear and careful reasoning of the adjudication panel was to describe it as 'mind-boggling'. Whatever Blunkett thought about the merits of the decision, his department was obliged to consider how to implement humanitarian protection for Afghan citizens. This obligation arose as they were at risk of persecution in their own country. Despite the need both to comply with the panel's decision and to have regard to the welfare of the Afghanis who were living in an uncertain legal limbo, Blunkett's department did nothing for a very long time. The panel's decision had been given in June 2004 and by March 2005 the Afghanis' solicitor complained about the 'inordinate delay'. Eventually, in September

2005 the Home Office wrote to the Afghanis to say that it was refusing discretionary leave to remain for a limited finite period. This decision was only taken after a warning by the Afghanis' solicitor that legal action might be taken if a decision was not forthcoming.

The reason for the delay, it seemed, was that the Afghanis' situation was extremely unusual and the Home Office had no settled policy on how to deal with such a case. The Home Office was playing for time. The solution the Home Office wanted was to place the Afghanis in a twilight zone of temporary admission, but Parliament had laid down that this status applied to certain defined categories which did not include the unusual case of the Afghani hijackers.

The hijackers' lawyers applied for a declaration in the High Court that the Home Office's inordinate delay made the decision an unlawful one. The case was heard by Mr Justice Sullivan. In addition to interpreting Britain's complex immigration laws, Mr Justice Sullivan was faced with an issue of power. Was it lawful for powerful executive bodies who have the futures of people under their authority to close their minds and decline to take a decision? Did this amount to an abuse of state power? During the course of the case Blunkett resigned as Home Secretary and was replaced by John Reid.

In a carefully considered judgment, the judge could find no reason why the Home Office had declined to carry out its responsibilities properly. 'The defendant's [the Home Office] conduct before the proceedings commenced was inexcusable. All the efforts of the claimants' solicitors to obtain an explanation for the delay, and to avoid proceedings, were met with a deliberate wall of silence.'[18] Even after the Afghanis had taken legal proceedings the Home Office failed to disclose their reasons and cobbled together a last-minute justification just days before the hearing. The judge condemned the behaviour of the Home Office as 'an abuse of power by a public authority at the highest level'. He wanted the full import of his decision to be clearly understood:

> Bearing in mind some of the newspaper headlines which reported the Panel's determination in 2004, it is important that there is no misunderstanding about the effect of this decision. The issue in this case is not whether the executive should take action to discourage hijacking, but whether the executive should be required to take such action within the law as laid down by Parliament and applied by the courts.

This was a stinging rebuke for the faceless bureaucracy that casts a gloomy shadow over the lives of many, but it was also a clear declaration of the vital importance of the rule of law being administered by an impartial judiciary. Instead of accepting the judge's verdict with humility and good grace, the Home Secretary, John Reid, insulted the judge in a combative public statement, calling his ruling 'inexplicable and bizarre', and in a populist flourish said that the judge had only 'reinforce[d] the perception that the system is not working to protect or in favour of the vast majority of ordinary decent hard-working citizens in this country'.[19] A few months later, in a speech in London, Reid said that certain people 'just don't get it' as he identified the judiciary for failing to understand the terrorist threat.[20] Reid had completely missed the point. The factual background to an 'inexplicable' ruling from a judge who 'just didn't get it' was the behaviour of the department of state over which he was now in charge. He was using the failings of his own department as the weapon with which to attack the judiciary in an unpleasant and personal fashion.

Perhaps the more concerning intervention in this hijacking case was the one from the Prime Minister, Tony Blair. A lawyer himself and in whose first administration the Human Rights Act 1998 had been enacted, Blair was not known for expressing dislike for lawyers or judges. But he had this to say about the decision of Mr Justice Sullivan: 'We can't have a situation in which people who hijack a plane, we're not able to deport back to their country. It's not an abuse of justice to order their deportation, it's an abuse of common sense frankly to be in a position where we can't do this.'[21]

Blair's memory may have deserted him when he made this comment, as it was his own government which had put in place legal processes to comply with the 'torture' dilemmas that were thrown up in the Chahal case. His government created the Special Immigration Adjudication Commission in 1997 and then enacted the Human Rights Act in 1998 to require English judges to have regard to decisions from the European Court of Human Rights. Tony Blair had an easy solution to putting right his dissatisfaction with the reasoning of Mr Justice Sullivan. His government could appeal the decision to the Court of Appeal. This it did, but Mr Justice Sullivan was unanimously upheld. The Court of Appeal observed that since the drama at Stansted Airport on 7 February 2000 there had been 'ample time' for the Home Secretary to obtain parliamentary authority to deal with the unique circumstances of the Afghani hijackers. But nothing had been done. Mr Justice Sullivan's ruling was upheld in August 2006.[22] So much for Jack Straw's promise to Parliament three days after the Stansted Airport siege in February 2000 that he would see the Afghanis removed 'as soon as reasonably practicable'.

CONTROL ORDERS

In the six and a half years during which the Afghani case proceeded through the courts, developments in the government's counter-terrorism strategy were advancing rather more quickly. Parliament passed the Prevention of Terrorism Act 2005 to substitute a regime of 'control orders' to replace 'indefinite detention', which the House of Lords had declared to be incompatible with the European convention.[23] The 2005 Act was an ingenious roadmap in navigating a strategy which was robust enough to tackle the terrorist threat with conviction, while at the same time making it compliant with acceptable legal procedures. It was also an intelligent attempt to remain true to Britain's endorsement of human rights as laid down in the European Convention on Human Rights. The 'control order' was an order restricting the movements and associations of a suspected terrorist which fell short of confinement to prison. In reality, house arrest had been substituted for imprisonment. The Act was passed just in time for the detainees in Belmarsh who had not voluntarily left the United Kingdom to be placed under a control order on their release. There was judicial oversight over the process. If the Home Secretary wanted to derogate from the convention right to liberty and security then the Home Secretary was obliged to obtain authorisation from a SIAC judge and a panel who would see the 'closed' material relied on by the security services. The Home Secretary could be overruled if their decision was 'obviously flawed'. This provided some measure of protection for the suspected terrorist, although only the special advocate, not his own lawyer, could see the sensitive material. The special advocate, however, could not reveal the material to the suspect. The 2005 Act was therefore a compromise. The liberty of suspected terrorists could be severely curtailed even though they were not charged with any offence, but the judiciary had a role in being able to overrule an executive decision.

The legality of the procedure and the distinction, if any, between a restriction of liberty and a deprivation of liberty soon occupied the attention of the Judicial Committee of the House of Lords, the predecessor of the Supreme Court. The judges took a pragmatic view and ruled that the distinction between 'restriction' of liberty under a control order and the unlawful 'deprivation' of liberty under the indefinite detention regime was a matter of degree. What governed the distinction was the exact length, duration and manner of implementation of the control order. Did it, in reality, mean confinement to prison or were the terms of the order such that the detainees' activities were curtailed and restricted to a degree which did not fall into the category of confinement?[24] The judges considered the exact facts of each case, without looking at the 'closed' material, to decide on which side of the line each case fell. In one case where the restrictions included an eighteen-hour curfew, the judges ruled that, together with other curtailments in the order, it did amount, in reality and substance, to a deprivation of liberty. In other cases, the judges ruled that the restrictions were compatible with convention rights.

A similar pragmatic approach was taken on the argument advanced by one suspect who was under restriction of a control order that by being denied access to the 'closed' material he had been denied a fair trial by the SIAC judge. The House of Lords ruled that in certain circumstances it is strictly necessary for certain material to be withheld from an accused person. For example, it is part of English common law that the identity of a police informer and the information provided by an informer does not feature in a criminal trial. The issue in control order cases was whether a significant injustice had been caused to the suspect by being denied access to closed material and whether this could be mitigated by other procedural safeguards. The judges decided that the presence of the special advocate and other measures involved in the SIAC hearings provided sufficient safeguards for the procedure to be fair.[25]

In all of the legal rulings discussed so far, English judges have rigorously applied reason, a respect for the dignity of persons and an awareness of international obligations, and followed, as far as it is possible to do so, the principles of the European Convention on Human Rights. An impartial observer would probably conclude that senior judges had approached their task in balancing the interests of security with the imperatives of liberty commendably and conscientiously. There was no proper reason for the thoroughly ill-informed attacks on the judiciary that followed the Belmarsh case and the Afghan hijack case, but the chasm between judges and politicians was to grow even wider during the long-running case of Abu Qatada.

THE CASE OF ABU QATADA

Abu Qatada al-Filistini, literally 'Abu Qatada the Palestinian' in Arabic, was born Omar Mahmoud Othman in 1960 in territory which was then ruled by Jordan. In the lengthy litigation in the courts which lasted many years he was sometimes referred to as Omar Othman. He arrived in the United Kingdom on 16 September 1993 on a forged United Arab Emirates passport. He claimed asylum after arrival for himself, his wife and his then three children. He had been living in Peshawar in Pakistan teaching Afghan children, he said, for two years but was forced to leave Pakistan and travelled via the Maldives and Singapore to London. The basis of his asylum claim was a fear that he would be tortured if he returned to Jordan, as he had been tortured in the past by the Jordanian intelligence services. They had objected to his Islamist political activities and he contended he would be tortured on return as he had left

Jordan illegally in breach of the terms of his house arrest. He was acknowledged to be a refugee by British immigration officials and was given permission to remain in Britain until 1998.

Within a short time of his refugee status being recognised Abu Qatada began expressing extreme and deeply disturbing views. Claiming to be a spiritual leader, he issued, in 1995, a fatwa justifying the killing of women and children of 'apostates' and another one claiming that it was permissible to commit fraud against unbelievers. He publicly insisted that there was no proof Osama bin Laden was a terrorist and he was in personal contact with bin Laden's London-based representative. He made these inflammatory remarks outside the Four Feathers Mosque near Regent's Park, where he gave unconditional support for Islamic separatists in Chechnya and called for their enemies to be destroyed. He advocated the killing of all Jews and a video of him making these revolting utterances was found in a flat in Hamburg, in premises once occupied by the team who carried out the 9/11 atrocity.

Qatada had been interviewed by the security services in 1995 and 1996 when he claimed to have exercised influence over Algerian terrorists not to mount attacks in the UK. He declared that violence against Jews in the UK was acceptable and he had assisted and en-couraged those in the UK who espoused the Al-Qaeda approach to world domination.

While Abu Qatada was under the watchful eye of the security services in London, he was also the centre of attention in Jordan. Two criminal trials took place within a short time of each other. The first, in 1999, was called the 'Reform and Challenge' trial and involved thirteen alleged terrorists who were on trial for attacks on the American School and the Jerusalem Hotel in Amman, the capital of Jordan. The second, called the 'Millennium Conspiracy', in 2000, was an alleged conspiracy to set off bombs during the millennium celebrations in Amman with the intention of killing many tourists. Abu Qatada, of course, did not appear at the trials as he was, at the time, in London making inflammatory speeches at the Four Feathers Mosque. He was tried in his absence. Of crucial importance to all the events that later unfolded in the courts of justice in the United Kingdom and in Strasbourg was the procedure adopted at these terrorist trials.

In both trials a co-accused, who was in the dock next to Abu Qatada's empty seat, had made incriminating statements to the state prosecutor about him which, if true, made Abu Qatada guilty. The co-defendants who had made damaging statements against Abu Qatada claimed that they were only made under torture. The judge at each of the trials rejected this claim, allowed the incriminating statements to be put in evidence against Qatada and, unsurprisingly, he was found guilty in both cases. He was sentenced, in his absence, respectively to life imprisonment and fifteen years' imprisonment. In one respect he was lucky. Other defendants were sentenced to death.

Meanwhile, in London Abu Qatada was arrested in February 2001 on suspicion of helping to plan a terrorist attack which had taken place at a Christmas market in Strasbourg, but he was released due to lack of evidence. In September 2001, he preached a sermon declaring that the 9/11 atrocity was part of a wider battle between Christendom and Islam. The security services in Britain regarded him as danger to the country and they wanted him removed. As soon as the Anti-Terrorism, Crime and Security Act came into force in December 2001, David Blunkett certified that the fiery and inflammatory preacher should be detained under powers granted to him by the 2001 Act. Qatada, however, outwitted the authorities. Anticipating that he might be imprisoned indefinitely, he disappeared and did not resurface until October 2002, when he was arrested and a stash of cash was found at his home labelled 'for the mujahideen in Chechnya'.

He was entitled to have the Home Secretary's decision to detain him indefinitely reviewed by the Special Immigration Adjudication Commission. Qatada, rather typically of his arrogance and sense of self-importance, boycotted the hearing on the grounds that the judge would be bound to be biased against him. Ironically, the SIAC judge had a reputation not only for scrupulous fairness but also for being diligent in checking the growth of ministerial power.[26] If Abu Qatada was to receive a fair hearing, Mr Justice Collins was the judge to provide it. His counsel had instructions not to withdraw but to seek to persuade the judge and the panel that he only gave spiritual guidance and advice to those who followed Al-Qaeda.

In the judgment of the panel 'there was no doubt' that Abu Qatada was heavily involved at the centre of terrorist activity in the UK associated with Al-Qaeda. He was pronounced a 'dangerous individual'. The judgment, in its assessment of Qatada's risk to the security of the country, stated:

We have no doubt that his beliefs are extreme and are indeed a perversion of Islam for the purposes of encouraging violence against non-Muslims and Muslims who are or have been supportive of the Americans in particular. It is no surprise that his speeches or sermons have been used in training of suicide bombers ... We are satisfied that the appellant's activities went far beyond the mere giving of advice. He has certainly given the support of the Koran to those who wish to further the aims of

Al-Qaeda and to engage in suicide bombing and other murderous activities ... He has assisted and encouraged many who have themselves espoused the Al-Qaeda approach and whom he knew or must have known to have been involved in terrorism. And after 11 September, in a sermon he stated that the attacks were part of a wider battle between Christendom and Islam and a response to America's unjust policies.[27]

The first stage of the government's concerns about the preacher with odious views and terrorist sympathies had been achieved. He was in custody in Belmarsh Prison. The second objective, to deport him back to Jordan, was to prove much more problematical. Following the *Chahal* case, described earlier, the government was obliged to consider Abu Qatada's rights under the convention when assessing the likelihood of him being tortured were he to be returned to Jordan. The co-defendants at the trials in Amman had specifically alleged that they were tortured to extract a confession and an incriminating statement against Abu Qatada. Amnesty International also had dossiers on torture being used by the Jordanian police. Abu Qatada's deportation would only be compliant with his convention rights if undertakings were given by Jordan in relation to his treatment once he arrived on Jordanian soil. A memorandum of understanding had been negotiated between British and Jordanian officials which stated that the authorities in each country would comply with human rights obligations under international law. This provided that if Abu Qatada was arrested and detained upon arrival in Jordan he would receive adequate nourishment and accommodation; he would be treated humanely in accordance with international law; he would be brought before a judge and informed of the charge against him; and he would be entitled to consult UK and Jordanian diplomats. In addition, if he was put on trial, an international monitoring body would be allowed to observe the trial. The memorandum between the two countries was signed on 10 August 2005 and the next day a deportation notice signed by the Home Secretary was served on Abu Qatada. The last piece of the jigsaw now appeared to be in place and the country could say good riddance to Abu Qatada.

This was certainly the opinion of much of the tabloid press and a large section of the political class, both Labour and Conservative. The Home Secretary issued a new certification that Abu Qatada must be deported for reasons of national security. As this was a new deportation notice, Qatada was entitled to challenge this certification before SIAC. This time the judge was Mr Justice Ouseley, another highly experienced judge in the field of asylum and immigration. The panel, which consisted of the judge and two lay members, could quash the deportation order if it concluded that the Home Secretary had no reasonable grounds for believing that Qatada was a threat to national security. As most of Qatada's disagreeable and offensive speeches had been delivered in public, much of the evidence against him was given in open session. With a self-confidence which bordered on the bizarre, his lawyers were not instructed to challenge the truth of his activities and no members of the security service were cross-examined in the hearing, which took place in 2006. The panel's judgment, which was not delivered until February 2007, was that the security risks were well-founded and that deportation was 'necessary as a measure of defence for the rights of those who live here'.[28]

Mr Justice Ouseley then had to wrestle with the difficult issue surrounding the use of evidence that may have been extracted under torture. It was obvious that the Jordanian authorities wanted Abu

Qatada to be put on trial again when his presence in the dock in Jordan could be achieved. The problem was that the memorandum of understanding signed in 2005 made no reference to the evidence in the first trial (from which he was absent) being excluded in the second. The brightest minds of the English judiciary in the Court of Appeal and the House of Lords had to grapple with this difficult point: given that Abu Qatada would be put on trial following his deportation, what test should the court apply as to whether deportation would breach a fundamental prohibition on the use of torture? Was it that he would suffer a 'flagrant denial of justice' unless an English court was satisfied that torture evidence would not be used? Or was it that the Jordanian trial process had such defects as fundamentally to destroy the fairness of the trial? In other words, was the real risk that evidence alleged to have been obtained by torture would be used against him enough to prohibit the removal of a person who was undoubtedly a security risk to this country? Mr Justice Ouseley took one view, the Court of Appeal took the other view and the House of Lords upheld Mr Justice Ouseley, who had decided that Jordanian legal processes were not so fundamentally defective as to deny Abu Qatada a fair trial. As it was the House of Lords which upheld the SIAC decision, it was inevitable that Abu Qatada would take his case to the European Court of Human Rights in Strasbourg. There was no consensus about the correct approach that should be taken within England's senior judiciary.

The Strasbourg Court allowed Abu Qatada's lawyers to present further 'compelling' evidence that his co-defendants had indeed been tortured into providing the case against him in the two trials which had taken place in his absence. Further, the court heard evidence that the Jordanian State Security Court (the tribunal who would retry Qatada) was incapable of properly investigating the allegations of torture in order to apply its own code, which prohibited the use of evidence so obtained. The Strasbourg Court had set the bar high. The burden was on Abu Qatada to adduce evidence that was capable of proving that there were substantial grounds for believing he would be exposed to a flagrant denial of justice if he was returned to Jordan. The Strasbourg ruling found that Qatada had succeeded in providing a 'sustained and well-founded attack on the State Security Court system that proposed to try him in breach of one of the most fundamental norms of international criminal justice, the prohibition of evidence obtained by torture.'[29] The court therefore concluded that Abu Qatada would be denied a fundamental right if he was deported.

By this time it was nearly twenty years since Abu Qatada had entered the United Kingdom illegally. He had provided succour and assistance to known terrorist groups, preached inflammatory encouragement to those contemplating terror, had become a danger to the nation's security and had caused immense distress to citizens of the Jewish faith. The frustration felt by a large segment of the population that he was still in Britain was now at boiling point. Michael Burleigh in the *Daily Mail* blamed 'radical lawyers and judges who do not give a wit for public safety' for allowing the case to go to Strasbourg in a piece entitled 'Abu Qatada: Get this creature out of our country'. He thought this 'racket' could be ended 'by moving towards an elected judiciary.'[30] *The Sun* took events into its own hands and, similarly to the petition that it launched in the Jamie Bulger case, organised one to demand that the government defy the European Court of Human Rights ruling and 'boot Qatada out'. Boris Johnson, who was Mayor of London, joined in, stating, 'Qatada does not belong here. *The Sun* is right to demand his expulsion.'[31] Here, Johnson is characteristically choosing his words carefully. He was reflecting public opinion by stating that Abu Qatada did not belong in Britain, but with a sleight of hand he was also associating himself with a populist call for the government to defy a judicial ruling and to deport Qatada whatever the law may say. It was an early sign of the populism that was to characterise his campaign to become leader of the Conservative Party some years later and the style of political leadership he adopted on becoming Prime Minister in 2019.

Fortunately, in government circles developments moved more circumspectly and a junior minister flew to Amman to try to gain further assurances from the Jordanian authorities about the use of torture in a retrial. The Home Secretary Theresa May, in a much-publicised visit, then went to Amman herself in March 2012. Meanwhile Qatada was released on bail with very onerous conditions, which included a 22-hour curfew, following the Strasbourg ruling. In April 2012, Qatada was rearrested and a new deportation order was served on him. May stated that she had received the necessary assurances from Amman and that he could now safely be deported. Abu Qatada's lawyers invited the Home Secretary to withdraw the order as it did not appear to be consistent with the Strasbourg ruling, but May refused to do so. He appealed this decision to SIAC. This time the case was heard by Mr Justice Mitting and a panel, who decided that the Home Secretary was wrong not to revoke the deportation order. The point that worried the judge and the panel was that the 'tortured' statements had been provided to a state prosecutor, who could not be relied upon to be entirely impartial when the retrial took place. In addition, the burden lay on the Home Secretary to satisfy SIAC that tortured statements would not be used in the retrial, and this she had not done.[32] This decision was handed down in November 2012.

By now most of the participants in the long-running saga were in a state of legal exhaustion. Edward Fitzgerald QC, Qatada's barrister, said, 'Enough is enough.'[33] The government, however, doggedly pursued their argument that Strasbourg and Mr Justice Mitting were both wrong and that, somehow, the Court of Appeal in London would come to their rescue. But however nit-picking and forensically detailed the government argument was becoming, the big picture could not be ignored. The big picture was not Qatada's activities in London, however disagreeable they undoubtedly were. The big picture was simple. As torture is universally abhorred as evil, a state cannot expel a person to another state where there is a real risk they will be tried on evidence where there was a real possibility that such evidence had been obtained under torture. The government lost. Abu Qatada's future now lay in diplomacy and a realisation by Jordan that to get Qatada back, their assurances to London would have to improve. Meanwhile, Abu Qatada remained on bail in London, although he soon breached these terms and was returned to prison, which was this time a high-security facility, HMP Long Lartin in Worcestershire.

Finally, on 24 April 2013, the Home Secretary told the House of Commons that the government had reached 'a comprehensive mutual legal assistance agreement with Jordan'. Abu Qatada would not be tried on evidence obtained under torture.[34] This paved the way for Abu Qatada's removal from the United Kingdom. Mr Fitzgerald QC told the SIAC tribunal that his client would return voluntarily providing Jordan ratified the treaty, which it did on 3 July 2013. Abu Qatada left Britain under police escort, watched by media photographers and television cameras, on 7 July 2013. He was acquitted by a Jordanian court at his retrial in June 2014.

In the long and exhausting series of events that comprise the case of Abu Qatada, it is easy to lose sight of three salient facts, which politicians chose, throughout the ten years of legal challenge and counter-challenge, to ignore. First, Abu Qatada was not charged with any criminal offence during his period in the United Kingdom. Distasteful and objectionable though his views and opinions undoubtedly were and the damage to national security his presence in the United Kingdom had caused, he had not transgressed UK criminal law as it then stood. Had he done so, he would have been arrested and put on trial. Second, in all the drawn-out legal proceedings, Abu Qatada was only pursuing remedies that the UK Parliament had created for cases like this. Third, the key point in the latter stages of the saga was not the danger he posed in this country, which had already been established, but whether fundamental international standards of a civilised legal system, the exclusion of evidence obtained by torture, would be observed if he were deported. This last point would apply if Qatada was *not* a danger in Britain. Civilised standards within legal processes are fundamental universal standards. Both Strasbourg and the English judges in SIAC and in the Court of Appeal who heard the latter stages in the saga kept their eye on this important legal ball.

Politicians, however, closed their eyes to principle and chose to blame 'the system' or 'human rights'. The day after Abu Qatada was deported, the Home Secretary told Parliament that the courts had adopted 'crazy interpretation of our human rights laws' and she blamed Strasbourg for moving the goalposts by establishing new legal grounds for blocking the deportation. She told MPs that the government would keep all options open, including withdrawal from the European Convention on Human Rights.[35] This wholly unjustifiable comment on the application of the rule of law was enthusiastically supported by many backbench MPs on the

Conservative side. Relations with the judiciary were at a low ebb and opposition to the application of the European Convention on Human Rights by courts of law, at home and in Strasbourg, was becoming a familiar refrain. Withdrawal from the convention entirely was now on the agenda.

CONCLUSION

Four important cases, the Chahal case, the Belmarsh case, the Afghani hijack case and the case of Abu Qatada, all established legal principles which protected the individual but at the same time altered the tenor of political debate. Three different Home Secretaries were, on separate occasions, in public disagreement with the courts. In the Belmarsh case, David Blunkett accused the judges of threatening the life of the nation; in the Afghani case, John Reid called a judicial decision 'inexplicable'; and in Abu Qatada, Theresa May deplored a judicial ruling as being 'crazy'. These utterances, always publicised prominently in the press and on television, have done much to promote a populist view that while politicians are accountable to 'the people', judges are unelected and out of touch. This rather puerile narrative that somehow terrorism is easy to deal with if only inconvenient laws, emanating from Europe, do not get in the way has helped sow the seeds of contemporary populism. The narrative is puerile because by being simplistic it ignores important features of our democracy which must be upheld. Home Secretary Charles Clarke said that his government could not fight terrorism with one hand tied behind its back, but he overlooked the point that if democracy is to survive governments may *have* to fight with one hand tied behind their backs. A responsible democracy does not give the executive all the powers it would ideally like. A responsible democracy respects the rule of law and the independence of the judiciary. 'The discipline of public and rationally justified decision-making is essential to the maintenance of the rule of law, and forms a powerful foundation for the legitimacy of decision-making independently of any consideration of democratic accountability.'[36] All of these rulings, castigated at different times by different Home Secretaries, were rationally justified with admirable logic and a fidelity to the principles of law. As the Council of Europe acknowledged in 2002, the evil of terrorism provides a temptation to fight fire with fire, but a state may not use indiscriminate measures which would only undermine the fundamental values they seek to protect.[37]

Terrorism presents a challenge to both politicians and judges. Lord Dyson, a judge who gave rulings in terrorist cases, has described the task of striking a balance between the need to do everything to reduce the threat on the one hand, while protecting the human rights of those potentially affected on the other as 'one of the biggest challenges of our time.'[38] It is a big challenge because at the heart of the challenge is a concept of ethics. How do we discharge our duties to those who have violated their duties to us? If your neighbour has been blown up by a terrorist, how should you react? Michael Ignatieff has addressed these ethical questions and has concluded that we believe in democracy because its procedures protect each of the individuals who belong to it and we care about rights because each human life is intrinsically worth preserving. He justifies the use of special measures by governments to tackle terrorism because a democracy must be able to defend itself, by force of arms if necessary. He then adds, tellingly, 'But even more with force of argument, for arms without argument are used in vain.'[39] In Britain the executive and the legislature have provided the arms to tackle terrorism, but the judges have, indubitably, provided the argument.

The last word should rest with Lord Bingham. He reminded his readers of the great Catholic thinker Christopher Dawson, who wrote in 1943: 'As soon as men decide that all means are permitted to fight an evil, then their good becomes indistinguishable from the evil that they set out to destroy.'[40] That wisdom, divulged during the height of the conflict between democratic nations and the evil of Hitler's Nazism, remains as true today as it was the day it was written.

CHAPTER 7

RECLAIMING THE PUBLIC DOMAIN AND DEFEATING POPULISM

In 2018, two books, one by American academics at Harvard University, the other by a retired US Secretary of State, were published almost simultaneously in the United States: *How Democracies Die* and *Fascism: A Warning* had similar themes.[1] Each warned of the signs to look out for if democracy, as we understand it in the United States and Europe, is in danger. Both books made copious references to countries in the world where democracies were, or have been, under threat. Both argued that democracy could be endangered by elected leaders. A seizure of power by decorated generals in uniform or by rioting mobs in the street is not the only way that democracies can die. Democracies can die at the hands of leaders who have gained power by democracy in the first place. The example of Hugo Chávez in Venezuela is the best-known case of an elected leader using power in an undemocratic way. But a similar route to undermining democracy by achieving power through it has happened in Georgia, Hungary, Poland, Russia, Ukraine and Turkey. Neither book singles the United Kingdom out for attention as a country whose democracy is under threat.

Two years later it is timely to look again at the warning signs that these authors have identified to see whether they have relevance to Britain. The Harvard professors Steven Levistsky and Daniel Ziblatt argue that the first sign of a democracy being in trouble is when those in power have only a weak commitment to democratic 'rules of the game'.

There have been three recent occasions when the Prime Minister, past and present, has not played by the rules. The first was Theresa May's attempt to begin the process of leaving the EU without a vote in Parliament. The second was Boris Johnson's attempt to frustrate Parliament by attempting to shut it down through prorogation, discussed fully earlier in this book. The third is Boris Johnson's relationship with the civil service and diplomats. His involvement in the resignation of Sir Kim Darroch was also discussed earlier, but there have been other threats aimed at the 'soft guardrails' of democracy. These are the informal rules of institutional forbearance, mutual tolerance and respect for others which are under threat in plans to reform the civil service. An impartial civil service, appointed on merit to provide stability within political volatility and bound by a code of neutrality, is essential to the functioning of British democracy.[2] These values are at the heart of our Constitution and prevent harm from being caused by too hasty and unthought-through policies.[3] Dominic Cummings, the Prime Minister's principal adviser, has recently contemplated replacing 'the blob' of civil servants with 'weirdos' who, he claims, would do a better job.[4] In February 2020, Sir Philip Rutnam resigned as permanent secretary at the Home Office on the grounds that he had been the target of a 'vicious and orchestrated briefing campaign'.[5] In June 2020, the Cabinet Secretary, Sir Mark Sedwill, was forced to resign his post as he was, apparently, perceived as being insufficiently identified with the Johnson style of government.[6]

The second sign that a democracy is in trouble is if there is a denial of the legitimacy of your opponents' arguments in political debate. Plainly, this happened throughout the fractious and disagreeable dialogue which occurred after the referendum vote in 2016. Those who had supported Leave traduced, insulted and demeaned anybody who either continued to argue that the result was wrong or who insisted that Parliament should debate the terms of leaving carefully, slowly and deliberately. The routine insult was to label them 'Remoaners'. Jeremy Corbyn, the Labour Party leader, was regularly labelled as being an illegitimate politician. A biography of him by the author Tom Bower hit a low point in character assassination.[7]

A third sign that a democracy is in trouble is if there is violence in the course of political disagreements which are not avowedly disowned by political leaders. This is more complicated to explain.

When the referendum campaign began, there were bitter disagreements between the pro-EU 'Remainers' and the anti-EU 'Leavers'. This disagreement split families, destroyed friendships and inflamed the language of political discourse. In the midst of all this, a hideous event occurred which shocked the nation. Jo Cox, a respected and much-loved Member of Parliament and mother of two young children, was brutally murdered as she went about her political business in June 2016. Her killer, who shouted 'This is for Britain' as he brutally stabbed her to death, was a white-supremacist Nazi sympathiser.

Unhappily, this incident was not isolated. On two occasions, in December 2018 and January 2019, Anna Soubry MP was harassed and intimidated outside Parliament by a group who shouted 'Nazi, traitor and scum' at her as she was on her way to do an outside media broadcast. In the year following Jo Cox's murder, MPs reported 111 crimes of harassment and malicious communications against them. This had more than doubled by August 2018. In the period of intense negotiations between Britain and the EU in which Parliament was as divided as the country about the terms on which Britain proposed to leave the EU, intimidation of MPs was still going up. The Assistant Commissioner of the Metropolitan Police said that Brexit had been a huge driver of the inexorable rise in threats against MPs. Between 2016 and 2018, spending on security for individual MPs increased from under £200,000 per year to over £4 million. Most of the targeted victims were women.[8]

In early September 2019, Boris Johnson, having become Prime Minister, told an audience of exhausted police cadets and the nation via television that he would rather 'die in a ditch' than postpone the date for leaving the EU, which had been fixed for 31 October. Four days later Parliament was prorogued, but it resumed on 25 September following the Supreme Court judgment. The atmosphere was intense. On the one side was the Prime Minister, whose party did not command a majority, who was determined, on the pain of death, to leave the EU, with or without a deal, on 31 October. On the other side were the opposition parties and some former Conservatives who wanted to delay Brexit if Johnson could not strike a deal by 19 October. This was a strategy which Parliament had devised in the Benn Act. Johnson appeared to be stuck by legislation passed in his own legislature.

This is the background to an extraordinary event which occurred on 2 October 2019 when 10 Downing Street let it be known that if MPs delayed Brexit beyond 31 October they would not be able to leave the comfort zone of SW1 (the postal address of Parliament) as they might be lynched if they did so.[9]

Although this shocking warning was not made by Johnson personally, and was uttered by a 'source' within Downing Street, the

Prime Minister had been in bullish form in Parliament a few days earlier, branding the Benn Act the 'surrender Act' more than fifteen times in the course fractious and inflammatory exchanges.[10] Given the background of actual violence, including the murder of Jo Cox and countless cases of threats of violence against MPs, the warning about violence issued from Downing Street amply fulfils the third test for judging whether democracy is in danger: violence which is not disavowed by a political leader.

Some will say that while our democracy might have been in danger, the danger has now passed. There was an election in December 2019 and political life can return to normal. This is to misunderstand how democracies may die. In another recent book, the British political scientist David Runciman has pointed out that democracies do not suddenly die.[11] There is seldom a single moment of catastrophe when some heavily medalled army chief emerges from his barracks, surrounded by lackeys and sycophants, to take up the role of dictator. Democracies die when trust in institutions begins to fade away. Democracies are in danger when the necessity of the bedrocks of democracy – democratic legislatures, independent law courts and a free press – start to be questioned. There certainly was a questioning of the legitimacy of our legislature when one Cabinet minister asked whether it could be possible for the Constitution to survive if there was a 'Remain' Parliament and a 'Leave' population.[12] Now, the government is taking this point seriously in setting out the reasons why a Constitution, Democracy and Rights Commission should be established.

DO WE NEED A NEW COMMISSION?

Three reasons are given for setting up a commission to examine aspects of our Constitution and they all touch on the rule of law.

First, the government has noted that the failure of Parliament to deliver Brexit revealed the 'destabilising and potentially damaging rift between politicians and the people'. Second, the government wishes to look at new ways to 'update human rights law' and thirdly the government wants to update judicial review proceedings so that the remedy is not used to 'conduct politics by another means'.[13]

The first question is to ask what the motivation is for such a commission at this time. The inability of Parliament to enable the result of the referendum to be delivered painlessly as many people wanted was because the electorate had chosen a hung parliament. Both Theresa May and Boris Johnson had to grapple with the fact that they were not mistress and master in their own house. However, that particular difficulty is now over; Johnson has a commanding majority in Parliament. Given the decisiveness of the 2019 general election, what is the rift now between politicians and the electorate? Or is the hidden agenda to forge a closer relationship between the leader and the people? This would certainly be consistent with populism, which thrives on a close affinity existing between what is described as a homogeneous body called 'the people' and a powerful charismatic leader.

The suggested terms of reference of the commission are so wide that they appear to be putting up for debate the values of core constitutional principles. This is a big step away from the sort of constitutional reform which has taken place in the recent past. Reforms to the House of Lords, devolution in Scotland and Wales and the creation of the Supreme Court did not put a dismantling of core foundations of liberal democracy in Britain on the table. The premises of such democratic values were accepted by the Labour Party when these changes were made.

It is not clear whether the motivation for the commission is to seek genuine objective views from obviously impartial experts or whether it has been created only to provide a semblance of objectivity to justify changes that the government has already decided are merited. The signs are not promising. One MP, Suella Braverman, who has been a Member of Parliament for five years and a barrister for fifteen years, commented on ConservativeHome, 'If a small number of unelected, unaccountable judges continue to determine wider public policy, putting them at odds with elected decision-makers, our democracy cannot be said to be representative.'[14] Within days of these comments being posted online, Braverman was appointed Attorney General, chief legal adviser to the Crown. Braverman had suggested that if judges are at odds with elected decision-makers, our, democracy is in danger. She misses the point. Judges are not 'unaccountable' because they are not elected. Judges are independent and accountable only to the law and to the Lord Chief Justice on matters of discipline. Judges may be 'at odds' with decision-makers but only if a decision is shown to have been unlawful.

The experience of past events provides warning signs of a danger to our democracy, and the plans to create the Constitution, Democracy and Rights Commission do not provide reassurance. There are few cogent alternatives within the arena of political debate. The Labour Party was so riven by internal wrangling and quarrels about its own ideological purity under the leadership of Jeremy Corbyn that there was little sign of any serious thinking from that quarter. It remains to be seen whether under Sir Keir Starmer the Labour Party will wish to make the Constitution and human rights a key element in his opposition to the Johnson government.

VALUE PLURALISM

Commentators outside the confines of party politics have made contributions to finding solutions to the decline in trust which poses a danger to democracy. John Gray is a political philosopher and his considerable contribution is available in one volume entitled *Enlightenment's Wake*, which was published in 2007.[15] Gray maintains that traditional conservatism is dead. On this he would, no doubt, have the support of Boris Johnson. Gray's solution to the rise of populism and its attendant dangers to democracy is something that he calls 'value pluralism'.

In order to understand 'value pluralism', some of Gray's starting points must be explained. One starting point is his insistence that nationhood is by far the most potent political force in modernity. It is within the nation state where common cultures exist and where political allegiances are formed. Stability can arise only if there is a shared common culture and this can only grow from the nature of humanity. This arises through living within a common culture which occurs historically through the passage of time. Usually a common culture is locally based. Gray argues that traditional liberal theory has gone wrong by attempting to impose theories of rationality and universalism to anthropological facts comprising the nature of human identity. He argues that the task of liberals is to attempt to reconcile the demands of a liberal form of life with the innate character of human identities and allegiances.

In this analysis, Gray has identified potent traits that have led to the appeal of populism. The fishermen of Grimsby whose stability and way of making a living from the sea are now threatened by fisherman from EU countries sailing in their environment. The steel workers of Sheffield had an identity and a pride which was expressed in trade union solidarity and this has been taken away from them by forces of rational economics and a universal world market.

Gray suggests that to deal with the anxieties and concerns of communities who have been 'left behind' is to admit that the Enlightenment project is dead and is incapable of providing solutions. These diverse claims of historic communities are never admitted by Enlightenment thinkers who are overwhelmed by the rights of individuals. Different communities may legitimately have different legal regimes to accommodate their 'distinctive exclusivities, hierarchies and bigotries'.

Modern liberalism needs a pluralist political theory which recognises that different legal and political institutions are desirable and legitimate in different historical and cultural milieu. It is the propensity to cultural difference which is the primordial attribute of the human species: human identities are plural and diverse and human nature is self-defining and self-transforming. It is a falsehood to believe that progress is achieved by abstract individualism 'at the service of a legalistic or jurisprudential paradigm of political philosophy'.[16]

It is here that Gray steps on controversial territory around the subject called the 'rule of law'. It is no longer realistic, Gray argues, to cling to a 'hubristic liberal ideology which succours the illusions of legalism and rationalism and spurns the historical realities of common culture for the sake of a mirage of universalism'.[17] To do so is to denigrate pluralism and cultural diversity as inessential or transitory and to elevate universalism and cosmopolitanism as the only rational choice for liberals. This is strong stuff and is guaranteed to raise the hackles clinging to the judges' wigs.

In place of a discredited liberalism Gray proposes 'value pluralism' as there can be no overarching standard whereby conflicts within societies can be arbitrated or resolved. Reason alone cannot resolve choices and it is a legalistic and formalist illusion to assume that right has priority over good. When individual liberties clash with one another they can only be resolved politically, not legally. These political resolutions often involve provisional settlements and compromises which will inevitably vary from place to place. Such settlements may be temporary or permanent. According to Gray, it is simply not possible to supplant the judgements reached via political discourse with disciplined legal decisions. He deplores modern liberal theory, most famously propounded by John Rawls in *A Theory of Justice*, which argued there were certain foundation principles of justice and liberty which stood separate and apart from politics.[18] Gray maintains that such a theory makes judicial institutions arenas of political struggle. The end result is the corrosion of political life itself.[19]

These ideas were written in a series of monographs in the mid-1990s and were consolidated in *Enlightenment's Wake* in 2007. In a recent article Gray drew comfort from the result of the 2019 general election by observing that the 'logic of events' was working in Boris Johnson's favour. He predicted that the new Conservative government would not have choices imposed upon it by 'legal fiat' and that the executive will be reassured that the British judiciary would be returned to a more modest role like the one it had before the creation of the Supreme Court.[20]

Gray's scepticism about 'legal fiat' and his view that political choices cannot be resolved by the discipline of legal decisions is not borne out by experience in Britain over recent years. It is simply not possible to resolve some disputes politically by recognising cultural diversity. What happens when there are conflicting values *within* communities having their own cultural identity? These can only be resolved by resorting to logic and the application of principles which Gray believes are long since dead. Modern experience does not support Gray's point that legalism is threatening the search for political solutions. Take the provision of schooling for those living in modern Britain who belong to distinct communities.

A Jewish man in north London wanted to send his son to JFS (formerly known as the Jewish Free School), which has a cultural history of Orthodox Judaism, which is taught and upheld in the school. The man was divorced from his wife, who was Italian, but she had converted to non-Orthodox Judaism before her marriage. Their son's line of descent was not recognised by the Office of the Chief Rabbi as providing their son with a status that the school accepted. The school gave priority to admitting boys whose Jewish status was recognised by the Office of the Chief Rabbi. As the school was oversubscribed, the boy was refused admission. The conflict therefore was one entirely within the Jewish community. How could it be resolved? Did the father's wish to have his son admitted to the school prevail over the school, who maintained that he did not have the relevant Jewish heritage to be admitted?

There could only be a legal resolution and the Supreme Court wrestled with the question of whether Jews were a racial or a religious group. If it was the latter, then the courts would not arbitrate as there would have to be a religious resolution. If, however, Jews were deemed to be a racial group then it would be possible to find a legal resolution by analysing whether there had been either direct or indirect discrimination by the school. The court decided that the boy had been treated less favourably than others by virtue of his racial group and therefore the Race Relations Act 1976 could be applied to provide a legal resolution to the impasse that this disagreement within the Jewish community had thrown up. In the event, the judgment went against the school.[21] The community of the school was at odds with the community of Jews beyond the school. Only a legal resolution was possible.

This decision does not mean that in some way legal solutions always favour the individual against a prevailing community culture. In another case the culture of a school prevailed over that of an individual. Denbigh High School in Luton, Bedfordshire, admits boys and girls and twenty-one ethnic groups are represented in the school. In 2006, the majority of the pupils at the school were from the Muslim community and four out of six parent governors were Muslim. The headteacher was a Bengali Muslim who believed that the wearing of a school uniform was integral to maintaining standards and promoting a sense of community identity within the school. Muslim girls were offered the option of wearing the shalwar kameez, a sleeveless smock, which allowed the collar and tie of the school uniform to remain visible, with loose trousers. After consultation with parents and governors, Muslim girls were permitted to wear a headscarf if they chose to do so. One day Shabina Begum, who was aged fourteen and embarking on puberty, arrived at the school wearing a long garment called a jilbab, which concealed the shape of her body and did not allow for any display of a school tie. She was sent home and told to change. She refused to do this and claimed, with the assistance of her elder brother and some family members, that she had been unlawfully excluded from school.

Was the school discriminating against her and declining her the right to express her Muslim convictions in the way she chose, exercising her personal autonomy? Other schools in the locality did permit the dresswear of Begum's choice, so why should Denbigh High School not do the same? This was a dispute about the expression of Muslim identity, but it could only be resolved legally. The judges read evidence from the Islamic Cultural Centre, whose scholars were not offended by the school policy on uniforms. They also considered the evidence from the headteacher and the governors, who stated that in the past too much discretion had been given to pupils to define themselves along racial lines. This had resulted in conflict within the school. The school wanted to foster cohesion, not the creation of sub-groups. The judges also heard from Muslim pupils who said they feared that they might be pressured into wearing the jilbab against their own wishes if Begum won the case. The House of Lords upheld the school and decided Shabina had not unlawfully been excluded from school.[22]

Cases like this are important. As the American sociologist Amitai Etzioni has observed, law has a function as part of a moral dialogue which shores up and revises core values, which is necessary to prevent the disintegration of communities by their pursuit of their own sub-set of values.[23] In the Denbigh High School case, the law, as expressed by the judges, reinforced essential values which existed already within the communities involved in the case.

John Gray has identified all the cultural forces that fuelled the rise of populism, but he has completely underestimated the necessity for judges to resolve problems that are incapable of resolution within cultural communities themselves. The community of the school was at odds with Shabina Begum's community beyond the school's walls. Gray also wants our constitutional arrangements to return to a better time of the past, before the creation of the Supreme Court. As has been argued in earlier chapters, it is an illusion to suppose that there was some better past time to which we could easily and painlessly return.

DEMOCRATIC PLURALISM

A similar analysis which seeks to downplay the role of the judiciary within society is put forward by the American academic Michael Lind. His book *The New Class War: Saving Democracy from the*

Managerial Elite argues that we should not be in denial about class divisions.[24] Instead we should recognise that a new 'managerial state' of university-educated people who run global and national corporations and government agencies have now replaced the bourgeoisie, the group so reviled by Karl Marx. This new class, the 'overclass' as Lind calls it, is pitted against grassroots politicians, trade unions, farmers and church leaders. These social delineations have produced a society of 'technocratic neoliberalism' which has replaced a society of 'democratic pluralism'. Power has shifted away from the working class. Lind argues that the solution lies in a return to a culture of 'democratic pluralism'. This is very similar to Gray's 'value pluralism'.

This viewpoint has a particular American slant to it which may not be relevant in Britain. For example, less than a quarter of the workforce in the United Kingdom are members of trade unions.[25] As for farming and church attendance, only about 1 per cent of the workforce in Britain works in farming, and church attendance has slumped to barely 5 per cent of the population.[26] The United States has huge farming communities in a large number of individual states and nearly 40 per cent of the US population attend church regularly. Applying Lind's ideas to Britain may not be straightforward; however, his opinions about the 'juristocracy' being part of the overclass must be considered carefully.

According to Lind, the new class war in both the United States and Europe has insulated the judiciary from voters, and judges are now part of the overclass pushing rights-based liberalism beyond its legitimate limits. The effect is that community interests are only represented by this or that individual right. This has had the consequence of weakening the voice of the working class, whose interests can only be represented in elected legislatures. Civic watchdogs have lost power to a new activism by a judicial overclass who have usurped power. This power grab by judges correlates with other college-educated elites who have roles in transnational bodies and executive agencies. An over-reliance on courts to solve problems in society will shift power from the working class to an overclass of judges. Lind implies that there is a hidden motivation within the overclass to shield themselves from democratic majorities as elites have an instinctive antipathy to strong government.[27]

This analysis does not apply to the United Kingdom. Britain does not have a federal system where state governors enjoy big power and where civic watchdogs in cities wield power in their office as mayors. Decentralised power bases are much weaker in Britain than they are in the United States. In fact, England is highly centralised and has no substantial regional devolution. Party government in Parliament, when commanding a big majority, can give a powerful executive enormous control over the lives of citizens.

Lind's solutions have won plaudits in the United Kingdom for the originality of his prescription for defeating populism. He blames the metropolitan overclass for provoking the populist rebellion from below and identifies Donald Trump and Boris Johnson as elitists who have exploited this rebellion for their own political advancement. The solution is to bypass elitist institutions and to delegate substantial areas of policy to rule-making bodies from below who can represent particular portions of the community. For example, organised labour and business should set wage levels together and representatives of religious and secular creeds should be charged with oversight of education and the media. The nation state should stand back and intervene only to protect individual rights or overall state interests. In this democratic-pluralist vision of democracy, the government should reign, not rule.[28]

When it comes to the 'rule of law', Lind argues that it has been absorbed into the neoliberal revolution from above, the provocative forces that caused populism. These forces comprise the most elite group of all and haunt the common rooms of universities and the courtrooms of the nation sharing a vision of social liberalism and economic conservatism. Such people have little place in Lind's ideas for democratic pluralism. 'Government by the judiciary tends to be a dictatorship of overclass libertarians in robes.'[29]

Here, Lind is way off the mark. He associates the judiciary with being an elite group 'in government' when, of course, the judiciary is separate and apart from government. He claims that unjust sexual and racial discrimination could have been dealt with by electoral coalitions in legislatures instead of in the Supreme Court in the United States. Perhaps they could have been, but they were not. His idea of devolving power away from elite libertarian judges to devolved community bodies overlooks the fact that any solutions reached by devolved bodies must carry authority. By what means is it suggested that there will be sufficient community cohesion for extra-legal resolutions to be honoured by the side that loses? If 'representatives' of certain community and regional bodies are to be given greater authority, what is to prevent these representatives from becoming a new elite?

A CONSERVATIVE CHALLENGE TO POPULISM

The ideas of Gray and Lind have been taken up by at least one Conservative thinker in Britain. Nick Timothy, who was Theresa May's chief of staff at 10 Downing Street, has written a provocative book, *Remaking One Nation: The Future of Conservatism*.[30] Unlike Gray, Timothy does not believe conservatism is dead; instead he proposes a radical rethink of what conservatism should mean in modern

Britain. His ideas have much in common with Michael Lind in that he argues that the power of ideological 'ultra-liberals' have so over-reached themselves that they threaten liberal democracies. This overreach has weakened Britain's largest demographic group, the white working class.

Timothy defines an 'ultra-liberal' as a person who may be on the right or the left of conventional politics: the former supporting market fundamentalism; the latter militant identity politics. Timothy has no time for the economic fundamentals of ultra-liberalism which promoted globalisation and caused hardship. He rejects much of what Margaret Thatcher believed. He argues that ultra-liberalism is kept alive by 'elite liberals' who believe personal autonomy is of principal importance. This 'elite liberalism' has allowed a culture of instant gratification to take over from relational humanity within communities who have obligations towards one another. His views are radical and extend to replacing the House of Lords with a wholly elected chamber and moving towards full devolution in England so that Britain would consist of four nations within a federation of Great Britain.

Timothy's prescriptions are important in proposing a strategy to defeat populism, but they are not ones that place the 'rule of law' high up on his agenda. He puts judges firmly in the same category as 'liberal technocrats', a cadre of unelected experts whose reports are nearly always implemented by the government or the civil service whose institutional 'groupthink' tried to subvert the referendum result. The conclusion, Timothy maintains, is that government by the people has become 'government by a certain kind of people'.[31] The kind of people who come into this category are the 'liberal judges' who can rely on quasi-constitutional laws like the European Convention on Human Rights to shape policies in ways

Parliament would never permit. The counter-argument to this has been set out in Chapter 5, but Timothy has further quivers to his bow when taking aim at judges. He claims that when Parliament passed the Human Rights Act in 1998 it bound future parliaments, so that the hands of ministers are tied and Parliament is prevented from changing direction. Judges use human rights, according to him, to close down future, legitimate, policy options. He gives the judgments in terrorist cases as an example of this claim. This fallacy has been discussed fully in Chapter 6. As earlier chapters have spelled out, the doctrine of parliamentary supremacy, whether defined in a modern way or in the way Dicey defined it in Edwardian times, remains the cornerstone of our Constitution. Parliament cannot bind its successors and judges may not strike down a law because it is 'unconstitutional'. If there is a need for a completely up-to-date restatement of the constitutional position of judges in relation to the executive then the evidence given by Lord Reed, President of the Supreme Court, to the Constitutional Committee of the House of Lords in March 2020, provided it.[32]

As with Gray and Lind, Nick Timothy does not like judicial lawmakers being too powerful. One way of reducing their power, he suggests, is to abolish the Human Rights Act. His arguments for doing so are weak and unimpressive. He claims that the Human Rights Act 'instructs' British judges to 'follow' case law 'established' by the European Court of Human Rights.[33] This is not the case. British judges are required to 'take into account' jurisprudence from the Strasbourg Court so far as it is relevant to the proceedings in the British court. Only a relatively few cases engage a British court's consideration of Strasbourg case law. It is only if 'it is possible to do so' that United Kingdom legislation should be read in a way which is compatible with a convention right.[34] Timothy's only concrete example for wishing to repeal the Human Rights Act is that the Act 'makes it harder to enforce immigration law'.[35] Again, he is on weak ground here. The Human Rights Act may make it harder for executive officers and employees of the UK Border Agency to enforce immigration law *unlawfully*, but the enforcement of law is an administrative act. The bulk of illegal entrants to the United Kingdom who are liable for deportation are overstayers who are long-term residents, mainly from China, Vietnam, India and Pakistan. It is not the judges, applying the Human Rights Act, who are responsible for the fact that they are still here, despite having no status to remain. There are also over 40,000 failed asylum seekers who have not been removed by the authorities.[36] The Human Rights Act is irrelevant to the failure to carry out actions to remove those who have exhausted their legal remedies.

John Gray, Michel Lind and Nick Timothy are united in concluding that the trust in law has broken down. They all identify strands of modern liberalism which have distorted the views of traditional liberalism to exclude the views of the majority in favour of unchecked individualism and unchecked market forces. If it is true that majority opinion is ignored by 'anti-democratic legalism', in Timothy's words, or by a judicial 'overclass' in Lind's or by 'legal fiat' in Gray's, then we are in trouble. But is a simple reliance on majority opinion always the way to protect a liberal democracy?

THE LIBERAL RESPONSE: RECLAIM THE PUBLIC DOMAIN?

One of the themes of this book has been to try to demonstrate that if the opinions of a bare majority were obediently followed at times when trust in law was breaking down, progressive reforms would never have taken place. A liberal democracy is a representative democracy, not an unqualified democracy where a directly expressed

opinion is acted upon by an executive which serves them. Representative democracy provides for the necessary filters so that any directly
expressed opinion is considered rationally and discussed in the context of the national interest generally and not simply obeyed as an
instruction. The most famous definition of representative democracy
was given by Edmund Burke in his speech to his electors in 1774:
'Your representative owes you, not his industry only, but his judgment; and he betrays, instead of serving you, if he sacrifices it to your
opinion.'[37] It is the application of this principle that allows the will of
the people to be reconciled with sound and stable government.

If our democracy had been unqualified, capital punishment
would never have been abolished, police malpractice would never
have been rooted out, misuse of executive authority would never
have been restrained and incidents of national crisis such as terrorism would have been tackled by inhibiting personal liberties
permanently. All these events are clear vindications of the merits
of representative democracy over unqualified, populist democracy. Maintaining the essential structures and building blocks of a
liberal democracy is essential even if, on occasions, maintaining
them does not reflect public opinion. Judges have to cling to their
independence despite their class origins, gender imbalance or the
unpopularity of their rulings. In any case, the judiciary is much
more representative of the community at large now than at any
time in the recent past. Over a quarter of High Court judges are
now women and over 30 per cent of the judiciary as a whole are
now women. More Black, Asian and minority ethnic (BAME) candidates are joining the bench than are retiring from it; 11 per cent of
the bench as a whole comprise BAME judges compared with 6 per
cent who had retired from judicial work.[38] In the period covered
in this book there were no women or BAME members of the High

Court bench until 1965, when Elizabeth Lane became a High Court judge. The first BAME judge of the High Court, Linda Dobbs QC, was not appointed until 2004.

Gray, Lind and Timothy all feel the need to reduce judicial power and yet they are unable to explain satisfactorily how this might be achieved, short of measures that would be fundamentally illiberal and would threaten judicial independence. For example, Timothy suggests the Human Rights Act should be scrapped and replaced with a Bill of Rights. This has been Conservative Party policy since 2014, when the party first published this proposal. Among other changes, a new Conservative Bill of Rights would abolish the requirement for judges to 'take account' of Strasbourg case law: 'In future, the UK courts will interpret legislation based upon its normal meaning and clear intention of Parliament, rather than stretch its meaning to comply with Strasbourg case law.'[39] Behind this bland language lies a sinister intent. This statement promotes the executive into a position more important than the independent judges because the proposal would compel judges to comply with executive demands, regardless of the meaning that years of interpretation had given to the words in previous cases. In addition, the Conservative Party proposed to confine legal arguments about convention rights to 'serious cases' only and to forbid the consideration by UK judges of Strasbourg law in trivial ones. Again, power is given to the executive over the judiciary as the definition of a 'serious case' would be something that Parliament would decide. If carried out, these proposals would diminish the power of judges and increase the power of the executive, but when this was the calibration of the scales between law and politics Britain was not a better place. This has been demonstrated by the real-life cases discussed in Chapters 2 and 3.

A completely different analysis of how to combat populism has been provided by the English historian David Marquand. His analysis is the one most in tune with the post-Covid-19 world in which we now have to live. He agrees with Lind and Timothy that populism is linked to the ravages of extreme neoliberalism, but he approaches the issue from a completely different perspective. Marquand maintains that neoliberalism devalues the concept of citizenship when every person is regarded as a customer of market-created enterprises. The 'market-mode' of neoliberalism has grown so powerful that it is infecting intermediate institutions like public service broadcasting at the BBC, the ethos of the civil service and the autonomy of universities with concepts such as proxy markets, performance indicators, privatisation and deregulation. This mania for markets drains society of the 'public domain', a precious but precarious commodity which was something that existed in late Victorian times but has since been lost. Marquand praises the outlook of Joseph Chamberlain, the Mayor of Birmingham from 1873 to 1876 and later a controversial imperialist politician who led the opposition to Henry Campbell Bannerman in Parliament. Chamberlain claimed that municipal enterprise was like a joint stock or cooperative company where every citizen was a shareholder of which the dividends provided better health and wellbeing for everybody.[40]

Chamberlain, when he was mayor, represented neither the overweening power of a centralised state nor the marketplace of commerce but civic activism, where a single individual spends time in the 'public domain'. Here, Marquand and Timothy have something in common. Nick Timothy has written a biography of Chamberlain and like Marquand is an admirer of 'civic capitalism', where the ethos is not merely complying with the law but extends to probity in paying taxes, contributing philanthropically and playing a part in community institutions. But now, Marquand and Timothy draw different conclusions. For Timothy, the lesson of Chamberlain's civic capitalism is that collective community rights are as important as individual workplace rights. For Marquand, Chamberlain represented a lost culture of civic activism, not simply civic capitalism. Civic activism is in the domain of the public.

Marquand argues that nowadays there are many occupations within this domain, such as policemen, soldiers, civil servants, nurses and judges. The domain is defined not by your employer or even your rank but by the outcomes of the work you undertake. These outcomes are equity and service. The notion that there is an important element to society other than markets or the operations of big government are to be found also in the notion of public goods like free public spaces, libraries and the delivery of justice, disinterested scholarship and the free access to the internet for information. This perception of the 'public domain' as Marquand has described it starts to look very like the sort of society we might become after the Covid-19 pandemic is over. There are several pointers to this conclusion.

At the start of the pandemic the headmaster of Eton College, Simon Henderson, observed that the arrival of Covid-19 on our shores would be a trigger for profound change as there would be a realisation that the values of compassion, community and civic responsibility – often practised by the least well-paid members of our society – are the key to our survival.[41] The contrast between politics before and after the arrival of the virus could not be more stark. During her general election campaign in 2017, Prime Minister Theresa May told a nurse working in the NHS who had not had a pay rise for eight years that there was 'no magic money tree' the government could pluck to place money into the health service.[42] Now, the Chancellor of the Exchequer has miraculously shaken the tree and found £350 billion to pump into the economy while we stand on our doorsteps or at our windows applauding those who work in the NHS. Before Covid-19, Home Secretary Priti Patel displayed all her populist credentials at the Conservative Party conference in 2019 by proclaiming, 'This is a Government driven by the people's priorities, hardworking, honest, law-abiding people whose needs are humble, whose expectations are modest and whose demands of their government are simple … They are the masters and we are their servants.'[43] This robust statement of populist belief is now woefully out of date. In a pandemic, the needs of the people are great, their demands of the government are considerable and the power of the state must be harnessed to save lives, protect the economy and promote civic responsibility.

The new agenda is already being forged by independent groups. The 'Krisis' manifesto (named after the Greek word meaning a turning point during an illness) signed by a number of prominent campaigners, lawyers and academics in May 2020 calls for a future where the value of care is properly recognised and rewarded and inequality within society is tackled by bold reforms to our political institutions. These include the creation of a United Kingdom citizens' assembly, made up of randomly selected members who would be able to deliberate on the basis of facts and which would be empowered to present three parliamentary Bills per session where MPs would not be whipped and there would be a genuine cross-party discussion in Parliament about the Bill's merits.[44] The cross-party thinktank Demos is planning a huge public consultation exercise, a 'People's Commission on Life After Covid-19', to find out how people believe daily life should change after the pandemic.

Nick Timothy is one of the leaders of this initiative, which wants to use social listening, polling and deliberation via virtual citizens' assemblies to identify solutions for a post-Covid-19 world.[45]

Marquand had anticipated much of this post-Covid thinking by not viewing contemporary problems within society as part of a class war, as Lind does, nor even as Gray does. Marquand views society as comprising three elements. First, there is the private domain of family life, friendships and hobbies. Second, there is the market domain of commerce, trade, banking and the wheels which provide for the circulation of money. Third, there is the public domain of citizenship and service. It is this domain which has become so relevant after the pandemic arrived in the United Kingdom.

The revival of the public domain which Marquand argues for is absolutely fundamental to any discussion about defeating populism. Gray, Lind and Timothy have identified a powerful judiciary as part of the problem, whereas for Marquand an independent judiciary and the rule of law are essential to the solution. For Marquand, the citizen should be in the driving seat of society in arguing, cajoling, debating and negotiating where the boundaries of the public domain should be erected. In this sense the individual citizen participates in forming rules which are legal. Most lawyers would probably accept, as Lord Bingham does, that legal rules are management agents for suppressing, confining, guiding, directing, standardising, integrating, adapting and changing behaviour.[46]

As Marquand has made clear, these rights of citizenship trump both market power and the bonds of clan and kinship. This is the opposite of the Conservative conclusion drawn by Timothy that the problems of the present partly arise because individualism has trumped community, legal rights have come before civic obligations and universalism has eroded citizenship. On the contrary,

Marquand maintains that notions of citizenship are universal in the sense that there are shared values in the modern world of liberal democracies. For Marquand, a vigorous and extensive public domain is fundamental to a civilised society, human flourishing and democratic citizenship. But there must be, within society, a belief that there is a public interest, as distinct from a private one, that is achievable. In the public domain citizenship rights trump both market power and ties of family, friendship and neighbourhood connections. The public domain is a domain of trust which is protected by an authoritative and independent judiciary and a non-partisan civil service.

The coronavirus pandemic called for exceptional measures to combat it and the experience of it has revived features of Marquand's vision of a public domain. Suddenly in June 2020, Boris Johnson began modelling himself on Franklin D. Roosevelt in his prescription for post-Covid politics.[47] Here, relying on facts, he appealed to the better natures of the population to use their own autonomy to help the interests of others. It was an example of the 'public domain' in action. Market power was abandoned in the interest of the citizen who might become infected. Private interests of clubs, parties, sports and family gatherings became less important than the public interest of valuing the life of a single individual. This had followed remarkable displays of public service by medical teams and participation by others in acts of kindness at the height of the crisis. Boris Johnson, once a disciple of Margaret Thatcher, was even able to declare that 'there is such a thing as society'.[48]

The coronavirus pandemic has brought into sharp relief how irrelevant and old-fashioned the ideas of F. A. Hayek are to our current predicaments. It was forty-five years ago that Margaret Thatcher announced to her Conservative colleagues that the ideas in Hayek's *The Constitution of Liberty* comprised her political philosophy. Now those ideas are in tatters. It was ideological ultra-liberalism which argued that market forces were the only conceivable way in which socialism could be held at bay. Few Conservatives now believe in Hayek's intellectually rigorous but utterly impractical solutions. The arrival of Covid-19 has resurrected doctrines of a strong state and a high level of public spending on socially worthwhile and necessary projects.

While Hayek's economic theories are well-known, it must not be forgotten that he also had a fixed opinion about the rule of law within society, which has been summarised in Chapter 3. According to Hayek, social justice was a mirage and the only role for law within society was to lay down rules to enable spontaneous order to flourish without restraint. Curiously, liberals like Gray and Lind or Conservatives like Timothy have chosen not to challenge Hayek's outdated legal theories at the same time as demolishing his economic ones. Hayek's economic prescriptions are now as irrelevant as his fixed view about the rule of law within societies.

CONCLUSION

In light of the coronavirus crisis, Marquand's vision provides the best long-term hope for defeating populism. His arguments have a cogency that Gray, Lind and Timothy do not confront. Support for Marquand's vision comes from Britain's leading Jewish scholar, Jonathan Sacks, who has argued that only the 'matrix of a civil society' can prevent populism taking hold.[49] He calls for a 'covenant' society where citizens dedicate themselves to a set of principles by an exchange of promises to uphold and advance certain commitments. This provides a shared belonging carrying with it collective responsibilities: 'Societies become strong when they care for the weak, rich when they care for the poor, invulnerable when they care for the vulnerable.' Such a society, Sacks argues, is the polar opposite to the populist one, which divides people into 'Us' and 'Them'.[50] Marquand and Sacks are correct to stress elements of active citizenship in their remedy for countering the rise of populism. There is an inconvenient fact that hangs over the conservative prescription for defeating populism. The inconvenient fact is that mankind has always strived for liberty.

The search for liberty in order to fully express personal autonomy has been a very powerful force in the history of humanity. A. C. Grayling, in his book *Towards the Light: The Story of the Struggle for Liberty and Rights That Made the Modern West*, argues that there are some ideas that are so central to humanity that they must be explained.[51]

Grayling maintains that there is literally a straight line from darkness into light during which 'enfranchisement' took place in step with scientific and social developments. This was an awakening by mankind that each individual possessed rights and claims which they could assert against the power of those in authority. The history of Western societies can be seen as a struggle to maintain and enlarge these basic rights. Grayling cites and prints in full the key documents which he claims produced democracy and with it personal enfranchisement: the Bill of Rights 1689; the United States Bill of Rights 1791; the Declaration of the Rights of Man and of the Citizen 1789; and the United Nations Universal Declaration of Human Rights 1948. Grayling argues that it is inconceivable that Britain, France, the United States and the United Nations would have each produced similar documents asserting basic human needs of empowerment unless there was a universalism about rights. The desire by mankind to be protected from tyranny and oppression in order for personal integrity and autonomy to be expressed freely is so ingrained within the human psyche that all generations must preserve the freedoms they have obtained for future generations to enjoy.

This is an idea that originated in the eighteenth century when David Hume famously said that a man was a slave to his passions. By this he meant the ability, unique to humans, to respond to the 'sentiments' or passions of others. Man had his own reasons, not given by God, for recognising all people are of equal worth, embracing some kind of common good in all. It is not true, as some critics of liberalism have tried to argue, that it is only rational self-interest which is the universal motivation of human action and behaviour. On the contrary, as Stephen Holmes has argued, the essence of liberal individualism is best expressed in the double imperative to take moral responsibility for oneself and to treat others as individuals, not just as members of a group.[52] These are Enlightenment ideas, as Anthony Pagden has explained: 'It [the Enlightenment] create[ed] a field of values, political, social, and moral, based upon a detached and scrupulous understanding ... of what it means to be human.'[53]

A. C. Grayling has taken up the same theme. In a later book, *Democracy and Its Crisis*, written shortly after the 2016 EU referendum, Grayling disagrees fundamentally with Gray about where 'the logic of events' is taking us. For him, hard-won struggles are in peril from a populist revolt against the core values of representative democracy and the rule of law.[54]

For Grayling, democracy can only survive if it is deliberative. This means that the forum of representation in any democracy must ensure that entrenched differences and opinions within society do not permanently fracture the system. The difference between democracy and dictatorship is that in a truly representative democracy we should have institutions and practices that 'filter' out from the tumult what is needful, what is right and what is good. Only through deliberative democracy can this be achieved.[55]

Defeating populism involves creating a strong, vibrant civil society where there are citizens' rights, mutual obligations underpinned by a strong and respected judiciary who occupy a public domain of equity. This route does not lie in judges admitting that they have overstepped the mark by intruding into politics. The tide of history and the social developments which have been hastened by individual expectations have moved the judiciary into a territory it did not previously occupy. The consequences of the Human Rights Act 1998 which obliged judges to add a new dimension to their reasoning have been evolving for over twenty years. It is a simple fact of legal history that judges have in a sense become more political than they used to be, but there is no need for judges to impose restraints upon themselves. As Lord Neuberger has pointed out, 'the safety valve in our democratic system is that Parliament has the last word'.[56] There is no obvious politically intrusive tendency among judges which cannot be explained by the tides of history, and judges should not feel obliged to clip their own wings.[57] There is no better yesterday when the judiciary behaved with the correctly calibrated decorum. As was argued in Chapter 3, the evolution of judicial activism coincided with society's expectations.

The progress of law-making by judges over recent years is, I have argued, a development to be welcomed, not feared. It is progress in the sense that the Enlightenment itself was progress. Populism, by contrast, is a kind of 'counter-Enlightenment movement'. The Canadian-American psychologist Steven Pinker traces populism to a push-back to elements of the human psyche that Enlightenment institutions were designed to circumvent. He cites tribalism, authoritarianism, demonisation and zero-sum thinking as human facets which unscrupulous populists have exploited.[58] In the process, elites, who try to protect hard-won knowledge and rule-based institutions that provide necessary checks and balances against the power of flawed human actors, are denigrated and despised. The checks and balances that the judiciary has provided against some flawed interventions in the field of human rights and terrorism have been described in earlier chapters, but those events bear out Pinker's observations.

Pinker is a scientist and his particular interests include trying to find out, with empirical evidence, how and why humanity wants to progress and make life better than it was for earlier generations. He has examined life expectancy, mortality, income inequalities, sustainability, education and a host of other features of human existence. His conclusions bear close reading. He waves 'good riddance' to the pre-Enlightenment era of 'starvation, superstition, maternal mortality, sadistic torture, slavery and witch hunts'. Instead his own scientific observations lead him to conclude that 'people flourish most in liberal democracies with a mixture of civic norms, guaranteed rights, market freedom, social spending and judicious regulation'.[59]

In a sense, too, this book has been an account of progress in the administration of justice and the refinements our historical experience has placed on the words the 'rule of law'. There were gloomy times for criminal law when the police had unaccountable power, mirrored by a judiciary which failed to make use of the power that the law could provide. The Enlightenment was not a perfect period in European and American history. Slaves worked for the powerful and wealthy, women could not participate in public affairs, and children had no rights whatsoever. There were elements of hypocrisy when the high-minded moral reasoning in the abstract so often conflicted with everyday life for the many. However, the values of universalism, rationality and a human autonomy in search of liberty provide the spur for a better protection for the rule of law than Gray, Lind or Timothy are willing to propose. Our democracy is in danger and its future cannot be guaranteed. If trust in law really does break down then the future is, indeed, bleak.

The former Chief Justice of Canada Beverley McLachlin reminded us in 2018 that the unwritten norms of the British Constitution must be preserved through independent judicial review. To do this, we must continue to remind the public about the benefits of a free society and the rule of law and speak out when the rule of law is threatened. The institution of the judiciary must be shored up against gratuitous attack and denigration, and judges must hold themselves to account by conducting themselves in a manner that inspires public confidence in the justice system.[60]

The American scholar Timothy Snyder has used his considerable experience of totalitarianism as a history professor at Yale University to provide a short *vade mecum* to remind us of what we must know to avoid tyranny. These are some of the lessons: 'Defend institutions. Beware the one-party state. Remember professional ethics. Believe in truth. Learn from peers in other countries. Listen for dangerous words. Be as courageous as you can.'[61] These lessons of the twentieth century are made from his perspective as a scholar of Marxism, Poland, the Ukraine, Hitler, Stalin and the Balkans. We would all be foolish not to heed his wisdom with care.

As David Feldman has commented, 'Our present system [the United Kingdom] for protecting rights against ill-judged legislative action remains somewhat unreliable.' He advocates rigorous debate, constant review and forceful protection to ensure we continue to enjoy what a modern 'rule of law' has given us. Writing in 2002, he said, 'The challenge is to plan for the future with ideals but without complacency, and have faith in democratic processes without ignoring the capacity of any political system to subvert the liberty on which it is founded.'[62] In present times, that is the challenge we must face with renewed vigour.

NOTES

INTRODUCTION

1 'The real anti-democratic outrage is the antics of the parliamentary Remainers', *Daily Telegraph*, 29 August 2019.

2 'Boris Johnson's suspension of parliament is an affront to democracy', *Financial Times*, 29 August 2019.

3 Sean Coughlan, 'Dissatisfaction with Democracy "at Record High"', BBC News, 29 January 2020.

4 Hansard Society, 'Audit of Political Engagement 16: The 2019 Report', https://www.hansardsociety.org.uk/media/coverage/the-public-think-politics-is-broken-and-are-willing-to-entertain-radical (accessed June 2020).

5 John Curtice, 'What UK Thinks', 31 January 2020, https://whatukthinks.org/eu/author/johncurtice/ (accessed June 2020).

6 Heather Stewart and Josh Halliday, 'House of Lords may move out of London to "reconnect" with public', *Sunday Times*, 19 January 2020.

7 Ferdinand Mount, 'Après Brexit', *London Review of Books*, 20 February 2020.

8 Boris Johnson, The Annual Margaret Thatcher Lecture, Centre for Policy Studies, 27 November 2013.

9 Steve Richards, *The Rise of the Outsiders: How the Anti-Establishment is on the March* (London: Atlantic Books, 2017).

10 James Slack, 'Enemies of the People', *Daily Mail*, 3 November 2016.

11 See generally, Albert Weale, *The Will of the People: A Modern Myth* (London: Polity Press, 2018).

12 Compare for example, Steve Richards, *The Rise of the Outsiders* and David Goodhart, *The Road to Somewhere* (London: Penguin Books, 2017).

13 Lord Hodge, 'Preparing Judicial Independence in an Age of Populism', lecture to the North Strathclyde Sheriffdom Conference, Paisley, 23 November 2018, https://www.supremecourt.uk/docs/speech-181123.pdf (accessed June 2020).

14 Beverley McLachlin, 'Where Are We Going? Reflections on the Rule of Law in a Dangerous World', The Sir David Williams Lecture, 19 October 2018, https://www.cpl.law.cam.ac.uk/sir-david-williams-lectures/rt-hon-beverley-mclachlin-where-are-we-going-reflections-rule-law (accessed June 2020).

15 Lord Neuberger, valedictory address at the Supreme Court, 28 July 2017; Frances Gibb, 'Give judiciary more support, says Supreme Court President Lord Neuberger', *The Times*, 29 July 2017.

16 Leslie Scarman, *English Law: The New Dimension* (London: Stevens and Sons, 1974).
17 Tom Bingham, 'Law in a Pluralist Society' in *The Business of Judging: Selected Essays and Speeches 1985–1999* (Oxford: Oxford University Press, 2000), pp. 103–15, p. 115.
18 Michael Lind, *The New Class War: Saving Democracy from the Metropolitan Elite* (London: Atlantic Books, 2020), p. 62.
19 John Gray, *Enlightenment's Wake* (London: Routledge Classics, 2007), p. 8.
20 Nick Timothy, *Remaking One Nation: Conservatism in an Age of Crisis* (London: Polity Press, 2020), p. 31.
21 Danny Kruger, 'Boris Johnson does have a vision but it is misunderstood', *New Statesman*, 19 February 2020.
22 *R (Bridges) v Chief Constable of South Wales Police* [2019] EUHC 2341 (admin) and *AAA v Associated Newspapers Ltd* [2013] EWCA Civ 554.
23 *Mandla v Dowell Lee* [1983] 2AC 548.
24 *R (Begum) v Headteacher and Governors of Denbigh High School* [2006] UKHL 15.
25 David Marquand, 'Counter-Attack' in *Decline of the Public: The Hollowing-Out of Citizenship* (Cambridge: Polity Press, 2004), pp. 116–48.

CHAPTER 1: WHAT IS POPULISM IN MODERN BRITAIN?

1 Ghita Ionescu and Ernest Gellner (eds), *Populism: Its Meanings and Characteristics* (London: Weidenfeld & Nicolson, 1969).
2 See generally, Robert Ford and Matthew Goodwin, *Revolt on the Right: Explaining Support for the Radical Right in Britain* (Abingdon: Routledge, 2014), pp. 1–20.
3 Tim Montgomerie, 'David Cameron ignores UKIP at its peril', *The Times*, 11 April 2012.
4 Glen Owen, 'Now UKIP leader Nigel Farage sets his sights on working-class Labour voters', *Mail on Sunday*, 25 May 2013.
5 John B. Judis, *The Populist Explosion* (New York: Columbia Free Press, 2018).
6 Roger Eatwell and Matthew Goodwin, *National Populism: The Revolt against Liberal Democracy* (London: Pelican, 2018).
7 For a further extrapolation of these generalisations, see Paul Taggart, *Populism* (Buckingham: Open University Press, 2000) and Marco Rivelli, *The New Populism: Democracy Stares into the Abyss* (London: Verso, 2019).
8 A. C. Grayling, *Democracy and Its Crisis* (London: Oneworld Publications, 2017), pp. 109–30.
9 Takis S. Pappas, *Populism and Liberal Democracy: A Comparative and Theoretical Analysis* (Oxford: Oxford University Press, 2019), p. 3.
10 The Brexit Party, 'Contract with the People', https://www.thebrexitparty.org/contract/ (accessed June 2020).
11 Timothy Peace and Parveen Akhtar, 'Postal votes and allegations of electoral fraud in Peterborough's by-election', Democratic Audit, 28 June 2019, www.democraticaudit. com/2019/06/28/postal-votes-and-allegations-of-electoral-fraud-in-peterboroughs-by-election (accessed June 2020).
12 Takis S. Pappas, 'How to Distinguish Populists from Non-Populists' in *Populism and Liberal Democracy*, pp. 41–78.
13 Pippa Norris and Ronald Inglehart, 'Understanding Populism' in *Cultural Backlash: Trump, Brexit, and Authoritarian Populism* (Cambridge: Cambridge University Press, 2019), pp. 3–25.
14 Matthew Goodwin, 'General election 2019: Corbyn's elite-bashing is naked populism', *The Times*, 3 November 2019.
15 A. C. Grayling, *The Good State: On the Principles of Democracy* (London: Oneworld Publications, 2020), pp. 11–34.
16 Takis S. Pappas, 'How do Populists Govern?' in *Populism and Liberal Democracy*, pp. 189–214.
17 Benito Mussolini, quoted in Robert Jackson, *Sovereignty: Evolution of an Idea* (Cambridge: Polity Press, 2007), p. 96.

18 Justin Collings, *Democracies Guardians: A History of the German Federal Constitutional Court 1951–2001* (Oxford: Oxford University Press, 2015), pp. 1–62.

19 George Orwell, 'England Your England' in *Selected Essays* (Harmondsworth: Penguin Books, 1962).

20 Vernon Bogdanor, 'On Popular Sovereignty' in D. J. Galligan (ed.), *Constitution in Crisis: The New Putney Debates* (London: I. B. Tauris, 2017).

21 John Gray, 'The Undoing of Conservatism', reprinted in *Enlightenment's Wake: Politics and Culture at the Close of the Modern Age* (London: Routledge Classics 2007), pp. 131–79.

22 Edward Luttwak, 'Why Fascism is the Wave of the Future', *London Review of Books*, 7 April 1994.

23 Takis S. Pappas, *Populism and Liberal Democracy*, pp. 40–78.

24 Yascha Mounk, *The People vs Democracy: Why Our Freedom is in Danger and How to Save it* (Cambridge: Harvard University Press, 2018), pp. 23–132.

25 Anthony Pagden, *The Enlightenment: And Why It Still Matters* (Oxford: Oxford University Press, 2013), p. 344.

26 Nigel Farage, quoted in John B. Judis, *The Populist Explosion*, p. 138.

27 Yascha Mounk, *The People vs Democracy*, p. 115.

28 David Maddox, 'Major leak from Brussels reveals NHS will be "KILLED OFF" if Britain remains in the EU', *Daily Express*, 3 May 2016.

29 Robert Booth, Alan Travis and Amelia Gentleman, 'Leave donor plans new party to replace UKIP – possibly without Farage in charge', *The Guardian*, 29 June 2016, quoted in Tom Baldwin, *Ctrl Alt Delete: How Politics and the Media Crashed Our Democracy* (London: Hurst and Co., 2018), p. 213.

30 Jennifer Kavanagh and Michael D. Rich, *Truth Decay: An Initial Exploration of the Diminishing Role of Facts and Analysis in American Public Life* (Santa Monica: RAND Corporation, 2018), https://www.rand.org/pubs/research_reports/RR2314.html (accessed June 2020).

31 Pippa Norris and Ronald Inglehart, *Cultural Backlash*.

32 Ian Harden and Norman Lewis, 'The Rule of Law: A Chequered History' in *The Noble Lie: The British Constitution and the Rule of Law* (London: Hutchinson, 1986), pp. 16–47.

33 Geoffrey Marshall, *Constitutional Conventions: The Rules and Forms of Political Accountability* (Oxford: Clarendon Press, 1984), p. 9.

34 Baroness Hale in *Ghaidan v Godin-Mendoza* [2004] 2 AC 557, at para. 132.

35 Baroness Hale in *A v Secretary of State for the Home Department* [2005] 2AC 68, at para. 237.

36 *Handyside v United Kingdom* [1976] 1 EHRR 737, at para. 49.

37 Aharon Barak, *The Judge in a Democracy* (Oxford: Princeton University Press, 2006), pp. 3–88.

38 Yascha Mounk, *The People vs Democracy*, p. 11.

39 Alan Travis, 'Blunkett to fight asylum ruling', *The Guardian*, 19 February 2003, quoting an interview on *The World at One*, BBC Radio 4, 12 February 2003.

40 'It's time for judges to learn their place', *News of the World*, 23 February 2003.

41 *R v Secretary of State for the Home Department, ex p. Q and others* [2003] EWCA Civ 364.

42 Aharon Barak, *The Judge in Democracy*, p. 77.

43 *Daily Express*, 13 June 2006.

44 Hansard, House of Commons Debate, 22 October 2013, vol. 748, col. 162.

45 William Davies, *Nervous States: How Feelings Took Over the World* (London: Vintage Digital, 2018), p. 52.

46 Peter Hennessy, *The Hidden Wiring: Unearthing the British Constitution* (London: Indigo, 1996), p. 127.

47 Isabel Oakeshott, 'Britain's man in the US says Trump is "inept"', *Daily Mail*, 6 July 2019.

48 Jane Dalton, 'Boris Johnson refuses to say he won't sack ambassador who criticised Trump', *The Independent*, 9 July 2019.

49 Michael Savage, 'Kim Darroch saga "is part of assault on civil service"', *The Guardian*, 13 July 2019.

50 George Parker, Sebastian Payne and Demetri Sevastopulo, 'Boris Johnson accused of throwing US ambassador "under a bus"', *Financial Times*, 10 July 2019.

51 Dominic Cummings, 'The Hollow Men' lecture, Institute for Public Policy Research, 2014, https://www.ippr.org/media-item/watch-dominic-cummings-hollow-men-lecture-2014 (accessed June 2020).

52 Iain Martin, 'Boris Johnson has proved his dependence on Dominic Cummings', *The Times*, 26 May 2020.

53 Jonathan Powell, 'The rise and fall of Britain's political class', *New Statesman*, 30 January 2019.

54 Pippa Norris and Ronald Inglehart, *Cultural Backlash*, p. 395.

55 Conservative and Unionist Party manifesto 2019, https://assets-global.website-files. com/5da42e2cae7ebd3f8bde353c/5dda924905da587992a064ba_Conservative%202019%20 Manifesto.pdf (accessed June 2020).

CHAPTER 2: THE NOT SO GOOD OLD DAYS: POWER, THE POLICE AND THE LAW

1   For a general discussion about the part trust plays in modern life, see Geoffrey Hosking, *Trust: A History* (Oxford: Oxford University Press, 2014); Geoffrey Hosking, *Trust: Money, Markets and Society* (London: Seagull Books, 2010); Russell Hardin, *Trust* (Cambridge: Polity Press, 2008); Anthony Seldon, *Trust: How We Lost it and How to Get it Back* (London: Biteback Publishing, 2009); Francis Fukuyama, *Trust: The Social Virtues and the Creation of Prosperity* (London: Penguin, 1995); Rachel Botsman, *Who Can You Trust? How Technology Brought Us Together and Why It Could Drive Us Apart* (London: Penguin, 2017); and Mark E. Warren (ed.), *Democracy and Trust* (Cambridge: Cambridge University Press, 1999).

2   Geoffrey Hosking, *Trust*, p. 28.

3   Niklas Luhmann, *Trust and Power* (Chichester: Wiley, 1979).

4   Clive Emsley, 'The English Bobby' in Roy Porter (ed.), *The Myths of the English* (Cambridge: Polity Press, 1992).

5   Patrick Devlin, 'Interrogation' in *The Criminal Prosecution in England* (London: Oxford University Press, 1960), pp. 26–66.

6   Ibid.

7   For a full account of the cases of John Christie and Timothy Evans, see Michael Eddowes, *The Man on Your Conscience: An Investigation of the Evans Murder Trial* (London: Cassell & Co., 1955) and Ludovic Kennedy, *10 Rillington Place* (London: Victor Gollancz, 1961).

8   Gisli Gudjonsson, *The Psychology of Interrogation and Confessions: A Handbook* (London: Wiley, 2009).

9   Hansard, House of Commons Debate, 14 April 1948, vol. 449, col. 1077.

10 Report by J. Scott Henderson QC, HMSO, July 1953, Cmnd 8896, para. 15.

11 For an insight into the mindset of the civil service in the 1950s, see Michael Coolican, *No Tradesman and No Women: The Origins of the British Civil Service* (London: Biteback Publishing, 2018).

12 HO 25662, National Archives, undated, October 1966.

13 *The Observer*, 15 January 1961.

14 HO 45/25656, National Archives, January 1961.

15 Hansard, House of Commons Debate, 4 February 1965, vol. 705, col. 1256.

16 'When "Yes Prime Minister" means anything but', *The Spectator*, 13 March 2010.

17 'Rillington Place, 1949: Report of an inquiry by the Hon. Mr Justice Brabin into the Case of Timothy John Evans', London, HMSO, Cmnd 3101, 1966.

18 HO 45/25662, National Archives, 9 October 1966.

19 *Mary Westlake v Criminal Cases Review Commission* [2004] EWHC 2799.

20 The sources for this account are M. J. Trow, *'Let Him Have It Chris'* (London: Grafton, 1992) and David Yallop, *To Encourage the Others* (Ealing: Corgi Books, 1990).

21 *R v Derek Bentley (deceased)* [1998] EWCA Crim 2516.
22 Earl of Kilmuir, *Political Adventure: The Memoirs of the Earl of Kilmuir* (London: Weidenfeld & Nicolson, 1964), p. 206.
23 Marcel Berlins, 'A Chief Justice got away with murder', *The Independent*, 2 August 1998.
24 David Pannick QC, 'Why Levin merits an honourable mention in our legal history', *The Times*, 7 September 2004.
25 David Ascoli, *The Queen's Peace: The Origins and Development of the Metropolitan Police 1829–1979* (London: Hamish Hamilton, 1979), p. 285.
26 Dick Kirby, *The Scourge of Soho: The Controversial Career of SAS Hero Detective Sergeant Harry Challenor* (Barnsley: Pen & Sword, 2013), p. 29.
27 Ibid., p. ix.
28 Ibid., p. 41.
29 James Morton, *Bent Coppers: A Survey of Police Corruption* (London: Little, Brown, 1993), p. 92.
30 Richard Davenport-Hines, *An English Affair: Sex, Class and Power in the Age of Profumo* (London: HarperPress, 2013), p. 107.
31 Dick Kirby, *The Scourge of Soho*, p. 91.
32 Mary Grigg, *The Challenor Case* (Harmondsworth: Penguin Books, 1965).
33 HO 287/919, memorandum of the permanent secretary, National Archives, 1 July 1964.
34 Hansard, House of Commons Debate, 2 July 1964, vol. 697, cols 1545–54.
35 'The episode concerning Donald Rooum', report of inquiry by Mr A. E. James QC (HMSO), Cmnd 2735, August 1965, pp. 102–19.
36 Ibid.
37 MEPO 2/11169, National Archives, files on DS Harold Challenor, held by the commissioner of the Metropolitan Police.
38 Paul O'Higgins, 'The Challenor Report, 1', *Criminal Law Review* (1965), pp. 633–6.
39 Mary Grigg, *The Challenor Case*, pp. 112–89.
40 MEPO 2/11169, memorandum of the commissioner, National Archives, March 1965.
41 David Ascoli, *The Queen's Peace*, p. 287.
42 Helena Kennedy, *Eve Was Framed: Women and British Justice* (London: Vintage Digital, 1993), p. 6.
43 Duncan Campbell, 'IRA groupie jailed for coach bomb sought folklore fame', *The Guardian*, 22 March 1991.
44 For a full account of the arrests and trial of the Birmingham Six, see Chris Mullin, *Error of Judgment: The Birmingham Bombings* (London: Chatto & Windus, 1986).
45 For a full account of the arrests and trial of the Guildford Four and Maguire Seven, see Robert Kee, *Trial and Error: The Maguires, the Guildford Pub Bombings and British Justice* (London: Hamish Hamilton, 1986).
46 *McIlkenny v West Midlands Police* ADD.
47 Patrick Devlin, 'Interrogation' in *The Criminal Prosecution in England*, pp. 26–66.
48 Mary Grigg, *The Challenor Case*, p. 91.
49 Barry Cox, Martin Wright and John Shirley, *The Fall of Scotland Yard* (Harmondsworth: Penguin Books, 1977).
50 Ben Whitaker, *Police in Society* (London: Eyre Methuen, 1979), p. 263.
51 Clive Emsley, 'The English Bobby' in Roy Porter (ed.), *The Myths of the English*, p. 135.
52 A full account of the case is provided in Christopher Price and Jonathan Caplan, *The Confait Confessions* (London: Maryon Boyars, 1977).
53 'Report of an Inquiry by the Hon. Sir Henry Fisher', 13 December 1977, https://assets. publishing.service.gov.uk/government/uploads/system/uploads/attachment_data/file/228759/0090.pdf (accessed June 2020).
54 Royal Commission on Criminal Procedure, London, HMSO, 1981, Cmnd 8092.
55 *R v Ward (Judith)* [1993] 96 Cr. App. R. 1.
56 Criminal Procedure and Investigations Act, 1996.

57 Pepita Barlow, 'The lost world of royal commissions', Institute for Government, 19 June 2013, https://www.instituteforgovernment.org.uk/blog/lost-world-royal-commissions (accessed June 2020).

58 Douglas Hurd, *Memoirs* (London: Abacus, 2004), pp. 351–2.

59 Roy Jenkins, 'On Being a Minister' in Valentine Herbert and James E. Alt (eds), *Cabinet Studies: A Reader*, (London: Macmillan, 1975).

60 William Belson, *The Public and the Police*, quoted in Dominic Sandbrook, *Seasons in the Sun: The Battle for Britain 1974–1979* (London: Penguin, 2013), p. 400.

CHAPTER 3: CLASS, DEFERENCE AND THE RISE OF JUDICIAL POWER

1 Cyril John Radcliffe, *The Problem of Power: The Reith Memorial Lectures 1951* (London: Secker & Warburg, 1952).

2 Wilfrid Greene, 'Law and Progress' in *Law Journal* (1944), vol. 94, p. 349.

3 TNA LC02 3827, National Archives, 'The Evershed memorandum', 23 January 1950.

4 Leslie Zines, *Constitutional Change in the Commonwealth* (Cambridge: Cambridge University Press, 1991), pp. 36–70.

5 Robert Stevens, *The English Judges: Their Role in the Changing Constitution* (Oxford: Hart Publishing, 2002), p. 47.

6 Ibid., p. 25.

7 Paul Addison, 'The Gentleman in Whitehall' in *No Turning Back: The Peacetime Revolutions of Post-War Britain* (Oxford: Oxford University Press, 2010), pp. 7–50.

8 For a cultural interpretation of the role of judges in the period before or just after the Second World War, see Stephen Sedley, 'The Crown in its Own Courts' in *Ashes and Sparks: Essays on Law and Justice* (Cambridge: Cambridge University Press, 2011), pp. 269–84, and 'Histories' in *Lions Under the Throne: Essays on the History of English Public Law* (Cambridge: Cambridge University Press, 2015), pp. 23–120.

9 Noel Gilroy Annan, *Our Age: A Portrait of a Generation* (London: Weidenfeld & Nicolson, 1995).

10 Roy Jenkins, 'On Being a Minister' in Valentine Herman and James E. Alt (eds), *Cabinet Studies: A Reader*.

11 Robert Stevens, '1900–1960, The Declining Role of the English Judiciary' in *The English Judges*, pp. 14–29.

12 Anthony Lester, 'English Judges as Lawmakers' in *Public Law* (London: Sweet & Maxwell, 1993).

13 *Magor v Newport Corporation* [1952] AC 189.

14 Stanley Alexander De Smith, *Judicial Review of Administrative Action* (London: Stevens, 1959), p. 8.

15 Professor Wade, quoted in Tom Bingham, *The Business of Judging*, p. 207.

16 Robert Stevens, *The English Judges*, p. 37.

17 Richard Davenport-Hines, *An English Affair*, p. 15.

18 Editorial, 18 February 1966, referenced in Michael Zander, *Lawyers and the Public Interest* (London: Weidenfeld & Nicolson, 1968).

19 *Anisminic v Foreign Compensation Commission* [1969] 2AC 147.

20 Lord Reid, 'The Judge as Lawmaker', *Journal of the Society of Public Teachers of Law* (1972), vol. 12, p. 22.

21 Leslie Scarman, *English Law*, pp. 7, 29.

22 Ibid., p. 17.

23 Simon Jenkins, *Accountable to None: The Tory Nationalisation of Britain* (Harmondsworth: Penguin Books, 1996), p. 1.

24 F. A. von Hayek, *Rules and Order*, reprinted in *Law, Legislation and Liberty* (London: Routledge, 1993), pp. 9–50.

25 F. A. von Hayek, 'Social or Distributive Justice' in *The Mirage of Social Justice* (Routledge Classics: London, 2013), pp. 227–66.

26 David Marquand, 'Kulturkampf' in *Decline of the Public*, p. 92.

27 Nigel Lawson, *The View from No. 11: Memoirs of a Tory Radical* (London: Bantam Press, 1992), p. 64.

28 Margaret Thatcher, speech to the American Bar Association, 15 July 1985 in *In Defence of Freedom: Speeches on Britain's Relations with the World 1976–1986* (London: Aurum Press, 1986).

29 Ibid.

30 Conservative Party manifesto, April 1979, available at: https://www.margaretthatcher.org/document/110858 (accessed June 2020).

31 Charles Moore, *Margaret Thatcher: The Authorized Biography, Volume 1: Not for Turning* (London: Allen Lane, 2014), p. 342.

32 Simon Jenkins, *Accountable to None*, p. 21.

33 Andy McSmith, *No Such Thing as Society* (London: Constable, 2011), p. 336.

34 Richard J. Terrill, 'Margaret Thatcher's Law and Order Agenda', *The American Journal of Comparative Law* (Summer 1989), vol. 37, no. 3, pp. 429–56.

35 Jeffrey Jowell, 'The Historical Development' in Harry Woolf, *Judicial Review of Administrative Action* (London: Sweet & Maxwell, 1995).

36 Stephen Sedley, 'The Moral Economy of Judicial Review' in *Ashes and Sparks*.

37 Lord Neuberger, 'Twenty Years a Judge; Reflections and Refractions', Neill Lecture 2017, Oxford Law Faculty, February 2017.

38 Boris Johnson, 'The Long Arm of the Law', *The Spectator*, 17 June 1995.

39 Noel Gilroy Annan, *Our Age*, p. 437.

40 Tom Bingham, speech at the Lord Mayor's Dinner, July 1996, quoted in Joshua Rozenberg, *Trial of Strength: The Battle Between Ministers and Judges Over Who Makes the Laws* (London: Richard Cohen Books, 1997), p. 91.

41 *R v Secretary of State for the Home Department, ex p. Moon* [1996] Amin. Law Reports 477.

42 David Faber MP, quoted in Joshua Rozenberg, *Trial of Strength*, p. 6.

43 Press release issued by Michael Howard MP, October 1993, quoted in Michael Crick, *In Search of Michael Howard* (London: Simon & Schuster, 2005), p. 276.

44 *The Sun*, 17 June 1993.

45 *The Sun*, 7 October 1993.

46 John Dyson, *A Judge's Journey* (Oxford: Hart Publishing, 2019).

47 Peter Hennessy, *Establishment and Meritocracy* (London: Haus Curiosities, 2014).

48 John Halliday, 'Making Punishment Work', July 2001, https://webarchive.nationalarchives.gov.uk/+/http:/www.homeoffice.gov.uk/documents/halliday-report-sppu/chap-1-2-halliday2835.pdf?view=Binary (accessed June 2020).

49 Joshua Rozenberg, *Trial of Strength*, p. 35.

50 Susan Ratcliffe (ed.), *Oxford Essential Quotations* (Oxford: Oxford University Press, 2016), https://www.oxfordreference.com/view/10.1093/acref/9780191826719.001.00 (accessed June 2020).

51 David James Smith, *The Sleep of Reason: The James Bulger Case* (London: Faber & Faber, 2017), p. 1.

52 *R (Thomson and Venables) v Home Office* [1997] UKHL 25.

53 Tom Bingham, *The Business of Judging: Selected Essays and Speeches*, p. 156.

54 See generally, Tom Bingham, 'The Exercise of Power' in *The Rule of Law* (London: Allen Lane, 2010), pp. 60–65.

55 John Major, '1993 Conservative Party Conference Speech', UKPOL Political Speech Archive, 30 November 2015, www.ukpol.co.uk/john-major-1993-conservative-party-conference-speech/ (accessed June 2020).

CHAPTER 4: POPULISM, THE LAW AND THE CONSTITUTION

1 *Jackson and Others v Her Majesty's Attorney-General* [2005] UKHL 56.

2 For a full explanation and discussion about the origins of parliamentary sovereignty,

see Jeffrey Goldsworthy, *The Sovereignty of Parliament: History and Philosophy* (Oxford: Clarendon Press, 2001), pp. 159–215.

3 Erskine May, *Erskine May's Treatise on the Law, Privileges, Proceedings and Usage of Parliament* (London: Butterworth & Co., 1971), pp. 29–30.

4 For a general discussion of the cultural aspects of the Constitution, see 'The Law Becomes You' in Robert Colls, *Identity of England* (Oxford: Oxford University Press, 2002), pp. 13–33.

5 For a full discussion of this point, see Nevil Johnson, 'The Waning of Constitutional Understanding' in *In Search of the Constitution: Reflections on State and Society in Britain* (London: Methuen, 1977), pp. 25–41.

6 Conservative and Unionist Party manifesto 2019.

7 Bentham manuscripts, University College London, p. cliii and p. 119, quoted in John R. Dinwiddy, *Bentham* (Oxford: Oxford Paperbacks, 1989), p. 54.

8 Jeremy Bentham, *An Introduction to the Principles of Morals and Legislation* (London: Pantianos, 1789), p. 11.

9 Jeremy Bentham, *The Handbook of Political Fallacies* (Baltimore: John Hopkins Press, 1952).

10 John Austin, *A Plea for the Constitution* (1859), quoted in Wilfred E. Rumble, *Oxford Dictionary of National Biography* (Oxford: Oxford University Press, 2004).

11 Tom Bingham, *The Rule of Law*, p. 3.

12 G. H. L. Le May, *The Victorian Constitution: Conventions and Contingencies* (London: Duckworth, 1979), quoted in Peter Hennessy, *The Hidden Wiring: Unearthing the British Constitution* (London: Indigo, 1996), p. 37.

13 See generally, 'The Peculiar Sentiment of Albert Venn Dicey' in Ferdinand Mount, *The British Constitution Now: Recovery or Decline?* (London: William Heinemann, 1992), pp. 47–65.

14 Ivor Jennings, *The Law and the Constitution* (London: University of London Press, 1943), p. 234.

15 Richard Crossman, Godkin Lecture, University of Harvard, quoted in Ferdinand Mount, *The British Constitution*, p. 206.

16 Tom Bingham, 'The Rule of Law', The Sixth Sir David Williams Lecture, 16 November 2006, https://www.cpl.law.cam.ac.uk/sir-david-williams-lectures2006-rule-law/rule-law-text-transcript (accessed June 2020).

17 Stephen Sedley, 'The Rule of Law' in *Lions under the Throne*.

18 Vernon Bogdanor, *Beyond Brexit: Britain's Unprotected Constitution* (London: I. B. Tauris, 2019).

19 Ibid., p. 261.

20 Vernon Bogdanor, 'The Referendum' in *The New British Constitution* (Oxford: Hart Publishing, 2009), pp. 173–96.

21 Hansard, House of Commons Debate, 11 July 2016, vol. 774, col. 29.

22 Hansard, House of Commons Debate, 7 December 2016, vol. 777, col. 301.

23 Joe Watts, 'Theresa May's pitch to the country: it's not racist to worry about immigrants', *The Independent*, 5 October 2016.

24 Vaughne Miller, Arabella Lang, Jack Simson-Caird, 'Brexit: How does the Article 50 process work?', Briefing Paper, 16 January 2017, http://researchbriefings.files.parliament.uk/documents/CBP-7551/CBP-7551.pdf (accessed June 2020).

25 The full reasoning of the judgment appears in *R(Miller) v Secretary of State for Exiting the European Union* [2016] EWHC 2768 (Admin).

26 Tom Bingham, 'The Rule of Law'.

27 James Slack, 'Enemies of the People: Fury over "out of touch" judges who have "declared war on democracy" by defying 17.4m Brexit voters and who could trigger constitutional crisis', *Daily Mail*, 3 November 2016.

28 Hansard, House of Commons Debate, 31 January 2017, vol. 780, col. 907, and Jack Maidment, 'Jacob Rees-Mogg compares Brexit to battles of Agincourt, Waterloo and Trafalgar', *Daily Telegraph*, 3 October 2017.

29 See for example, *R (Wilson and others) v The Prime Minister*, 'Legal challenge to European Union withdrawal without merit', *The Times*, 6 May 2019.

30 Liam Fox MP, *The Andrew Marr Show*, BBC One, 20 January 2019.

31 Constitutional Reform Act 2005, Section 6A, http://www.legislation.gov.uk/ukpga/2005/4/section/17?view=plain (accessed June 2020).

32 Harriet Agerholm, 'Liz Truss may have broken law in failing to defend Brexit judges, warns former lord chief justice', *The Independent*, 19 November 2016.

33 Ben Wright, 'Brexit ruling: Lord Chancellor backs judiciary amid row', BBC News, 5 November 2016.

34 See Pippa Norris and Ronald Inglehart, *Cultural Backlash*, particularly Part III, Chapter 11, pp. 394–8.

35 Anthony Seldon with Raymond Newell, *May at 10* (London: Biteback Publishing, 2019), p. 577.

36 'Brexit: "Tired" public needs a decision, says Theresa May', BBC News, 20 March 2019.

37 Hansard, House of Commons Debate, 25 September 2019, vol. 664, col. 660.

38 See Robert Saunders, 'The Rise and Fall of British Democracy', *New Statesman*, 10 April 2019.

39 Jason Stanley, *How Fascism Works: The Politics of Us and Them* (New York: Random House, 2018).

40 Jacob Rees-Mogg, 'Our constitution is robust. No harm will come from respecting the will of the voters', *Daily Telegraph*, 28 August 2009.

41 Will Hutton, 'The sheer scale of the crisis facing Britain's decrepit constitution has been laid bare', *The Observer*, 1 September 2019.

42 Paul Craig, 'Prorogation: Constitutional Principle and Law, Fact and Causation', Oxford Human Rights Hub, 31 August 2019, https://ohrh.law.ox.ac.uk/prorogation-constitutional-principle-and-law-fact-and-causation/ (accessed June 2020).

43 *The Times*, 3 September 2019.

44 *R (on the application of Miller) v The Prime Minister* [2019] UKSC 41.

45 Ibid., para. 31.

46 *New York Times*, 11 September 2019.

47 Hansard, House of Commons Debate, 25 September 2019, vol. 664, col. 663.

48 David Davis, 'Brexit is the writing on the wall for our "constitution"', *Sunday Times*, 6 October 2019.

49 Jonathan Sumption, *Trials of the State: Law and the Decline of Politics* (London: Profile Books, 2019), p. 34.

50 Paul Craig, 'Paper on the Rule of Law' submitted in evidence to the House of Lords 6th Report of Session 2006–07, 'Relations between the executive, the judiciary and Parliament', Appendix 5, https://publications.parliament.uk/pa/ld200607/ldselect/ldconst/151/151.pdf (accessed June 2020).

51 *Woolwich Building Society v Inland Revenue Commissioners* [1993] AC 70.

52 *A(FC) and Others v Secretary of State for the Home Department (the Belmarsh Case, no. 1)* [2005] 2AC 68.

53 For a full discussion of the meaning of the word 'politics', see Bernard Crick, *In Defence of Politics* (Harmondsworth: Penguin, 1962).

54 Jonathan Sumption, 'The Limits of Law', 27th Sultan Azlan Shah Lecture, Kuala Lumpur, 20 November 2013, https://www.supremecourt.uk/docs/speech-131120.pdf (accessed June 2020).

55 Stephen Sedley, 'Judicial Politics', *London Review of Books*, 23 February 2012.

56 Lord Dyson, 'Are the Judges Too Powerful?' in *Justice: Continuity and Change* (Oxford: Hart Publishing, 2018), p. 59.

57 Jonathan Sumption, 'Anxious Scrutiny', Lecture given to the Administrative Law Bar Association, September 2014.

58 Ibid.

59 Stephen Sedley, 'A Boundary Where There Is None', *London Review of Books*, 12 September 2019.

60 Tom Bingham, 'The Exercise of Power' in *The Rule of Law*.

CHAPTER 5: HUMAN RIGHTS: WHY WE NEED THEM AND WHY POPULISTS HATE THEM

1   Meeting with the Master of the Rolls, Lord Dyson, 30 January 2013, discussed in John Dyson, *A Judge's Journey* (Oxford: Hart Publishing, 2019), p. 153.

2   Will Woodward, 'Cameron promises UK bill of rights to replace Human Rights Act', *The Guardian*, 26 June 2006.

3   Conservative Party manifesto 2015, https://issuu.com/conservativeparty/docs/ge_manifesto_low_res_bdecb3a47a0faf/75 (accessed June 2020).

4   Jon Swaine, Christopher Hope and Duncan Gardham, 'Renounce European Court, Britain Urged', *Daily Telegraph*, 9 April 2012.

5   James Slack, 'End of human rights farce', *Daily Mail*, 3 October 2014.

6   Ian Drury, 'Five-year human rights farce over the "killer too depressed to be deported"', *Daily Mail*, 16 April 2015.

7   William Blackstone, *Commentaries on the Laws of England* (London: Cavendish, 2001), Book IV, Chapter 27.

8   Martyn Brown, 'Fury at European Court as terrorists win human rights', *Daily Express*, 19 August 2015.

9   For a general discussion about the treatment of human rights in the media see Michelle Farrell, Eleanor Drywood and Edel Hughes (eds), *Human Rights and the Media: Fear or Fetish* (London: Routledge 2019).

10 For a general history of the debate about human rights in the United Kingdom from 1968 to 1996 see 'The History of the Bill of Rights Debate' in Michael Zander, *A Bill of Rights?* (London: Sweet & Maxwell, 1997).

11 Hansard, House of Commons Debate, 6 February 1987, vol. 109, col. 1224.

12 Hansard, House of Commons Debate, 6 February 1987, vol. 109, cols 1271–1289.

13 Tom Bingham, 'The European Convention on Human Rights: Time to Incorporate', *Law Quarterly Review* (1993), 109, pp. 390–411.

14 Anthony Lester, *Five Ideas to Fight For: How Our Freedom is Under Threat and Why it Matters* (London: Oneworld Publications, 2016), p. 34.

15 'Rights Brought Home: The Human Rights Bill', October 1997, CM 3782, https://assets.publishing.service.gov.uk/government/uploads/system/uploads/attachment_data/file/263526/rights.pdf (accessed June 2020).

16 Conservative Party manifesto 1997, http://www.conservativemanifesto.com/1997/1997-conservative-manifesto.shtml (accessed June 2020).

17 Hansard, House of Commons Debate, 16 February 1998, vol. 306, col. 790.

18 For a general discussion of the fundamentals of human rights see David Feldman, *Civil Liberties and Human Rights in England and Wales*, 2nd edn (Oxford: Oxford University Press, 2002), especially 'Part I: Some Basic Values: Civil Liberties, Human Rights and Autonomy', pp. 3–113.

19 Isaiah Berlin, 'Two Concepts of Liberty' in *Four Essays on Liberty* (Oxford: Oxford University Press, 1969), p. 165.

20 Joseph Raz, *The Morality of Freedom* (Oxford: Clarendon Press, 1986).

21 David Feldman, 'Part I: Some Basic Values: Civil Liberties, Human Rights and Autonomy', *Civil Liberties and Human Rights in England and Wales*, pp. 3–112.

22 David Feldman, 'Rights, Democracy and the Rule of Law', *Civil Liberties and Human Rights in England and Wales*, pp. 31–2.

23 Anthony Lester, *Five Ideas to Fight For*, p. 16.

24 Hannah Arendt, *The Origins of Totalitarianism*, 2nd ed. (San Diego: Harcourt, 1968), p. ix.

25 Lord Irvine of Lairg, *Human Rights, Constitutional Law and the Development of the English Legal System: Selected Essays* (Oxford: Hart Publishing, 2003).

26 Ibid., p. 36.

27 Ibid., p. 54.

28 Human Rights Act 1998, Section 19, http://www.legislation.gov.uk/ukpga/1998/42/section/19 (accessed June 2020).

29 Ibid., Section 3.

30 Tom Bingham, speech on the seventy-fifth anniversary of the Foundation of Liberty, National Council for Civil Liberties, June 2009.

31 Lord Dyson, 'Are Judges too powerful?' in *Justice, Continuity and Change*, pp. 39–65.

32 Lord Mance, 'Destruction or Metamorphosis of the Legal Order?', speech at the World Policy Conference, Monaco, 14 December 2013, https://www.supremecourt.uk/docs/speech-131214.pdf (accessed June 2020).

33 Jonathan Sumption, *Trials of the State: Law and the Decline of Politics*.

34 See the arguments set out in Chapter 4.

35 Jonathan Sumption, 'Lessons from America', *Trials of the State: Law and the Decline of Politics*, p. 91.

36 Bernard Crick, *In Defence of Politics*.

37 Jonathan Sumption, *Trials of the State: Law and the Decline of Politics*, p. 60.

38 *R (Purdy) v Director of Public Prosecutions* [2009] UKHL 45.

39 Anthony King, *Who Governs Britain?* (London: Pelican Books, 2015), p. 273.

40 Jonathan Sumption, 'Law's Expanding Empire', 1st Reith Lecture, broadcast by the BBC on 21 May 2019, http://downloads.bbc.co.uk/radio4/reith2019/Reith_2019_Sumption_lecture_1.pdf (accessed June 2020).

41 *R (F) v Secretary of State for the Home Department* [2010] UKSC 17.

42 Lord Dyson, 'What is Wrong with Human Rights?' in *Justice, Continuity and Change*, pp. 199–219.

43 Conor Gearty, 'Protecting the Exposed' in *On Fantasy Island: Britain, Europe, and Human Rights* (Oxford: Oxford University Press, 2016), pp. 131–60.

44 *Gammans v Ekins* [1950] 2 KB 329.

45 *Dyson Holdings v Fox* [1976] 1 QB 503.

46 Lord Nicholls of Birkenhead in *National Westminster Bank v Spectrum Plus* [2005] AC 680.

47 *R v Horncastle* [2009] UKSC 14.

48 Lord Justice Leveson, 'Leveson Inquiry – Report into the culture, practices and ethics of the press', Department of Culture, Media and Sport, 29 November 2012.

49 Jonathan Sumption, *Trials of the State: Law and the Decline of Politics*, p. 59.

50 Ibid., p. 57.

51 Chris Grayling, 'Our plan to protect human rights – while making the European Court advisory only', ConservativeHome, 3 October 2014, https://www.conservativehome.com/platform/2014/10/chris-grayling-mp-our-plan-to-protect-human-rights-while-making-the-european-court-advisory-only.html (accessed June 2020), and Gordon Rayner, 'How Labour's Human Rights Act morphed into a privacy law', *Daily Telegraph*, 19 May 2016.

52 Nina Peršak, *Legitimacy and Trust in Criminal Law, Policy and Justice: Norms, Procedures, Outcomes* (London: Routledge, 2016).

53 *Hirst v United Kingdom* [2006], 42 EHRR 41.

54 Richard Littlejohn, 'Now get us out of the human rights racket, too', *Daily Mail*, 15 July 2016.

55 Conor Gearty, *On Fantasy Island: Britain, Europe, and Human Rights*, pp. 180, 181.

56 Richard Littlejohn, 'Democracy? No, Britain's now a judicial dictatorship – and it's time for revolution', *Daily Mail*, 13 August 2014.

57 Emma Glanfield, 'Drug-dealing killer jailed for nine years for manslaughter can't be deported because he's illegitimate', *Daily Mail*, 19 July 2014.

58 *Johnson v Secretary of State for the Home Department* [2014] EWHC 2386.

59 Conor Gearty, *On Fantasy Island: Britain, Europe, and Human Rights*, p. 218.

60 Tom Bingham, speech on the seventy-fifth anniversary of the Foundation of Liberty, National Council for Civil Liberties, June 2009.

CHAPTER 6: ARMS OR ARGUMENTS? TERRORISM AND THE RULE OF LAW

1   See generally, Ancieto Masferrer and Clive Walker (eds), *Counter-Terrorism, Human Rights and the Rule of Law: Crossing Legal Boundaries in Defence of the State* (Cheltenham: Edward Elgar Publishing, 2013), pp. 17–36.

2   Paul Wilkinson, *Terrorism versus Democracy: The Liberal State Response* (London: Routledge, 2011), p. 119.

3   William A. Galston, *Anti-Pluralism: The Populist Threat to Liberal Democracy* (New Haven: Yale University Press, 2017), p. 56.

4   Conor Gearty, *Human Rights in an Age of Counter-Terrorism* (Oxford: Amnesty Lecture, February 2006).

5   Alan Travis, 'Anti-terror critics just don't get it, says Reid', *The Guardian*, 10 August 2006.

6   'In full: John Reid speech', BBC News, 28 September 2006.

7   George Jones, 'We must put safety before liberty, says Blair', *Daily Telegraph*, 24 February 2005.

8   Hansard, House of Commons Debate, 26 October 2005, cols 325–8.

9   Lord Atkin, dissenting speech in *Liversidge v Anderson* [1942] AC 206.

10 Michael Ignatieff, *The Lesser Evil: Political Ethics in an Age of Terror*, 2nd ed. (Oxford: Princeton University Press, 2004).

11 Tom Bingham, 'Terrorism and the Rule of Law' in *The Rule of Law*, pp. 133–59.

12 *Chahal v United Kingdom* [1996] 23 EHRR 413.

13 Dominic McGoldrick, 'Terrorism and Human Rights Paradigms', in Andrea Bianchi and Alexis Keller (eds), *Counterterrorism: Democracy's Challenge* (London: Bloomsbury, 2008).

14 Lord Hope in *A (FC) and Others v Secretary of State for the Home Department* [2004] UKHL 56.

15 Ibid.

16 Clare Dyer, Michael White and Alan Travis, 'Judges' verdict on terror laws provokes constitutional crisis', *The Guardian*, 17 December 2004.

17 Hansard, House of Commons Debate, 10 February 2000, col. 418.

18 *S and Others v Secretary of State for the Home Department* [2006] EWHC 1111.

19 'Government appeal over hijackers', BBC News, 11 May 2006.

20 Alan Travis, 'Anti-terror critics just don't get it, says Reid', *The Guardian*, 10 August 2006.

21 'Blair dismay over hijack Afghans', BBC News, 10 May 2006.

22 [2006] EWCA Civ 1157.

23 *A (FC) and Others v Secretary of State for the Home Department* [2004] UKHL 56.

24 *R v Secretary of State for the Home Department, ex p. JJ* [2008] AC 385.

25 *R v Secretary of State for the Home Department, ex p. AF and MB* [2008] AC 440.

26 Alan Travis, *The Guardian*, 18 March 2004.

27 *Abu Qatada v Secretary of State for the Home Department*, http://siac.decisions.tribunals.gov.uk/Documents/outcomes/documents/sc152002qatada.pdf (accessed June 2020).

28 *Omar Othman (AKA Abu Qatada) v Secretary of State for the Home Department*, http://siac.decisions.tribunals.gov.uk/Documents/QATADA_FINAL_7FEB2007.pdf (accessed June 2020).

29 *Case of Othman (Abu Qatada) v United Kingdom* [2012] 55 EHRR 1.

30 Michael Burleigh, 'Abu Qatada: Get this creature out of our country', *Daily Mail*, 18 January 2012.

31 Tom Newton Dunn, 'Fury as Abu Qatada is freed', *The Sun*, 14 February 2012.

32 *Omar Othman (AKA Abu Qatada) v Secretary of State for the Home Department*, http:://siac.decisions.tribunals.gov.uk/Documents/Othman_substantive_judgment.pdf (accessed June 2020).

33 Allan Travis, 'Abu Qatada wins appeal against deportation', *The Guardian*, 13 November 2012.

34 Hansard, House of Commons Debate, 24 April 2013, col. 888.

35 Alan Travis, 'Theresa May criticises human rights convention after Abu Qatada affair', *The Guardian*, 8 July 2013.

36 David Feldman, 'Terrorism and Risk' in *Public Law* (London: Sweet & Maxwell, 2006), pp. 364–84.

37 Council of Europe, 'Guidelines on Human Rights and the Fight against Terrorism', July 2002, quoted in Bingham, *The Rule of Law*, p. 159.

38 Lord Dyson, 'Human Rights in an Age of Terrorism' in *Justice, Continuity and Change*, p. 235.

39 Michael Ignatieff, *The Lesser Evil*, pp. 145–70.

40 Christopher Dawson, *The Judgement of the Nations* (London: Shed & Ward, 1943), quoted in Tom Bingham, *The Rule of Law*, p. 159.

CHAPTER 7: RECLAIMING THE PUBLIC DOMAIN AND DEFEATING POPULISM

1 Steven Levitsky and Daniel Ziblatt, *How Democracies Die* (London: Viking, 2018) and Madeleine Albright, *Fascism: A Warning* (London: William Collins, 2018).

2 Steven Levitsky and Daniel Ziblatt, *How Democracies Die*, pp. 100–101; see also the Constitutional Reform and Governance Act 2010.

3 See Vernon White, Stephen Lamport and Claire Foster-Gilbert, *Truth in Public Life* (London: Haus Curiosities, 2020) and John Major and Nick Clegg, *The Responsibilities of Democracy* (London: Haus Curiosities, 2019).

4 Rajeev Syal, 'Dominic Cummings calls for "weirdos and misfits" for No 10 jobs', *The Guardian*, 2 January 2020.

5 'Philip Rutnam resignation: his full statement', *The Guardian*, 29 February 2020.

6 Rachel Sylvester, 'This pin-stripe purge is political vandalism', *The Times*, 30 June 2020.

7 Tom Bower, *Dangerous Hero: Corbyn's Ruthless Plot for Power* (London: William Collins, 2019).

8 'Security costs for MPs total £3.5m', BBC News, 19 December 2019.

9 Paul Withers, '"People could get killed!" MPs fear being "lynched" on streets if second referendum called', *Daily Express*, 2 October 2019.

10 Hansard, House of Commons Debate, Prime Minister's Statement, 25 September 2019, vol. 664, cols 785–824.

11 David Runciman, *How Democracy Ends* (London: Profile Books, 2018).

12 Liam Fox MP, *The Andrew Marr Show*, BBC One, 20 January 2019.

13 Charley Coleman, 'Constitution, Democracy and Rights Commission', House of Lords Library Briefing, March 2020, https://lordslibrary.parliament.uk/research-briefings/lln-2020-0089/ (accessed June 2020).

14 Suella Braverman, 'People we elect must take back control from people we don't. Who include the judges', ConservativeHome, 27 January 2020, https://www.conservativehome.com/platform/2020/01/suella-braverman-people-we-elect-must-take-back-control-from-people-we-dont-who-include-the-judges.html (accessed June 2020).

15 John Gray, *Enlightenment's Wake: Politics and Culture at the Close of the Modern Age* (London: Routledge, 2007).

16 Ibid., 'Against the New Liberalism', p. 8.

17 Ibid., 'Agnostic Liberalism', p. 128.

18 John Rawls, *A Theory of Justice* (Cambridge, Mass: Belknap Press, 1971).

19 John Gray, 'Agnostic Liberalism', pp. 114–15.

20 John Gray, 'The New Battleground', *New Statesman*, 23 January 2019.

21 *R (E) v Governing Body of JFS* [2009] UK HL 15.

22 *R (B) v Governors of Denbigh High School* [2007] 1 AC 100.

23 Amitai Etzioni, 'Forging New Legitimacy' in *Law and Society in a Populist Age: Balancing Individual Rights and the Common Good* (Bristol: Bristol University Press, 2018).

24 Michael Lind, *The New Class War: Saving Democracy from the Managerial Elite* (London: Atlantic Books, 2020).

25 Daniel Clark, 'Trade union density in the United Kingdom 1995 to 2018', Statista, https://www.statista.com/statistics/287232/trade-union-density-united-kingdom-uk-y-on-y/ (accessed June 2020).

26 'United Kingdom – Employment in Agriculture', Trading Economics, https://tradingeconomics.com/united-kingdom/employment-in-agriculture-percent-of-total-employment-wb-data.

html (accessed June 2020) and 'Christianity in the UK', Faith Survey, 25 June 2020, https://faithsurvey.co.uk/uk-christianity.html (accessed June 2020).

27 Michael Lind, 'The Neoliberal Revolution from Above', *The New Class War*, pp. 45–66.

28 Ibid., 'Countervailing Power', pp. 121–45.

29 Ibid., p. 63.

30 Nick Timothy, *Remaking One Nation: The Future of Conservatism* (Cambridge: Polity Press, 2020).

31 Ibid., pp. 42–9.

32 Lord Reed, oral evidence before Constitutional Committee of the House of Lords, 4 March 2020, https://parliamentlive.tv/Event/Index/eobdb9ad-cd56-441c-b5e3-2f979225ea51 (accessed June 2020).

33 Nick Timothy, *Remaking One Nation*, p. 221.

34 Sections 2 and 3 of the Human Rights Act 1998.

35 Nick Timothy, *Remaking One Nation*, p. 139.

36 Richard Ford, 'Britain has most illegal immigrants in the EU', *The Times*, 14 November 2019.

37 Edmund Burke, speech given on 3 November 1774, quoted in A. C. Grayling, *Democracy and Its Crisis*, p. 155.

38 'Judicial Diversity Statistics 2019', Courts and Tribunals Judiciary, 11 July 2019, https://www.judiciary.uk/publications/judicial-diversity-statistics-2019-2/ (accessed June 2020).

39 'Protecting Human Rights in the UK: The Conservatives' Proposals for Changing Britain's Human Rights Laws', BBC News, 3 October 2014.

40 David Marquand, *Decline of the Public*.

41 Alice Thompson, 'This crisis is much harder on the poor … Eton must step up', *The Times*, 2 May 2020.

42 *Question Time*, BBC Two, 3 June 2017.

43 Speech to the Conservative Party conference, 1 October 2019, https://www.conservativehome.com/parliament/2019/10/priti-patel-i-will-give-the-police-the-powers-they-need-to-defeat-crime-full-text-of-her-conference-speech.html (accessed June 2020).

44 'The "Krisis" Manifesto is the petition we should sign to stop business-as-usual-post-covid', The Alternative UK, 24 May 2020, https://www.thealternative.org.uk/dailyalternative/2020/5/24/krisis-manifesto (accessed June 2020).

45 'Renew Normal: The People's Commission on Life After Covid', Demos, https://demos.co.uk/project/about-the-peoples-commission-on-life-after-covid-19/ (accessed June 2020).

46 See Chapter 3.

47 Mark Landler and Stephen Castle, 'A Surprising Role Model for Boris Johnson: F.D.R.', *New York Times*, 29 June 2020.

48 PA Media, 'There is such thing as society, says Boris Johnson from bunker', *The Guardian*, 29 March 2020.

49 Jonathan Sacks, 'Democracy in Danger' in *Morality: Restoring the Common Good in Divided Times* (London: Hodder & Stoughton, 2020).

50 Ibid., Chapter 23, pp. 321–36.

51 A. C. Grayling, *Towards the Light: The Story of the Struggles for Liberty and Rights that Made the Modern West* (London: Bloomsbury Academic, 2007).

52 Stephen Holmes, *Passions and Constraint* (London: University of Chicago Press Ltd, 1995), p. 269.

53 Anthony Pagden, *The Enlightenment and Why It Still Matters* (Oxford: Oxford University Press, 2013), p. 343.

54 A. C. Grayling, *Democracy and Its Crisis*.

55 Ibid., p. 163.

56 David Neuberger in Claire Foster-Gilber (ed.), *The Power of Judges: A Dialogue Between David Neuberger and Peter Ridell* (London: Haus Publishing, 2018), p. 33.

57 Jonathan Sumption, 'Meddling by judges is a problem only they can fix', *Sunday Times*, 16 February 2020.

58 Steven Pinker, 'The Future of Progress' in *Enlightenment Now: The Case for Reason, Science, Humanism and Progress* (London: Allen Lane, 2018), pp. 322–45.

59 Ibid., p. 365.

60 Beverley McLachlin, 'Where Are We Going? Reflections on the Rule of Law in a Dangerous World'.

61 Timothy Snyder, *On Tyranny: Twenty Lessons from the Twentieth Century* (London: Vintage Digital, 2017).

62 David Feldman, *Civil Liberties and Human Rights in England and Wales*, pp. 1090–91.

INDEX

INDEX